W. E. B. DU BOIS' AFRICA

W. E. B. DU BOIS' AFRICA

Scrambling for a New Africa

Taharka Adé

Anthem Press
An imprint of Wimbledon Publishing Company
www.anthempress.com

This edition first published in UK and USA 2026
by ANTHEM PRESS
75–76 Blackfriars Road, London SE1 8HA, UK
or PO Box 9779, London SW19 7ZG, UK
and
244 Madison Ave #116, New York, NY 10016, USA

First published in the UK and USA by Anthem Press in 2023

© 2026 Taharka Ade

The author asserts the moral right to be identified as the author of this work. All rights reserved. Without limiting the rights under copyright reserved above, no part of this publication may be reproduced, stored or introduced into a retrieval system, or transmitted, in any form or by any means (electronic, mechanical, photocopying, recording or otherwise), without the prior written permission of both the copyright owner and the above publisher of this book.

British Library Cataloguing-in-Publication Data
A catalogue record for this book is available from the British Library.

Library of Congress Control Number: Submitted
A catalog record for this book has been requested.

ISBN-13: 978-1-83999-801-0 (Pbk)
ISBN-10: 1-83999-801-6 (Pbk)

Cover Photograph: W.E.B Du Bois Collection, Special Collections and University Archives, UMass Amherst Libraries

Cover Design: Zoey Adé

This title is also available as an eBook.

Dedicated to My Little Brother and Oldest Friend
Eric De'Airius Flott

CONTENTS

Acknowledgments   ix

Preface   xiii

Introduction   1

1. The Situation   15
2. Du Bois on African History and Classical Antecedents   47
3. Du Bois and the Formation of Contemporary African History   75
4. Locating Du Bois   107
5. "Pan-Africa"   123

Conclusion   139

References   143

Index   151

ACKNOWLEDGMENTS

I must begin by stating that this publication is my first academic book and many people and events in my life have led me to this moment. It may perhaps be a bit unconventional to begin by listing those who had no direct involvement with this work, but I will do so nonetheless for without those influences in my life this work would not exist. There are not many who have the opportunity to immortalize themselves and those who have helped them in their life's journey in a book of academic scholarship. I feel honored and overjoyed to be able to do so. While there are many more people who I could name that have added to my life in various ways and are of no less importance, I hope that you can understand and forgive me for not including you for the sake of brevity. Please consider your representation under the fold of the matriarchs and patriarchs I shall soon name.

I must first acknowledge my wife, Zoey Adé (née Mallard), for possessing grace, patience and emotional wherewithal during this lengthy process. She has been my Ọṣun, as we, just as so many others in this tradition, have sought to create a life and, by extension, a world that facilitates the African renaissance. To my mother, Rhonda Peters (née Flott), thank you for your continued and unconditional love and support, and for your own everyday patience to understand the person your son is growing to be. To my father, William Lipscomb II, thank you for your encouragement, and for always seeing the best in me. I have certainly appreciated our long talks on history and world politics over the years and hope to continue to have them for many more decades. To my grandmother, Leola Flott, who calls every week to ask the weather and fulfill the advising duties of the family matriarch; our daily competitions on the Nintendo as a child formulated within me early the understanding and respect of the adaptiveness, dexterity, ingenuity and grace of eldership. I thank the entire Flott clan for my amazing childhood. All of you have supported me in your own way, and I am eternally grateful.

I also thank the Lipscomb clan, headed by grandma Shirley Lipscomb and the late grandpa William (Bill) Lipscomb Sr., for never allowing our geographical distance to prevent me from understanding how loved I am by you all. To my great aunt, Carolyn Phillips, thank you for placing me in my very first dashiki. You also brought me to my very first Pan-African event, and the rich taste and aroma of your peanut butter and chicken stew will never be forgotten. Perhaps someday my own kids will visit you and Uncle Tony at the "Phillips Bootcamp."

I would also like to thank four very influential family ancestors: To my grandfather, Cleveland Anthony Flott, thank you for setting me on this journey of self-discovery and love for African people. Thank you also for raising us all to be unapologetically proud of our heritage and to strive for integrity in all circumstances. To my great aunt and uncle, Ida and Willie Triplett, thank you for instilling in me the lessons of giving back to one's community and how one should cherish family. Finally, to my little brother, Eric D. Flott, whose recent passing has changed my life forever. You were my oldest and dearest friend and our childhood together cemented in me some of the guiding principles of my life. Together we learned the importance of loving and protecting family and friends, the importance of forgiving no matter how difficult that forgiveness may be and the importance of helping those in need. My academic journey has come at the grave price of not being able to spend enough time with you in our adult years. Therefore, I dedicate this entire work to you. Words cannot express the emptiness we have all felt since your passing.

To the faculty, students, alumni and colleagues in the Department of Africology at Temple University, I thank you immensely for your guidance, acceptance and friendship. I cherished our time together and hope that we may all remain in great health and continue to work toward the unified goal of African liberation. To the outstanding first reviewers of this manuscript, I am very grateful to you. Dr. Molefi Kete Asante, you took me in as a mentee, and have often treated me as a son. I appreciate you for all your words of wisdom, your reprimand when I fall short of excellence and your continued affirmation. Dr. Kimani S. K. Nehusi, thank you for the strict guidance of my scholarship, for always expecting excellence and for the many inspiring anecdotes you have shared from your times as a scholar-activist. Dr. C. Amari Johnson, thank you also for your guidance as well as your many words of advice whenever I am in need. Dr. Kehbuma Langmia, I thank you for your belief in this humble bit of scholarship and your continued encouragement to get it published.

There are still too many to name who have had a profound effect on me. I am certainly the product of a village-raising, and my village is quite extensive. I will however attempt to name a few more. For moral and academic support, I sincerely appreciate and thank Dr. Dorothy Autrey, Dr. Kimberly Brown Pellum, Dr. Aaron Horton, Dr. Bertis English, Dr. Carlos Morrison, Dr. Stephen Redmond, Dr. Byrdie Larkin, Dr. Ralph Bryson, Dr. Adisa

Alkebulan, Dr. Frank Moorer, Professor Anthony Browder, Professor Robert White, Professor Corie Muhammad, and Mr. Kenneth Dean. For emotional support during this process, I sincerely thank and appreciate Oshunde Shango Oshun, Victor Revill, Mark Overall, Darius Caldwell, Michael Bean, Myesha McCants, Thomas Anthony McCants, Brandon Hayes, Jasmine Flott, Darnisha McCants, Erica Flott, Anthony Flott, Deloris Flott, Kristopher Dotson, Carl Moorer Jr., Ronald Broussard Jr., Mary Thrash, Chucky Grant, and Charles "Bobo" Grant.

PREFACE

This work has in so many ways been a personal journey for me as years before the inception of this volume I began a journey of intellectual self-discovery in which the life and work of Du Bois remained a central muse. So intertwined with my personal story, I ask the reader to indulge me as I break from the traditional means of penning a preface and walk you through portions of that journey as I find it necessary in understanding the soul of this work before you.

The 2009–2010 academic year presented interesting turning points in my life. I was a student at Alabama State University at the time, majoring in history and performing disastrously. Many who supervised my novice scholarship expressed that while I was naturally gifted in history and philosophy—a trait I inherited from my grandfather who taught history for over thirty years—I was unfortunately very undisciplined. However, in the fall of 2009, a chance meeting with Dr. Stephen Redmond, the newly installed director of Alabama State University's branch of the Wesley Foundation, set off a series of events that put me on the right course. Redmond had just moved three doors down from me in the same apartment complex. He was a recent graduate of Emory University's Candler School of Theology, receiving the degree Master of Divinity.

I, much like Du Bois throughout his life, had begun to question the historicity of biblical events as well as the historical effects of African people's adoption of this culturally foreign religious faith. However, I was neither informed enough nor intellectually mature enough to provide any serious cultural-historical assessment of the Hebrew religion that could serve to ease my growing discontent with Christian dogma. On the night of our meeting, Redmond was quite welcoming and conceded to my inquiries though, unbeknownst to me at the time, did so in the tradition of a good scholar of biblical apologetics. He would in later years inform me that this was a ruse to shield his own theological standings while at the same time discovering for himself my intellectual potential.

With a slight smirk and wide-eyed gaze, he questioned me on my own thinking about the world, particularly the state of African people within it. This turn in discourse was refreshing, and I began to offer my humble thoughts. I suppose he soon found me worthy and, though still withholding his true thoughts about my initial inquiries, decided instead to bring up the life and work of Dr. John Henrik Clarke. Clarke is known in some African American intellectual circles as the dean of African American historians, and more broadly as the "master teacher." I learned that night, among other things, that Dr. Clarke was a Pan-Africanist and activist-scholar who had dedicated nearly the entirety of his adulthood to the study of African history and culture as well as to the social, political, cultural and economic advancement of African people.

After Redmond briefed me of Dr. Clarke's life history, he handed me a copy of *John Henrik Clarke: A Great and Mighty Walk*, a documentary about the life and philosophy of this master teacher. Forgetting the very reason why I came, I immediately went home and excitedly began to watch the film. It was through watching this documentary—narrated by Wesley Snipes and directed by St. Claire Bourne, the prominent documentary filmmaker of important figures in African American history—that I first learned of Du Bois' association with Pan-Africanism. It was also my first thorough introduction to Pan-Africanism as a concept. Prior to this, everything that I had been taught in reference to Du Bois had been from a few sparse speeches and essays penned during his early adulthood, though I had no recollection of hearing anyone until that point mention Du Bois and Pan-Africanism within the same sentence.

My initial introduction to Du Bois was perhaps as early as my freshman year in high school as there were posters of the great sociologist hanging in several classrooms of John L. Leflore Magnet High School, the historically Black high school in which I attended. At Alabama State University, there existed a little white building that housed the W. E. B. Du Bois Honors Program, and every year during Black History Month there were many speeches and symposia in which a number of people would discuss Du Bois in some capacity. Nevertheless, as the Clarke documentary had illuminated for me, there were vast gaps in my DuBoisian education. To be sure, I learned in the ensuing years that there are a number of professors at my alma mater who are quite familiar with the totality of Du Bois' life and scholarship. However, despite their presence, the principal ideas of Du Bois impressed on me through classes and other events on campus revolved around his notion of a *talented tenth*, and perhaps even more attention was given to the theory of *double consciousness*. Clarke, however, had framed Du Bois as "the leader and theoretician of Pan-Africanism." A visit to my campus library yielded

David Levering Lewis' two-volume biography on Du Bois. After a cursory read through of the first few chapters of the first text, I realized that the very little I knew of Du Bois still only encompassed the first one-third of the life of a man who had lived until he was 95 years old.

In the fall of 2009 I began in earnest to understand the intellectual journey of Du Bois beyond *The Soul of Black Folk*, which at that time in my undergraduate career was being touted as his most seminal work. Interestingly, where I began was with Du Bois' 1906 activities at Harpers Ferry. Du Bois, along with William Monroe Trotter, had just the year before become one of the principal founders of the Niagara Movement, a group that opposed the racial accommodationist ideals of Booker T. Washington, and sought immediate redress to issues surrounding racial injustice and disenfranchisement. The members of the Niagara Movement decided to hold their second conference meeting, the first on United States soil, at Storer College, an historically Black institution located in Harpers Ferry, West Virginia, and now part of the Harpers Ferry National Historical Park. The conference took place between August 16 and 19. Indisputably, the highlight of this conference was the morning pilgrimage from Storer College down to what is now known as John Brown's Fort to commemorate the historic 1859 antislavery raid led by John Brown, which had its bloody conclusion at that very fort.

Reading about this event, I came across "An Address to the Country," which was ostensibly penned by Du Bois, and upon its reading at the conference, had been met with great enthusiasm, essentially becoming the manifesto of the Niagara Movement. In the spring of 2010, I decided to recite this manifesto for a Black History Month speech competition being held by the Department of Communication at Alabama State University. This competition was created and principally sponsored by Dr. Carlos Morrison who, having arrived at the university just two springs prior, quickly took a liking to me and encouraged me to compete.

Having read that the members of the Niagara Movement made their pilgrimage to the fort barefoot in consideration of the supposed "hallowed ground" on which they stood, I was inspired to deliver my speech barefoot in hopes that it would lend me a memorable presence. In an attempt to replicate the well-known dandy appearance of Du Bois, I donned a black suit, white button shirt, black bowtie and wool overcoat. I had also prepared myself by listening to a few of the available recorded speeches of Du Bois, and thus attempted to mimic what David Levering Lewis refers to as Du Bois' "clipped diction." When my speech concluded, the large crowd before me in the lecture hall located in the John L. Buskey Health Science Building gave a standing ovation. I won first prize and for years afterward some faculty and students associated me with being a "DuBosian scholar." A dubious assertion as I, of course, was far from that, but was nonetheless inspired by these events to continue to pursue my understanding of Du Bois and his work.

An interesting, albeit tangentially related, event occurred not long after the speech competition that has remained a prominent memory since that time. I invited a young lady I was interested in dating to dinner and somehow Du Bois came up in conversation. This progressed into me mentioning winning the contest, which she was excited to hear about as she was an ardent fan of Du Bois. However, things went sour as I went on to mention that I had of late made somewhat of a game out of trying to discover errors in some of Du Bois' writings. To be clear, I had been told by Dr. Ralph Bryson, professor of English at Alabama State University and someone who also knew Du Bois in his lifetime, that there were some writings in which Du Bois purposefully included typographical errors and structural problems to see if his editor was exercising due diligence. According to Bryson, this unfortunately led to a few works being published with the unedited typos. I apparently did not explain this situation very well to the young lady and she promptly ended the dinner before calling later to inform me that she was not interested in someone of our age who could be "so arrogant as to think he could critique the work of Du Bois." Though I could hardly consider what I was doing at that time a "critique," that is now quite an amusing sentiment given the aims of this very volume.

Not long after the speech competition, I came across an article written by John Henrik Clarke entitled, "W. E. B. Du Bois: The Scholar Reconsidered." Clarke's article was essentially a *gedenkschrift*, memorializing Du Bois in a way that celebrated the Pan-Africanism of his later life rather than his earlier Americanism. Clarke quoted these words from Du Bois spoken in April 1957: "From the fifteenth through the seventeenth centuries, the Africans imported to America regarded themselves as temporary settlers destined to return eventually to Africa. Their increasing revolts against the slave system, which culminated in the eighteenth century, showed a feeling of close kinship to the motherland and even well into the nineteenth century they called their organizations 'African,' as witness the 'African Unions' of New York and Newport, and the African churches of Philadelphia and New York. In the West Indies and South America there was even closer indication of feelings of kinship with Africa and the East."

This passage re-enforced Clarke's assertion that Du Bois was the leading theoretician of Pan-African thought. Though over the years I came to greatly appreciate the grassroots organizing of Marcus Mosiah Garvey and still consider his brand of Pan-Africanism the most interesting, I nevertheless have always respected Du Bois and particularly for his interpretation of the intellectual heritage of enslaved Africans who, according to him, perceived their sojourn in the Americas as largely transient as Africa would never leave their hearts—and evidently neither did it leave the hearts of their progeny. Emphasizing this history of unified struggle, Du Bois essentially placed the heritage of Pan-Africanism in a time before the coining of the phrase itself by the Trinidadian barrister, Henry Sylvester Williams in 1900. This understanding, I would not doubt, became paradigmatic for Du Bois as early as the 1896 publication of his doctoral thesis, *The Suppression of the African Slave-trade to the United States of America, 1638–1870*.

Nevertheless, the realization of Du Bois' words in this passage had a profound impact on my consciousness. Though I was already quite interested in the history and social circumstances of those of African descent, I was inspired by Du Bois to become a more disciplined scholar in order to be of actual use to *our* people. Furthermore, it was also at this time that I learned from Du Bois the value of having intellectual rivals. Upon completing my undergraduate degree, Redmond insisted that I read more of the works of Dr. Carter G. Woodson. Doing so, I soon developed the opinion that Du Bois' true intellectual rival was neither Booker T. Washington nor Marcus Garvey. I argue that it was instead Woodson who, through his largely self-funded scholarship, challenged the very approach, and many times the lack of an approach, being taken to educate African Americans about their African heritage. Woodson staunchly opposed white philanthropy, understanding the "gifts of the Greeks" to be followed always with unwanted consequences. An in-depth comparison of both their scholarly work coupled with an analysis of their criticism of each other, and even their silent discontent toward one another, is a scholarship worth undertaking that will undoubtedly yield interesting results.

In the summer of 2010, having not yet realized the autobiographical nature of *Darkwater*, I decided to read, among other things, Du Bois' two later autobiographies, *Dusk of Dawn* and *The Autobiography of W. E. B. Du Bois*. I researched figures Du Bois mentioned such as Mark Hopkins and his wife, Mary Frances Hopkins Searles, the latter of whom, following Hopkin's death, was thought by publications of her day to have become the wealthiest widow in America. In researching, I discovered that in *Dusk of Dawn* Du Bois had confused some details of the Hopkins family lineage, an error that was transplanted over to the 1968 autobiography as well. Another very minor thing that perplexed me is that while Du Bois replicated large parts of *Dusk of Dawn* into his last autobiography, there was a typographical error in the latter book that did not exist in the former. I remember this distinctly as I questioned in *Dusk of Dawn* Du Bois' use of the word "pored" instead of "poured" only to discover that the former was the correct usage within the context of Du Bois' discussion. However, by the publishing of the 1968 autobiography this had been erroneously replaced with "poured." As I pondered this, I thought of Bryson's words and figured perhaps the fault lies more with Herbert Aptheker as editor than with Du Bois.

Regardless, in reading these autobiographies I also became fascinated with Du Bois' evolving view on religion. His family was quite religious and, though Episcopalian, as a child Du Bois and his mother often attended the Congressional Church which was theologically Calvinistic. However, there also existed in Du Bois' childhood town of Great Barrington, Massachusetts a small African Methodist Episcopal Church which he and his mother sometimes visited. Despite those visits, Du Bois longed for a social setting, religious or otherwise, in which the primary demographic shared his African heritage. He realized this even in childhood when a surprise visit from the Hampton Quartet who sung "Negro folk songs" moved him to tears in the pew of the lily-white Congressional Church. For me personally, having grown up in a church environment where the whole congregation was of my own heritage, I sympathized with Du Bois' lamenting of an upbringing that afforded him only rare glimpses of African-influenced religious culture. My church upbringing afforded me a foundational understanding of the great spirituality of African Americans, something that Du Bois perhaps could only somewhat appreciate for the first time upon arriving at Fisk.

It was within the setting of Mt. Olive Primitive Baptist that I matured into a person capable of forgiveness, unconditional charity, unwavering social ethics and diligence and courageous rhetoric. I have mostly fond memories of my upbringing in that institution, though naive I was of the commitment others made to ensure I developed with an ethical character. Prompted by Du Bois' analysis of Black Church culture and the role of Black women within, I reflected on the burdens, sacrifices and joys of the Black women churchgoers of my youth. I understand now in hindsight that my childhood church in particular would have been devoid of its soul without the dedication and sacrifices of its women who in their capacity headed the usher board, ran the Sunday school, organized field trips to social gatherings, wrote and directed plays, developed Black History Month programs, governed vacation bible school, choreographed praise dances, conducted the choir and heralded free-lunch programs available to all the town's children—among many other things too numerous to list. Du Bois characterized the Black Church as a "social institution first, and religious afterwards," but without the dedication of its women it is neither. I also fully empathize with Du Bois' discontent with the church as it comes to the dishonesty and immorality of some of its leadership. Further, like Du Bois, I question our very relationship and compatibility with Judeo-Christian ethos as from the very beginning it was the Trojan horse that led to the conquest of Africa and the enslavement of our ancestors.

After graduating from Alabama State University, I was admitted into graduate school in the Department of Africology at Temple University. By this time, my expressed intent was to shift my scholarly focus to the life and work of the Honorable Marcus Mosiah Garvey. Du Bois had taken up enough of my attention, and I wanted now to research the Pan-Africanism and Black Nationalism of Garvey, also known as Garveyism, and help to advance his theories and philosophy. I attempted to accomplish this somewhat in my little treatise on Black nationalism that I crafted as a master's thesis, albeit sophomorically written. "Very good student of history, but poor at theory," I was told by my advisor, Dr. Molefi Kete Asante, though approving the thesis nonetheless so that I may finish the degree. Dispirited, I spent that summer rereading a few old works that had given me inspiration in the past. I came across the beat-up old copy of Du Bois' *The World and Africa*, a book that had traveled with me from my home in Alabama to as far as Luxor, Egypt.

As I rediscovered my notes scribbled in the page corners of this book, it dawned on me that what I had attempted in my thesis was clearly more DuBoisian than it was an expansion of Garvey's philosophy. In fact, I had failed to actually incorporate the philosophies of Garvey at all, as the parts where I mentioned him were more akin to hagiography than theory. However, after rereading Du Bois' *World and Africa*, I began to think of the limitations to Du Bois' arguments for Pan-African unity. From there, I developed what I now call African World Antecedent Methodology (AWAM), a methodology which largely employs methods of comparative analysis to cultural-historical phenomena throughout the African world. Initially, I intended to write my dissertation using this methodology as the sole basis. This would have involved comparing the cultural-historical realities of African societies as ancient as Kemet (Ancient Egypt) with their contemporaries as well as with the overlapping cultural histories of societies that declined as each subsequent society began to rise.

When it came time to draft my dissertation proposal, I expounded on this idea and presented it to Asante with much enthusiasm. Alas, I again experienced dejection as I was advised that not only was the proposed work cumbersome, but it would take ages to complete. However, he did very much like AWAM and inquired how I came to develop the idea. Intrigued by my explanation, he suggested that I instead attempt to apply the methodology as part of a larger engagement with Du Bois' approach to African history. This, he correctly surmised, was a much more reasonable task to accomplish. I was initially amused by this suggestion. I was to once again take on the "arrogance" of my undergraduate days that the aforementioned young lady found so unsuitable for romantic affection 10 years prior. Nevertheless, over the next few years I pored over a litany of scholarship related to my dissertation, gradually building my appraisal and criticism of Du Bois' historical and social writings on Africa and Pan-Africanism. In the earlier drafts, Asante must have thrown out over fifty pages of writing as he demanded edits and revisions. Eventually, he informed me that he was pleased with the work and that I could then begin editing for clarity. A date for the dissertation defense was set and I went on to successfully defend, earning, with distinction, a PhD made possible by the more than a decadelong engagement with the life and work of William Edward Burghardt Du Bois.

In the years since that time, I have continued to develop that final draft into the work you have before you today. Along with a revisional overhaul of all original chapters, the removal of a chapter and the addition of two new chapters, this is a much more sophisticated work than its modest beginnings. Nevertheless, what follows is still but a humble entry within the vast body of works in praise and criticism of DuBoisian thought. Furthermore, what's before you partially fulfills what is assuredly a lifelong quest to impress upon future generations the importance of understanding the totality of the life and scholarship of Du Bois. A quest that I have not been personally unaffected by, as those who know the work of Du Bois will certainly recognize the DuBoisian-esque liberty I have taken with the breadth and errantness of this very preface. To conclude, while this text focuses primarily on the writings of Du Bois in his later years, especially his *The World and Africa*, there are numerous references to earlier writings and speeches in attempt to reveal Du Bois' intellectual maturation, particularly as it relates to his political Pan-Africanism and his scholarship on African and African diaspora history and culture.

Taharka Adé
San Diego, CA.
March 2023

INTRODUCTION

In the late 1940s, the African world was in utter turmoil. Many factors led up to this condition, and most, if not all, stemmed from the adverse effects of the history of European encroachment and colonialism. The European trade of enslaved Africans brought not only cultural instability and foreign ideological immoralities to the African continent but drained it of both valuable human and natural resources. The Portuguese, specifically, ruined the ancient Indian Ocean trade network, while simultaneously opening up the Kongo Kingdom in modern-day Angola to the trade of human bondage that would ensure that over a quarter of Africans taken to the so-called Americas came from its shores.

Further, the ending of the trade by the very same European powers brought even more economic havoc to major kingdoms and territories that had incautiously grown dependent on its resources. In the late nineteenth and early twentieth century, Africa began to be ravaged by colonial forces. Ancient cities like Benin were burned to the ground by the British, the French would subjugate the last of Dahomey's brave warriors, and the mighty Oyo empire under the rule of Adeyemi Alowolodu came completely under the vassal-ship of Britain's Victoria. The 1884–1885 Berlin Conference carved up the African continent and separated people into colonial territories without regard for cultural and political affiliation.

The twentieth century continued this trend. Masses of African people were affected by two large-scale European wars, usually referred to under the misnomers World War I and World War II, in which millions of Africans found themselves to be little more than cannon fodder. Two decades before the second war, a pandemic known as the Spanish Flu infected over a third of the world's population, as well as killing millions of African people on the continent. In the United States, African Americans were far more likely to die from the disease than whites.

A decade before the second war there was a worldwide economic crisis, retroactively referred to as the Great Depression, which greatly affected African peasant farmers and miners, still under the thumb of European trading companies. It is also reported that during the Great Depression, African Americans, already no strangers to hardship, were under such economic duress that nearly 40 percent of the African American population could not support themselves without government assistance.[1]

This is all to say that by the late 1940s many factors had impacted the state of the African world. W. E. B. Du Bois, who by this time is the leading African American intellectual, took all of this into consideration when he decided to write his text, *The World and Africa*. I analyze the scholarship of Du Bois as he attempted to pen an argument for a historical construction of African people. I argue that his statement, "[…] here is a history of the world written from the African point of view; or better, a history of the Negro as part of the world which now lies about us in ruins […],"[2] presents an understanding of himself and all people of African descent within the same historical matrix. Du Bois' attempt at presenting this relationship was to begin first by describing the need for such an assessment as his due to the state of the world caused by Europe's apparent evils.

In 1945, Du Bois decided to take a position with the National Association for the Advancement of Colored People (NAACP) that would allow him to do further research on the colonial conditions of African people. He used this opportunity to do research that would allow him to eventually publish *The World and Africa*, which details the historical, social, political, and cultural reasoning for Pan-African struggle. This book was a profoundly significant contribution to African history and Pan-African sociopolitical thought. However, I contend that there doesn't seem in his scholarship to be a robust appreciation for the cultural dimension of Pan-Africanism. Further, there exists some elitist and Eurocentric attitudes that had not yet been completely worked out in Du Bois' own mind.

Du Bois' evolving approach to Pan-African theory and practice is worthy of greater evaluation. Early in Du Bois' Pan-African advocacy, he attempted an audience at the 1918 Peace Conference in Paris. A dispatch from the *Chicago Tribune* would quote him stating, "We can, if we will, inaugurate on the *dark continent* a last great crusade for humanity. With Africa redeemed, Asia would be safe and *Europe indeed triumphant*" (emphasis mine).[3] Du Bois was beseeching the European colonial powers to "redeem" Africa,

---

1 Cheryl Lynn Greenberg, *To Ask for an Equal Chance: African Americans in the Great Depression* (Rowman & Littlefield Publishers, Inc., 2011), 21.
2 William E. B. Du Bois, *The World and Africa; Color and Democracy*, ed. Henry Louis Gates, (New York, NY: Oxford University Press, 2017), xxxi.
3 Ibid, 6.

or more Eurocentrically, "the Dark Continent," by allowing the *"natives,"* as he described them, a Western education and a chance at involvement in the Western systems of government that Europeans had brought to Africa.

Du Bois would believe that "self-determination cannot be applied to the *uncivilized* people," and, therefore, those who are "civilized" are those who have adopted the West's false universal humanism. However, this was in 1918, and this particular line of thinking of Du Bois certainly evolved to some degree by the time he published *The World and Africa*. To be clear, by the late 1940s Du Bois did not see the European world the same as he did at the turn of the twentieth century. He describes the West as a domain of decadence and on the brink of collapse. He offers it up as the "pattern of human culture" which has led to the aforementioned disastrous conditions that he had seen in his lifetime.

However, though Du Bois is very clear about the "pattern of human culture" that encompasses the European world, despite his penning a history of African people, he seems much less clear about the "pattern of human culture" that is the African world. Perhaps it missed him on more theoretical levels the understanding that while he was profoundly associated with the ideals, customs and cultural connectivity of Europeans that made up for Pan-European politics, African people's pattern of culture also needed to be clearly illustrated in order for there to be a deeper connection for Africans engaged in Pan-African struggle. Though, certainly, the superficial connections based on the racial paradigm, as well as racial oppression, were enough to both kick-start and continue Pan-African initiatives, I argue that even deeper, and more influential ties can be established by positioning a cultural paradigm as paramount.

The purpose of this book is to address the problem of Du Bois' Eurocentric subjectivity and the lack of an African cultural-historical matrix in his analysis. The primary issue is that there is some confusion on the part of Du Bois in understanding the deeper possibilities and necessities in framing Pan-African struggle along cultural-historical lines. This is an important issue not only in general academic discourse but for me personally and politically, as I seek to further the discourse on the cultural and political identity of my people, African Americans, by relocating and centering the arguments and perspectives toward African ontology and Pan-African politics. Therefore, I seek to further Du Bois' discourse that frames the epistemology of African Americans regarding our own history and culture. This involves illuminating the cultural-historical matrix missing from Du Bois' historical analysis.

Further, much like the sociological aims of Du Bois, what I seek in this book is to advance the perspectives and agency of African people in the telling of our own history. The deep study of African cultural history being done by Africologists[4] and non-Africologists alike should empower and invigorate both a domestic ethnic unity as African Americans, as well as a general intracultural unity as African people. However, there is still much work to be done in order to disseminate information among the African people of the Americas, as well as provide proper pedagogy for African Americans to understand and relate to the information.

By producing clearer Afrocentric analyses of Pan-African intellectuals like Du Bois, we may further our understanding of African conditions as well as further the discourse on African liberation. Thus, analyzing Du Bois' *The World and Africa* and other writings assists in African empowerment as well as ideological and cultural centering. As aforementioned, Du Bois is considered one of the most important intellectuals of the American twentieth century, especially as it pertains to African and African diaspora issues. In investigating the reality that Du Bois saw in the African world, it is imperative to highlight Du Bois' limitations. Likewise, it is also important to emphasize his intellectual development during the era in which he wrote *The World and Africa*, as much of the academy is focused on the idealism of "double consciousness" that he penned 50 years before.

In 1935, Du Bois penned an essay entitled "A Negro Nation within the Nation" in which he argued, "the colored people of America are coming to face the fact quite calmly that white Americans do not like them, and are planning neither for their survival, nor their definite future."[5] In this essay, Du Bois heralded some of the hallmarks of Black nationalist and Pan-African ideology: cooperative economics, autonomy over education and elevation of the arts and aesthetics of African American culture. Du Bois had begun to abandon the idealism he once held for America and African Americans' chances for advancement under American democracy. But, again, I contend that without a cultural-historical methodological approach to his work that informed his activism, Du Bois was unable to produce more meaningful answers in relation to identity that would have better served his advocacy for Pan-Africanism.

I argue that Du Bois was acknowledging some notion of a composite African ontology comprised of history of various past and contemporary African groups. Du Bois would attempt in the last chapter of *The World and Africa*, and in several works following this text, to use this argument of the historical achievement and character of the composite African identity in order

---

4 Africologists are scholars who utilize the theoretical model that is Afrocentricity, also known as the Afrocentric Paradigm.
5 William E. B. Du Bois, *A Negro Nation within the Nation*. New York, NY: *New York Times*.

to argue for Pan-African unity. Nevertheless, Du Bois failed to capitalize on the cultural argument regarding African people and instead focused on arguments that could valorize Africa to the Western world. This effectively weakened his contention that African people should seek to "save" Africa. An Afrocentric approach to saving Africa is an approach that values the restoration of African cultural and social norms. However, instead of Afrocentric norms, and regardless of the fact that Du Bois seemed to be advocating for the right of Africans to govern their own affairs, Du Bois' argument for saving Africa would see the further imposition of Eurocentric in Africa though governed by African people in a fashion reminiscent of arguments made by Frantz Fanon in *Black Skin, White Masks*.

I have offered this work as one of many in a growing body of Afrocentric scholarship. It is primarily an analysis of Du Bois' approach to the process of historiography and questions of identity in relation to African people. As aforementioned, much of this culminated in his major work, *The World and Africa*. Through my analysis of *The World and Africa* and other works of Du Bois, I have offered a critique as well as a methodology that centers both African agency as well as highlights the importance of African cultural cosmology. The desired result of which is to advance DuBoisian scholarship, better understand the work that must be done in advancing Afrocentric awareness in academic scholarship relating to African identity, history and culture, as well as to advance what I term the African world cultural project.

****

This book is an inherently Afrocentric work, being so theoretically guided by the Afrocentric Paradigm. Some principal scholars whose theories and methodologies I use are Molefi Kete Asante, Maulana Karenga, Ama Mazama, Cheikh Anta Diop and Marimba Ani. As Afrocentricity provides the foundational paradigm for this analysis, I focus on two major influences on Afrocentric theory. The father of Afrocentricity, Molefi Kete Asante, in his major work, *The Afrocentric Manifesto*, advances the idea of "Diopian historiography."[6] The namesake of which, Cheikh Anta Diop, emphasized often and effectively the cultural unity of African people. In his many works, Diop would meticulously lay out the evidence for such a claim. During his years at the Sorbonne, Diop would become proficient in the sciences of history, Egyptology, physics, linguistics, anthropology, economics

---

6 Asante, *Afrocentric Manifesto*, 118–119.

and sociology.⁷ This would of course aid him in his pursuit to recapture the truth of the African past and assist those who look to his work in re-invoking African agency.

Diop would begin his analysis of African culture with Kemet (otherwise known as Ancient Egypt). He theorized, and later set out to prove, that African cultural expressions share foundational antecedents that can be traced back as far as the ancient Nile Valley civilizations. According to Diop, "The history of Black Africa will remain suspended in air and cannot be written correctly until African historians dare to connect it with the history of Egypt."⁸ He would further suggest, "The African historian who evades the problem of Egypt is neither modest nor objective [...] he is ignorant, cowardly, and neurotic."⁹ Du Bois shared the same sentiments decades before Diop:

> The Egyptians, however, regarded themselves as African. [...] It was due to the fact that the rise and support of capitalism called for rationalization based upon degrading and discrediting the Negroid peoples. It is especially significant that the science of Egyptology arose and flourished at the very time that the cotton kingdom reached its greatest power on the foundation of American Negro slavery. We may then without further ado ignore this verdict of history, widespread as it is, and treat Egyptian history as an integral part of African history.¹⁰

In his pivotal work, presented to the English-speaking world as *The African Origin of Civilization* (a synthesis of several theses), Diop asserts that African people have inherent commonalities, and in subsequent works argued Africans should unify on the bases of these linguistic, cultural, genetic, economic and social commonalities. Diop understood well that the unifying factors of African cosmology were more fundamental than the externally imposed notions of what makes African people diverse.¹¹

Contrary to claims of essentialism, or of assuming African culture as a monolith, it is important to note that Diop did not deny any African society their own distinctive aspects, cultural variety or even unique cultural dynamism, but insisted on foundational and unifying aspects of what can be

---

7   John G. Jackson, *Introduction To African Civilizations* (New York: Citadel Press, 2001), 13.
8   Cheikh Anta Diop, *The African Origin of Civilization: Myth or Reality* (Chicago: Chicago Review Press, 1974), xiv.
9   Ibid.
10 Du Bois, *World and Africa*, 64.
11 Cheikh Anta Diop, *The Cultural Unity of Black Africa: The Domains of Patriarchy and Matriarchy* (London: Karnak House, 1989), x.

termed *African culture* based on ancient antecedents and contemporary social-cultural reality. Further, Diop's notion of complementary domains of African matriarchy and patriarchy remains an influential method of reconstructing an Afrocentric social history of Africa. The scholarship of Diop was another primary influence on my creation of African World Antecedent Methodology (AWAM), which I will discuss later in this introduction.

The second influence on Afrocentricity by which this analysis is framed is Maulana Karenga's Kawaida theory. Kawaida finds itself responsive to culture and its seven core elements, being, "history; spirituality and ethics; social organization; political organization; economic organization; creative production (art, music, literature, dance, etc.) and ethos."[12] The term Sankofa is used in this research within the context of Kawaida theory, thus being, "an ongoing synthesis of the best of African thought and practice in constant exchange with the world."[13] The need for a paradigm shift in African-American cultural dynamics has been the call of many, but this is perhaps best illuminated by Maulana Karenga when he states that we have a "popular culture" and not a "nationalistic" one.[14] Mazama explains Karenga's assertion by stating:

> What Karenga is speaking to is the reciprocal relationship that exists between a people and its culture. While it is clearly understood that culture determines one's outlook on life, it is also necessary to understand that people are ultimately the makers of culture. It is possible, and often necessary, as Karenga would argue, to consciously and deliberately affect the course of culture to make it reflect the best that is within us, as well as serve as a source of inspiration and guidance while we thrive to become the best that we can be. Thus, to reinforce ourselves as a people, as a nation, Africans must identify ourselves culturally. More specifically, we must rebuild our national culture.[15]

Nationalistic cultures have nationalistic histories that are cosmologically centered and politically instrumental. Throughout the ages, the writing of people's history has proven to be an inherently political project. The utility of history for the purposes of distinguishing a group, justifying engagement in war and/or the continuation of cultural, religious and political homogeneity

---

12 Maulana Karenga, "Philosophy, Principles, and Program," http://www.us-organization.org, US Organization, Last Modified: February 25, 2020, http://www.us-organization.org/30th/ppp.html.
13 Ibid.
14 Ama Mazama, *The Afrocentric Paradigm* (Trenton: Africa World Press, 2003), 19.
15 Ibid.

has been the primary aims of many an annal. For Du Bois, I argue that he emphatically displayed his understanding of this when he expressed the aforementioned sentiments, "[…] here is a history of the world written from the African point of view; or better, a history of the Negro as part of the world which now lies about us in ruins […]"[16] To be clear, though undoubtedly a Pan-Africanist, Du Bois was not a Black nationalist, or at least not to the degree as that of *Garveyism*.[17] However, though Du Bois fell short of centering culture as a paradigm, it is clear that his attempt with the *World and Africa* was one which fell in line with the objectives of deliberately affecting "the course of culture to make it reflect the best that is within us, as well as serve as a source of inspiration and guidance" for African people.

As early as Du Bois' publication of *The Negro*, which in its last three chapters he focused on people of African heritage in the Caribbean and in the United States, it is obvious Du Bois was primarily engaging with praxis as he encouraged the involvement of African people in the realization of Pan-Africanism, an idealism he would later apotheosize as *Pan-Africa*. This is also clear in the last chapter of the main text of *The World and Africa*, as well as the *Writings on Africa* (1955–1961) essays added at the end of the text in later editions. The use of scholarship from Afrocentric theorists has been quite useful in framing Du Bois' ideologies. In *The Afrocentric Paradigm*, Ama Mazama imparts that "from an Afrocentric perspective, where knowledge can never be produced for the sake of it but always for the sake of our liberation, a paradigm must activate our consciousness to be of any use to us."[18] She concludes this thought by astutely submitting, "The ultimate test will be our praxis."[19] Mazama's essay, "Cognitive Hiatus and White Validation Syndrome: An Afrocentric Analysis," introduces the concept of cognitive hiatus as "a break in the continuity of logical reasoning, a missing logical step in one's thinking. Cognitive Hiatus is easily recognizable because it produces discursive and behavioral incoherence."[20] This theory serves well in differentiating the ideologies which embody either cognitive hiatus or cognitive dissonance, while also highlighting how such could be, or is, an exercise in white validation.

---

16 Du Bois, *World and Africa*, xxxi.
17 Asante, *Afrocentric Idea*, 134.
18 Mazama, *Afrocentric Paradigm*, 8.
19 Ibid.
20 Ama Mazama, "Cognitive Hiatus and the White Validation Syndrome: An Afrocentric Analysis," in *Black/Africana Communication Theory*, eds. Kehbuma Langmia and Ronald L. Jackson. 25–38 (Cham, Switzerland: Palgrave Macmillan, 2018), 29.

Another scholar whose theory I utilize is Marimba Ani and her concept of *asili*.[21] The theories and critique of Eurocentric ethos presented in her text, *Yurugu*, are essential in order to delineate between the African and European cultural ethos that form the differences in their interpretations of history. Ani's concept of *asili* is useful in particular as it not only provides the means to historically, philosophically and empirically establish what is of European ethos, but also, as a parallel with Afrocentricity, provides analysis for making clearer what truly encompasses the ethos of the African.

Finally, I have developed a methodology based on the antecedent hypothesis presented by Diop. Being Pan-African in scope, I have utilized three African terms, *Kanna*, *Fanna* and *Naani*, to develop a methodology in which to use in order to further understand, as Victor Okafor put it, the "matrix" of African history and culture.[22] This methodology I have tentatively termed African World Antecedent Methodology (AWAM).

****

African-World Antecedent Methodology

The first aspect or method of approach in AWAM is *Kanna* (sameness). This approach is developed from the Yoruba phrase, "ti kanna ọrọ," or "of the same matter." It involves the gathering of data garnered from the field of Africology, as well as various other fields of interest and synthesizing it using Afrocentric methodology in order to show clear antecedent sameness between various African ethnic groups and cultures. Examples could include the use of oral tradition and oral history in order to reconstruct antecedents between regional groups, Afrocentric analysis of written accounts of various ethnic groups or Afrocentric analysis of the material culture of various African societies (especially if they help to formulate social histories or examples of past lifeways).

The more nuanced concept of *Fánna* (similarity) derives from the Xhosa/Zulu term "Kuyafana," or "in the same way; it is just the same." This method assists with the notions of cultural continuity stemming from ancient precedents argued to be exemplified throughout Africa and the African diaspora. *Fánna* may somewhat overlap with the *Kanna* method as investigations into

---

21 Marimba Ani, *Yurugu: An African-centered Critique of European Cultural Thought and Behavior* (Trenton: Africa World Press, 1994), xxv, 11.
22 Victor Oguejiofor Okafor, "Toward an Africological Pedagogical Approach to African Civilization," *Journal of Black Studies* 27, no. 3 (1997): 305.

cultural phenomena such as water rites, circumcision, libation, domains of matriarchy and a variety of other cosmological similarities become central. However, Fánna recognizes that similar African phenomena may not present ready antecedents. It is simply a bridge in assisting in the possible discovery of antecedents or the acknowledgment of African phenomena that appears inherent throughout multiple groups despite any clear origin.

The concept of *Naanị* (uniqueness) derives from the Igbo phrase, "naanị ebe," or "only place/source." The use of the Naani method involves the distinguishing of cultural phenomena which shows no clear antecedents or similarity with other groups. This would involve first the identification and investigation of the unique phenomena before also investigating other groups in proximity, and/or regional and diaspora groups, in order to determine if either *Kanna* or *Fánna* is, indeed, not present. The utility of such may also serve to secure the agency and intellectual autonomy of individual African societies.

Data collected from these three approaches are to then be analyzed in a manner that lists all clear cultural antecedents and suggestible antecedents while simultaneously distinguishing between foundational cultural aspects as well as unique cultural phenomena among the various groups being compared. In this case, I am doing a comparative analysis between the various African civilizations that Du Bois discusses and African Americans. However, I will also look at ancillary groups that we know are immediately related to African Americans (such as the Igbo, Yoruba, Bakongo, etc.). Doing so yields knowledge on cultural antecedents to African American culture that were severely impacted by way of the great calamity that was the European trade of enslaved Africans, or Maafa.

In *The World and Africa*, Du Bois makes a clear political and social case for African Americans to involve themselves in Pan-African struggle. It is clear that his intention in turning the attention of the reader to the African past is so that connections could be made with the African present. However, as aforementioned, he fails at connecting past and present African cultural ontology. Certainly, Du Bois understands the importance of culture as he makes clear the particular cultural ethos of Europeans that seeded Pan-European political unity. However, while he places forth a history of African people, he does not illustrate to the reader a cultural-historical matrix that, in my opinion, would strengthen his arguments for a Pan-African political imperative.

Therefore, AWAM is especially salient as it provides frame-working for reconstructing the past lifeways of African people transgenerationally and transcontinentally. Doing so assists in further reconstructing the cosmological rationale and utility of various aspects of African cultural continuity and unity among African Americans, enriching the collective comprehension of our own *Africanity*. In Chapters 3 and 4, I analyze Du Bois' historical construction of African people from an Afrocentric standpoint. I also end the chapters using AWAM to piece together past and present African cultural ontology and cosmology. Doing so, I provide an example illustration of the cultural connectivity between African Americans and the African world.

****

Outline of This Book

Chapter 1, "The Situation," discusses the necessity for an Afrocentric critique of Du Bois' engagement with African history and the African people of his era, particularly the "natives," as he described them. Du Bois' first three chapters of *The World and Africa* deals primarily with his critique of European cultural decadence, Eurocentric historiography and the historical effects on African people. While largely providing a positive appraisal of these various assessments of Du Bois, I also offer some critique of his own Eurocentric ideological entrapments. This chapter also introduces the use of Marimba Ani's concept of *asili* as a useful parallel with Afrocentricity in delineating between that which consists of African and European ethos.

Chapter 2, "Du Bois on African History and Classical Antecedents," examines chapters 4 and 5 of *The World and Africa*, which deals primarily with the peopling of Africa and the civilization of Kemet. Du Bois uses the scholarship of those he considered in his day to be the primary scholars on Kemet to formulate his discussion about the cultural history of this ancient Nile Valley civilization. He provides a somewhat chronological assessment that briefly covers Kemetic history up until the period of the New Kingdom. I also analyze Du Bois' chapter on Kush, which he referred to as ancient Ethiopia, or, "Land of the Burnt Faces." In which, Du Bois challenges the erroneous notion that Africans were incapable of building the civilizations in the ancient African world. These were feats which many racist scholars had speculated belonged instead to non-Africans, particularly Europeans. Du Bois utilizes Greek writings and other sources to combat this narrative. He also uses the work of scholars such as Flinders Petrie and Randal McIver, two British scholars who once had a student-teacher relationship that apparently grew contentious. However, for this chapter in particular, Du Bois states he most heavily relied on the work of African American historian William Leo Hansberry. I provide some commentary on the importance of the use of Hansberry's work. I also note Frank Snowden's rejection of the use of his work for Du Bois' text.

Chapter 3, "Du Bois and the Formation of Contemporary African History," assesses Du Bois' discussion of West Africa in his chapter, "Atlantis," as well as provides an assessment of Du Bois's approach to the history of Bantu migration discussed in the chapter "Central Africa and the March of the Bantu." Du Bois begins his discussion on West Africa by relaying the exploits of Leo Frobenius. Frobenius gained fame after announcing to the Western world that he had discovered the mythical land of Atlantis in the sprawling forests of West Africa. In actuality, Frobenius had stumbled upon the kingdom of Benin. Nevertheless, Frobenius believed the Benin Kingdom to be the result of the migration of an ancient and advanced European people and the African people then living there to be some degenerate form of that once great ancient civilization. To this end, I provide commentary on the belief in Western society that African people were ostensibly incapable of developing complex societies so therefore any evidence of civilization existing prior to modern European contact would have to have been the result of foreign intervention in the ancient past. I also argue that Du Bois does not go far enough in his own critique of the same.

Chapter 4, "Locating Du Bois," tackles the last three chapters in *The World and Africa*, being "Asia and Africa," "The Black Sudan" and "Andromeda." In which, Du Bois gives historical context for the encroachment of Asiatic groups (especially Muslim) and their invasion of Africa, influencing many different cultures throughout the continent. In the final chapter, *Andromeda*, Du Bois continues his discussion about invasion but shifts the focus to Europe. Interestingly, while in the preceding chapters there is some critique on Islam, Arabs and their effects on African people, there's hardly any critique on Christianity. Though it may be valid to argue that Christendom as a tool of imperialism in Africa is implied, I address the issue with some of Du Bois' ancillary writings. Further, I critique Du Bois' use of the Andromeda myth for his arguments as I view it as antithetical to his early contention that this text is primarily from "the African point of view."

Chapter 5, "Pan-Africa," begins by highlighting what I believe to be an important early strand of Afrocentric thought, namely the coining of the word "Afrocentric" itself. Though the record is not clear as to who first coined this phrase, Du Bois or Nkrumah, it was meant to serve as the guiding theoretical framework for the creation of Du Bois' *Encyclopedia Africana*. I then address Du Bois' appraisal of Russia's Marxism-Leninism and offer a brief analysis of the germinating matrix, or *asili*, of Marxism and its applicability to Africa. The chapter ends with an investigation into Du Bois' philosophy of "Pan-Africa," in which I argue that *Pan-Africa* should be viewed as a DuBoisian theory that should be considered more significant than even double *consciousness*. In laying out the ideological parameters of *Pan-Africa*, I detail further reasoning to support the contention that Du Bois lacks a cultural-historical matrix in which to frame his arguments.

Chapter 1

THE SITUATION

Africa is, of course, my fatherland. Yet neither my father nor my father's father ever saw Africa or knew its meaning or cared overmuch for it. My mother's folk were closer and yet their direct connection, in culture and race, became tenuous; still, my tie to Africa is strong.

—W. E. B. Du Bois[1]

William Edward Burghardt Du Bois explains in his posthumously published autobiography that many non-African people in his day thought that all African Americans regarded Africa as their motherland. However, Du Bois makes it clear that they were mistaken. Due to the effects of enslavement and colonialism, many of the descendants of the millions of kidnapped Africans in the Americas had turned their backs on their heritage. "This was true in the 17th and early 18th centuries, when there actually were, in the United States, Negroes who either remembered Africa or inherited memories from their fathers or grandfathers,"[2] explained Du Bois before continuing that "among Negroes of my generation there was not only little direct acquaintance or consciously inherited knowledge of Africa, but much distaste and recoil because of what the white world taught them about the Dark Continent."[3] Du Bois would also highlight a growing perception of identity among his generation. He explains that resentment arose whenever someone would suggest "that a group like ours, born and bred in the United States for centuries, should be regarded as Africans at all. They were, as most of them began gradually to assert, Americans."[4]

---

1 W. E. B. Du Bois, *Dusk of Dawn: An Essay Toward an Autobiography of a Race Concept* (New York: Harcourt, Brace and Company, 1940), 116–123.
2 W. E. B. Du Bois, *The Autobiography of W.E.B. Du Bois: A Soliloquy on Viewing My Life from the Last Decade of Its First Century* (New York, NY: International Publ., 1968), 343.
3 Ibid.
4 Ibid.

Du Bois would however conclude that African Americans, or *Negros*, as described in his day, are indeed African people. In 1945, he would leave Atlanta and return to New York to become the director of Special Research for the NAACP. He took the post to better concentrate his study toward the history of colonized people in general, and the history of African people specifically. The result of which produced the book, *The World and Africa*.[5] Within the book, Du Bois begins by critiquing Europe as the "pattern of human culture" which has left the world in ruin.[6] He then presents an historical account of African people which includes the classical examples of Kemet and Nubia, the history of Bantu migration, the Sudanic Empires, as well as histories of Western, West-Central and Southern African societies. He ends the text with a chapter dedicated to "the future of the darker races and their relation to the white peoples."[7] Based on the preponderance of assuredly obscure or gate-kept sources that Du Bois employed, for the late 1940s, the book was a magnificent achievement.

However, despite Du Bois' profound intellect and insight, the understanding that much of his thinking was predominantly Eurocentric has also been laid bare.[8] Du Bois' critique shows similarity with, and in many ways perhaps a forerunner to, that of later African and Afrocentric theorists such as Chekh Anta Diop,[9] Marimba Ani,[10] Molefi Kete Asante[11] and Ama Mazama.[12] All of whom have critiqued the cultural ethos of Europe so far as to express the differences with African ethos. Like Du Bois, each of these individuals also embraced some pan-African philosophy of resistance and liberation of African people and African cultural agency. Consequently, each has also called for African Americans to reassess our political and cultural-historical ties to Africa.

In this chapter, I will discuss a few texts to reveal evolutionary links in Eurocentric thought toward Africa. I begin with Du Bois' critique of the European world and their general ambivalence toward their exploitation of

---

5 Ibid.
6 William E. B. Du Bois, *The World and Africa; Color and Democracy*, ed. Henry Louis Gates (New York, NY: Oxford University Press, 2017), 1–51.
7 Ibid, 143.
8 Asante, *Afrocentric Idea*, 136.
9 Mario H. Beatty, "W.E.B. Du Bois and Cheikh Anta Diop on the Origins and Race of the Ancient Egyptians: Some Comparative Notes." *African Journal of Rhetoric*, 8, no. 1 (2016): 45–46.
10 Marimba Ani, *Yurugu*, 448.
11 Asante, *Afrocentric Idea*, 138.
12 Mazama, *Afrocentric Paradigm*, 10.

African people in his day, and how such ambivalence and exploitation continue to play out in varying ways today. Within this discussion, I also frame Du Bois' own Eurocentric ideological entrapments as well as what I perceive as the primary avenues by which Eurocentric ideology becomes embedded in the minds of African people. The two principal culprits I argue are Western education and religion, particularly Christianity, which both largely stem from the same epistemological paradigm that espouses Eurocentric supremacy. I argue that both Western education and Christendom, or the politics of Christian Europe (and Christian America by extension), are closely intertwined and that one cannot exist in the Western world, nor its imperial domains, without being socialized by way of the confluence of Western education and Christianity.

In the opening chapters of *The World and Africa*, Du Bois weaves together the cultural variances and cultural connections between several European nations such as Germany, France, Russia, Britain, Belgium and the United States. He makes it clear the major currents that make up the cultural ethos of European Civilization, or "the pattern of human culture" that, according to him, is at that time in collapse. Based on his assessment of Europe, his efforts then to pen a history of African Civilization was necessary in order to expose the existence of a different pattern of human culture. However, to expose this he had to make it clear that Europe has attempted to position itself as not simply a pattern of human culture but the universal standard by which human culture should operate.[13] I have termed this false universal humanism the *Eurocentric Masquerade*, a term I arrived at after reading the works of Molefi Kete Asante who states in his text, *The Afrocentric Idea*, that his work represents "a radical critique of the Eurocentric ideology that masquerades as a universal view."[14] Within this context, I contend that Europe has imposed on Africa and the rest of the non-European world a war of cultural dominance. It has been a war of attrition, as they quietly, and yet also boisterously, assert Eurocentric perspectives as standard through various mediums of propaganda in which they have power over. This has over time worn down the defenses of cultural autonomy which exists among all other world cultures. Du Bois himself provides anecdotes that sum up how this cultural war operates from the European side of the battlefield.[15]

However, while Du Bois makes clear what entails the particular cultural ethos of Europe, I argue that he fails at connecting past and present

---

13 Du Bois, *World and Africa*, 78.
14 Asante, *Afrocentric Idea*, 1.
15 See: Du Bois, *World and Africa*, 41–43; 63–78.

African cultural ontology and cosmology. Certainly, he places forth a history of African people, but he does not illustrate to the reader a cultural-historical matrix that would strengthen his arguments for a Pan-African political imperative. This is why I have advanced my own methodology, African World Antecedent Methodology (AWAM), which seeks to provide the discipline of Africology an apparatus in which to more easily display the cultural matrix of the African world. Particularly for the purpose of this book, the information to be presented by the use of AWAM would provide African Americans empirical, analogical and demonstrative evidence in which to see ourselves and our cultural history within the African cultural-historical matrix. Further, my aim for AWAM is for it to be expanded and used by any African-world ethnic group in need or want of such methodology for the purposes outlined.

The Collapse of Europe

In this modern time, we have come to see that the collapse of the European world during the era of the early Cold War, as related to us by Du Bois, was but among the first of many gasps for air that European civilization has made in order to stay afloat as the masters of the world. As aforementioned, Du Bois, who was born just three years after the end of the Civil War and the subsequent emancipation of millions of African Americans, would by the writing of his *The World and Africa* had lived to see the rise of industrial America, two large-scale European wars referred to by the West under the misnomers World War I and World War II, a pandemic that infected over a third of the world's population, a world economic crisis we retroactively refer to as the Great Depression, as well as the beginnings of the aforementioned Cold War.

The Western world certainly appeared to be on the very precipice of collapse. However, the West recovered to some degree. As the Cold War raged on, the *Space Race* ensued with the launch of Sputnik in 1957. To compete, much finance and focus went toward education in American society, as well as in Europe. This was however headed off by the push for Civil Rights by African Americans which saw its height of popularity on August 28, 1963, when over two hundred and fifty thousand men, women and children marched to the United States' capital in demand of equal social and economic liberties. Du Bois died the day before this historic event, marking the end of a 95-year legacy that saw him as a contemporary of the likes of Booker T. Washington and Marcus Garvey, as well as a figure of considerable intellectual authority during the rise of Martin Luther King, Jr.

Nevertheless, European Civilization is still very much so in the process of collapse. Du Bois contends that the collapse of Europe is "the greatest tragedy that has ever overtaken the world."[16] As such collapse would have a series of implications for nations formerly colonized, and those of which under the hegemony of Western imperialism, Du Bois is perhaps right to consider the whole world to be in the midst of tragedy. However, I would argue that, assuredly, the greatest tragedy to have overtaken the world was the rise of Western powers which set the world into such disarray in the first place. The collapse of Europe may indeed have dreadful repercussions in the immediate future, but the removal of the boot of Western hegemony from the throats of other world cultures is something that is to be anticipated with solace.

Du Bois analyzed the nature of the catastrophe his world has found itself in and again, as he puts it, "to which pattern of human culture does it apply."[17] Indeed, the greater contention is that the catastrophe in which Du Bois speaks of is a result of the cultural war that has since its beginning had the central premise of "which culture will prevail." Du Bois could have perhaps also been alluding to such when he quoted Felix von Luschan in stating that "nations will come and go, but racial and national antagonism will remain."[18] Du Bois' primary reason for quoting von Luschan was to suggest that he may have unintentionally prophesied the coming of war between von Luschan's native Germany against Britain and other European powers in 1914. However, Du Bois makes it clear that the control over Africa remained a clear objective of Europe as he states, "When Germany invaded Belgium [...] it must be remembered that by that same token Germany was invading the Belgium Congo and laying claim to the ownership of Central Africa."[19] Whether ruled by Germany or ruled by Belgium, it was a war to decide whose particular set of Eurocentric cultural subjectivity will prevail in dominating Central Africa.

Du Bois argues that during this war the colonies of Africa were called upon in order to "save Europe." I argue that in the general process of saving Europe, Africa was losing itself as it had to, before the war, indoctrinate itself in Eurocentric thinking in order to contend with Europe and, because of the war, indoctrinate itself even further. Thus, Africa was also involved in a cultural war, not against one European power but all that had aims of colonizing

---

16 Du Bois, *World and Africa*, 1.
17 Ibid.
18 Ibid, 3.
19 Ibid, 4.

its lands and indoctrinating its people. To that end, Du Bois mentions the fervent French nationalism of the Senegalese political leader Blaise Diagne. Diagne had become Commissaire-Général and oversaw the recruiting of Africans into the French army.

Diagne perhaps epitomizes the way in which African people were conditioned to value the culture of Europe above that of their own homelands. Du Bois describes Diagne as, "more patriotic in his devotion to France than many of the French."[20] Indeed, Diagne often encouraged African people to accommodate themselves to French domination, as well as adopt French customs and culture. In a very early edition of *Foreign Affairs* magazine, Du Bois criticized Diagne as, "[…] a Frenchman who is accidentally black. I suspect Diagne rather despises his own black Wolofs."[21] However, despite his shortcomings, it would be Diagne who approved Du Bois' first Pan-African Congress held in Paris on that cold February day in 1919. Thus begins the earliest primary setting of Du Bois' Pan-African leadership as well as the setting in which this book will begin framing Du Bois' Eurocentric ideological entrapments.

Framing Du Bois' Eurocentricity

Du Bois, of course, is not without criticism for his own Eurocentric entrapments both in writing and in action. In *The World and Africa*, Du Bois presents an article written by a reporter who interviewed him for the *Chicago Tribune* for his attempt to convince members of the December 1918 Peace Conference held in Versailles of the need for a Pan-African Congress. His initial hope was to hold a meeting with Woodrow Wilson, but he failed at this endeavor. The dispatch from Paris was dated December 30, 1918, just less than two months prior to Du Bois' first Pan-African Congress. In it relays Du Bois' sentiments that "the principle of self-determination cannot be applied to uncivilized peoples, yet the educated blacks should have some voice in the disposition of the German colonies [of Africa]."[22] At the end of the article, Du Bois is quoted as stating, "We can, if we will, inaugurate on the *dark continent* a last great crusade for humanity. With Africa redeemed, Asia would be safe and *Europe indeed triumphant*" (emphasis mine).[23]

---

20 Ibid.
21 "Worlds of Color," *Foreign Affairs, an American Quarterly Review*, New York, Vol. Ill, No. 3.
22 Du Bois, *World and Africa*, 6.
23 Ibid.

There is much to unpack about such sentiments. Perhaps it can be argued that some veil of appeasement to Western egotism is being utilized by Du Bois in order to garner the support he is seeking. Perhaps too it is simply a layover of attitude about the superiority of Europe, encompassing what some have argued as the first of three stages of Du Bois' intellectual development. Reiland Rabaka, in *Against Epistemic Apartheid*, challenges the notion of fixed stages in Du Bois' development though he does submit that Du Bois' writings before this time at least were sometimes plagued by Eurocentric imperial ideology.[24] Nevertheless, the very existence of such a monumental text as *The World and Africa*, which begins with a scathing indictment of the European world, presents a later contradiction with such sentiments, evidencing Du Bois' intellectual evolution.

After all, Du Bois states therein *The World and Africa* that he is presenting "a history of the world written from an African point of view."[25] Although he was undoubtedly an African person, and one of the greatest intellectuals of the twentieth century (African or otherwise), his view was both an African perspective and one that was authoritative. But the structuring of some of his arguments do present ailments that Molefi Kete Asante describes as *lynched texts*. As such, some of the arguments are "strung up with the tropes and figures of the dominating [European] culture."[26] His work requires both lexical and ideological refinement in order to tease out more of the agency of African people that Du Bois ultimately seeks to provide.

The most paradoxical ideology that he presents is the insistence that "self-determination cannot be applied to the uncivilized people," suggesting those who are *civil* have adopted Western culture, and yet Du Bois is penning a history of African civilization meant precisely to correct the perpetual lie that Africa and African people have not contributed to human civilization. In fact, in sections of the text he becomes rather emphatic that what was to be understood in his day as civilization was quite old among African people before the coming of Europeans. For Du Bois to refer to Africa as the "dark continent" and speak of Europe as being "triumphant" in "redeeming" Africa is a terrible offense to African agency. However, if such agency was to be afforded, as offensive as this perception of agency may be, then why is there no language in the resolutions of the first Pan-African Congress that

---

24 See: Reiland Rabaka, *Against Epistemic Apartheid: W.E.B. Du Bois and the Disciplinary Decadence of Sociology* (Lanham, MD: Lexington Books, 2010).
25 Ibid, xxxi.
26 See: Molefi Kete Asante. "Locating a Text: Implications of Afrocentric Theory," in *Language and Literature in the African American Imagination*, ed. Carol Aisha Blackshire-Belay (Westport, CT: Greenwood, 1992).

suggests inquiring upon the "native" their opinion on the matter?[27] I contend that this is because for Du Bois at this time the use of the term "native" was largely synonymous with uncivilized.

To be sure, of the 57 delegates present at the first Pan-African Congress, 12 delegates were native to nine African countries. Du Bois explains that since America and other colonial powers refused to issue visas, most delegates who attended already resided in Paris at the time. We can surmise that their presence in Paris during this era already places them among men who were socialized by Western education and norms. I should also point out that although 12 of these men were from 9 African countries, neither of them were referred to by Du Bois as natives. This is interesting as the only real difference between these men and the "natives" in Africa they are referring to would be their Western socialization and, thus, recognition as civilized men. Nevertheless, with reliable translators, if the delegates had thought to ask the native ethnic groups of Africa such as the Yorùbá, Wolof, Bambenga, Bambara, Akan, Zulu, Shona or Maasai and particularly those of which who had no Western socialization, what their thoughts were on decolonization and self-governance, would perhaps a vastly different array of perspectives had been produced?

Perhaps the Eurocentric paternalism of these *civilized* men would not have afforded the native an audience, or much less considered their uncivil perspective to be of value. This stands at the very crux of my argument. Du Bois claims to be attempting in *The World and Africa* a history of the world from an African point of view, yet gives no context for the inclusion of the events surrounding this meeting of delegates held nearly thirty years prior whose worldview were clearly affected by their socialization in Europe. Instead, Du Bois has centered what were then his and others' Eurocentric ideological proclivities toward African people and, ironically, done so with the message of African liberation.

To be sure, this is after all the Pan-African Congress and the list of resolutions Du Bois and the subsequent congresses place forth do evolve. For that matter, Du Bois' use of the term "native" and his opinion on their epistemology tends to evolve as well (as I will cover later in this volume). But if we take into consideration the resolutions produced by this first Congress, we nonetheless find the language problematic: "The natives of Africa must have the right to participate in the government *as fast as their development permits.* [...] They shall at once be allowed to participate in local and tribal government, according to ancient usage, *and this participation shall gradually extend, as education*

---

27 Du Bois, *World and Africa*, 7–9.

and experience proceed, to the higher offices of State" (emphasis mine).²⁸ We must consider here, by whose standards do we measure the "development" of the so-called natives? Further, from whose pedagogical ethos are the natives to proceed with *their* education?

It is clear that Du Bois and company considered the cultural, political and educational ethos of Europe to be the standard of measurement. For them, it is fine for the natives to immediately be *allowed* to participate in their "local and tribal government" but matters of the state require a level of education they do not have naturally and ostensibly can only be provided by the European powers that dominate them. Nowhere in the resolution is there consideration that perhaps the native epistemologies of African people should be brought to the fore and exist as the primary measurement by which the natives should "develop" themselves. After all, Europe's reign of terror in Africa interrupted these dynamics, and prior to this interruption Africans had always existed and governed themselves without the need for the European's epistemological and pedagogical subjectivities. This is not to say that the people of Africa did not need to have some understanding of the historical and geopolitical circumstances of Europe in order to contend on the world stage. After all, the unmitigated power of these European nations was indeed a reality. But this did not mean that Africans should see their cosmological perspective as hierarchically less than the Europeans.

For example, the young samurai of nineteenth-century Japan took it upon themselves to dissolve the shogunate and restore power to the empire. With emperor Meiji as figurehead, a series of reforms were implemented which Westernized the nation. But these *natives* of Japan did so without sacrificing the cultural and epistemological ethos of Japan. To this day, the educational system of Japan continues this pluralism but, as Japan is an ethnically homogenous project, Japanese culture and education rightfully remains the national epistemological paradigm. Certainly, Japan was an independent nation and, though the possibility of Western colonialism was looming, this was an internal struggle. However, my contention is that Japan did not consider the cultural paradigm that informed its systems of governance less than Europe, it merely drew inspiration from European nations in order to both defend itself and compete on the world stage.²⁹ Interestingly, this all occurred during Du Bois' lifetime. In fact, he was born in the first year of the Meiji restoration.

---

28 Ibid, 7.
29 See: Robert Hellyer and Harald Fuess, ed., *The Meiji Restoration: Japan as Global Nation* (Cambridge: Cambridge University Press, 2020).

I should note that, unlike Japan, Du Bois and company were dealing with the circumstances of an already colonized Africa and so their methods of approach to liberation would have to be different.[30] Further, the condition of being colonized presents a psychological burden sometimes manifesting in an unconscious inferiority complex which, in this case, would assume the natural superiority of Western epistemology. Nevertheless, it is important to acknowledge the Eurocentric language of their resolutions as the history of Pan-Africanism in the twentieth century, save for Garveyism, is primarily framed around the five congresses occurring between 1919 and 1945 of which Du Bois was a central figure. Those who study this history today may not understand the Eurocentric nature of these positions. Thus, the Afrocentric interrogation of this history becomes a necessity.

The resolutions as promoted by this first congress appear to have influenced the language of the resolutions of subsequent congresses. Phrases such as "the recognition of *civilized men* as *civilized*" and "self government for *backward* groups" continued to shape the ideals of the next three congresses. To be clear, in taking such a position as to consider the native to be underdeveloped and Western education the key for them to run their own affairs one must then insinuate the natural superiority of Western ways of knowing. Japan's answer during the Meiji era was not to replace their epistemological approach to governance with Western approaches but instead to supplement their knowledge in order to better strengthen their nation against Western encroachment. As pointed out by Hellyer and Fues in their book *The Meiji Restoration*, "Japanese leaders and intellectuals did not simply imitate established Western methods and practices. Rather, as they found inspiration in an idealized Japanese antiquity, the leaders of the new Meiji state simultaneously moved in conjunction with unfolding global trends in nation-state construction."[31]

The language of the resolutions by Du Bois could be construed as an endorsement of the Western-style system of governance in Africa, except that they wanted Africans to one day run these systems. There is no hint, as far as state formation is concerned, of drawing inspiration from an idealized African antiquity that moves in conjunction with unfolding global trends of their day. There is however the hint of Eurocentric conditioning that would,

---

30 While Japan was never formally colonized, it has since this time suffered semicolonial experiences. I find it also responsible to point out that while these were the goals of Japan's Westernization, this process led soon after to Western-style imperialism directed at neighbors, particularly Korea, present-day Taiwan and Manchuria. They even made a failed bid to conquer China entirely, leading to the loss of over twenty million souls in the bloody conflict that ensued during the Second Sino-Japanese War.
31 Ibid, 6.

in the minds of Du Bois and company, consider the so-called native to be underdeveloped—as well consider indigenous African epistemology underdeveloped by extension. To be sure, there too in the resolutions exists language which holds some Afrocentric possibility. For example, some of the resolutions contain the language "education in self-knowledge" and, perhaps the most promising, "freedom in their own religion and social customs and with the right to be different and non-conformist."[32]

In ways perhaps not apparent to the authors, these words present a contradiction with the request for Western education as a seemingly foundational epistemological paradigm for running a nation. I would argue that nations, when formed naturally, are based primarily on the "self-knowledge" of the people who form those nations. Thus, in my estimation, the natural line of thinking for African decolonialists would be to restructure national boundaries based on a *self-knowledge* that informs the cultural relationships and organizational abilities between various ethnic groups, and not to simply keep in place the same arbitrary national boundaries and systems of Western governance. Further still, to continue to educate the people in the maintenance of these governments based on Western epistemology is to continue to socialize people based on European values including their religious beliefs, social norms and cultural aspirations. Unfortunately, the African pursuit of "self-knowledge" and "freedom of religion and social customs" continue to clash with the cultural ethoses of Europe and Southwest Asia, as well as their dogmatic religions.

Nevertheless, Du Bois was not without any critiques of Eurocentricity and general history of European supremacy in Africa. In fact, he made some of the most damning arguments against *euromodernity*[33] among many of his ilk in the early- to mid-twentieth century. But this critique had to mature to become what it had by the publishing of *The World and Africa* as well as that of his thinking beyond this time. But Du Bois and many others suffered from the often invisible effects of what I term the *eurocentric masquerade*. The eurocentric masquerade is the standardizing of ways of knowing, or epistemology, under a type of false universalism. It is a set of Eurocentric epistemological subjectivity which places European cultural ethos as hierarchically preeminent. However, through the history of colonialism and neocolonialism, the deployment of missionaries, the development of European-ran international institutions like the League of Nations of Du Bois' day or today's United Nations,

---

32 Du Bois, *World and Africa*, 7–8.
33 See: Sabelo J. Ndlovu-Gatsheni, *Epistemic Freedom in Africa: Deprovincialization and Decolonization* (New York, NY: Routledge, 2018), 243–247.

and their international recognition for housing the world's leading academic institutions and other methods of socialization, Europe has been able to project their subjectivities onto the world and hide these subjectivities behind a masquerade which presents them as universal human values.

The Eurocentric Masquerade

In *The World and Africa* Du Bois' intensity of righteous assault against the systems of white superiority is near palpable. It is clear that by this moment in time he has evolved in his thinking in regard to Western Civilization and done so to such a degree that one could use this critique to measure his ideas drafted around the phrase *double consciousness* as near sophomoric. Du Bois is now of the mind that America, and the European world in general, does not have "too much to teach the world and Africa"[34] except for corruption, decadence and decay. Du Bois is slowly awakening to the fact that a war between cultures and cultural epistemologies has been the crux all along. Perhaps he has come to the conclusion that what has made the West capable of dominating others is not any manner of intellectual or cultural superiority, but plainly a matter of power.. With this realization, Du Bois acknowledges that though the accumulation of wealth and power is particularly important to observe among the leisurely elite, he further contends that the European worker idolizes the elite and wishes to emulate such accumulation of wealth for themselves.

Du Bois believed that this idolizing of the elite seriously affected the mind of European worker as he stated, "he did not love humanity and he hated 'niggers'." In discussing the opinions revolving around the American Civil War, Du Bois suggests that the South's philosophy of domination over African people was favorable in Europe. He argues further that even for those who might be sensitive to the inhumane treatment of the colonial subjects of African and Asian descent, efforts were made by way of social engineering that would keep many of such minds ignorant to the truth of the circumstances. Du Bois argues:

> This philosophy had sympathizers in Europe. Without doubt, a large majority of influential public opinion in England, and possibly in both France and Germany, favored the South at the outbreak of the Civil War and sternly set its face against allowing any maudlin sympathy with

---

34 W. E. B. Du Bois and Brent Hayes Edwards, *The Souls of Black Folk* (Oxford, UK: Oxford University Press, 2008), 9.

"darkies," half monkeys and half men, in the stem fight for the extension of European domination of the world. Widespread insensibility to cruelty and suffering spread in the white world, and to guard against too much emotional sympathy with the distressed, every effort was made to keep women and children and the more sensitive men deceived as to what was going on, not only in the slums of white countries, but also all over Asia, Africa, and the islands of the sea. Elaborate writing, disguised as interpretation, and the testimony of so-called "experts," made it impossible for charming people in Europe to realize what their comforts and luxuries cost in sweat, blood, death, and despair, not only in the remoter parts of the world, but even on their own doorsteps.[35]

It has been more than 70 years since this writing, and the truth remains no less the same. Social engineering has evolved to desensitize the masses to even the most grotesque of European atrocities. To be sure, many texts a year are printed with grave and gritty detail about the past and contemporary horrors of the domination of African people. One of the most famous of which is Adam Horchschild's *King Leopold's Ghost*, that chronicled the horrendous and murderous activities of Belgium's Leopold II in the Congo during the early half of the twentieth century. While Leopold projected to the world a campaign of civilizing the native in Africa, he had actually enacted military measures in which enslaved the Congolese people, forcing them to rend the earth asunder in search of natural resources such as rubber latex.

Du Bois, naturally, mentions this event in *The World and Africa*. After all, this occurred during his lifetime and certainly existed as an occurrence that helped to mold his ever-evolving opinions of European imperialism. Of this event he states that the "[Congo Free State] became the worst center of African exploitation and started the partition of Africa among European powers."[36] But the supposed point of a text like Hochschild's is for it to be seen as a call to action. It should be seen as such particularly because of ongoing exploitation of African labor for the purpose of mining raw materials in the Congo such as coltan, which is increasingly used in electronic devices, especially cellular phones. Further, texts such as Jason Stearns' *Dancing in the Glory of Monsters* and Tom Burgis' *The Looting Machine* have, since Horchschild, added further depth to the story of ongoing crises in Africa. Regardless, as with *King Leopold's Ghost*, such texts find an audience among an already desensitized Western population, done so by the popularity of earlier works such

---

35 Du Bois, *World and Africa*, 14–15.
36 Ibid, 22.

as Joseph Conrad's *Heart of Darkness*, which places such atrocities in the realm of otherworldliness. This is harmful to the degree that the average European with no direct hand in oppressing African people, though be the witting or unwitting benefactors, could add to their comfort and ignorance a veil of fiction to any overarching sentiment about the Congo.

Due to the degree in which Africa, and what it means to be African, has such a monolithic stance in the Western imaginary, such literature contributes to the desensitization of readers toward atrocities committed against African people. This is done first and primarily by centering the stories around the white explorer. For Conrad, this was in the personage of the fictional Charles Marlow, who relates his supposed experiences in witnessing the atrocities occurring in the so-called "place of darkness," an otherworldly place which the reader is left to assume is the heart of Africa, or, at the time, the Belgian terrorized Congo. This fixation on Africa as the imaginary and the association with otherworldliness is elaborated by Nigerian scholar Chinua Achebe when he states, "*Heart of Darkness* projects the image of Africa as 'the other world,' the antithesis of Europe and therefore of civilization, a place where man's vaunted intelligence and refinement are finally mocked by triumphant bestiality."[37]

Achebe, a novelist himself, who spent a great deal of his literary career focusing on the agency of the African characters in his novels, argues further that Conrad places "Africa as setting and backdrop which eliminates the African as human factor. Africa as a metaphysical battlefield devoid of all recognizable humanity, into which the wandering European enters at his peril," and concludes this sentiment with the thought, "Can nobody see the preposterous and perverse arrogance in thus reducing Africa to the role of props for the breakup of one petty European mind?"[38] To that end, this use of Africa as "setting and backdrop" occurs too in the nonfictional literary realm.

Think now of the implications of titling a book *King Leopold's Ghost*. Does doing so place Africans as a "human factor"? Does it center their agency in the midst of the terror brought down upon them? On the contrary, to galvanize sympathizers in America to the plight of Congolese people, Horchschild sees it most befitting to begin his narrative by first exploring the efforts of the French-born British journalist, Edmund Morel. Similar to the fictional Marlow in Conrad's tale, in Horschild's story Morel becomes the "wandering European" who "enters at his peril" both Africa and the political climate

---

37 Chinua Achebe, "An Image of Africa: Racism in Conrad's Heart of Darkness," *The Massachusetts Review* 57, no. 1 (2016): 14–27. https://doi.org/10.1353/mar.2016.0003.
38 Ibid.

of African domination. To be sure, Morel should be considered a man of morality to bring light to the condition of the Congolese. For if it were not for his efforts, perhaps Leopold's lie of philanthropy at the expense of human life would have continued to hoodwink some of those who had the power or influence to assist in intervening yet needed the word of a white man to do so. Nevertheless, in beginning with such an approach, Africans are yet again reduced to mere props in the narrative of European morality assailing European immorality. Certainly, Horchschild mentions the efforts of African Americans such as Booker T. Washington, William Sheppard and George Washington Williams, but only as an afterthought to the grand narrative of Morel. Though Hochschild briefly admits that Morel was not the first to bring attention to the situation, as indeed it was Williams and Sheppard who preceded him.[39]

An orientation to the history that would have afforded a centering of Williams and Sheppard, two men of African descent, and surely partial heritage that stems from the Congo area due to the historical circumstances of the European trade of enslaved Africans, as they make their efforts to liberate their distant relatives in what they obviously considered a motherland, would have been a less Eurocentric endeavor. Better still, beginning with the narratives of past and present Congolese people about the horrors of that day, would have naturally afforded agency to Congolese people specifically. Nevertheless, this is the paradigm from which African narratives, fiction or nonfiction, are related by the Western world. In Stearns' little book, *Dancing in the Glory of Monsters*, he makes it clear early on that the Congolese are not without grievance of the removal of their humanity in Western narrative as he opens his introduction with this anecdote:

> This is how it usually worked: I would call up one of the people whose names I had written down in my notebook, and I'd tell him I was writing a book on the war in the Congo and that I wanted to hear his story. [...]We would typically meet in a public place, as they wouldn't feel comfortable talking about sensitive matters in their offices or homes, and they would size me up: a thirty-year-old white American. Many asked me, "Why are you writing this book?" When I told them that I wanted to understand the roots of the violence that has engulfed the country since 1996, they often replied with a question, "Who are you to understand what I am telling you?" The look of bemusement would

---

39 Adam Hochschild, *King Leopold's Ghost: A Story of Greed, Terror, and Heroism in Colonial Africa* (London, UK: Pan Books, 2002), 4.

frequently appear in the eyes of interviewees. An army commander spent most of our meeting asking me what *I* thought of the Congo, trying to pry my prejudices out of me before he told me his story. "Everybody has an agenda," he told me. "What's yours?"[40]

This is what would seem to be an earnest attempt to express the concerns and perspectives of the Congolese that he interviewed. Interestingly, however, in the very next sentence he states,

A local, *illiterate* warlord with an amulet of cowries, colonial-era coins, and monkey skulls around his neck shook his head at me when I took his picture, telling me to erase it: "You're going to take my picture to Europe and show it to other white people. What do they know about my life?" He was afraid, he told me, that they would laugh at him, think he was a *macaque*, some forest monkey.[41]

The contradictions in Stearns' use of words are glaring. Why would Stearns begin his description of this man as an "illiterate warlord" if only to supposedly be presenting the man's statements for the purpose of garnering reader's sympathy toward his frustrations with how the Western world often misrepresents African people? Was it vital to the story that the man was illiterate? To that end, by what epistemological standard is Stearns measuring illiteracy? Clearly, Stearns had no trouble communicating with him and there's no indication that Stearns himself spoke the man's language. Also, was it really essential for Stearns to point out that the man was a warlord? Does it somehow lend some texture to the man's character? Or perhaps this was to somehow texturize Stearns' character that a supposed African "warlord," a word that sparks the ideas of aggressiveness and brutality in the popular imagination of the West, sat down to have a conversation with a "thirty-year old white American"?[42] The description of the Congolese man with cowries, coins and monkey skulls, also plays into the Eurocentric biases of Stearns as such description without any context is often an exercise in sensationalism. Stearns did not mention the manner of dress of the other individuals interviewed. Could this be because they were wearing European-standard attire? Paradoxically, later in the chapter Stearns critiques the caricatures created

---

40 Jason K. Stearns, *Dancing in the Glory of Monsters: The Collapse of the Congo and the Great War of Africa* (New York, NY: PublicAffairs, 2012), 1.
41 Ibid.
42 Ibid.

by Western news reports such as a "brutal African warlord with his savage soldiers."[43]

To be fair, Stearns' book does its best to center the narrative around the Congo and its war history. Nevertheless, it is ripe with Eurocentric interpretations while also veiled by the paradoxical innocence of white guilt. This is all the same for Burgis' *The Looting Machine*. Burgis opens the text with an author's note in which he presents a metaphor of seeing connecting threads of African oppression and European exploitation as an allegorical prop. Burgis had traveled to Jos, a city located in the middle belt of Nigeria, and witnessed a horrific scene of violence in which many men, women and children were murdered. He then states he suffered PTSD because "the ghosts of Jos" would "haunt" him. He would later come to the realization that his own guilt is what really haunted him. The guilt that he had survived as well as the guilt that such violence is perhaps, as Du Bois would put it, a "frightful paradox" that would see people like Burgis as "the foundation on which is built the poverty and degradation of the world."[44]

Burgis states he now sees "the thread that connects a massacre in a remote African village with the pleasures and comforts that we in the richer parts of the world enjoy."[45] Du Bois would help this statement further as he posits, "This is the modern paradox of Sin [...] a group, a nation or a race commits murder and rape, steals and destroys, yet no individual is guilty, no one is to blame, no one can be punished."[46] It can be certain, however, that the surviving people of Jos have for their lives been aware of the bloody ends of the threads that Burgis is only just aware of existing. Interestingly, we do not hear the voices of those men and women. In fact, other than that of major political figures, we don't hear the direct voices of any African person in Burgis' *Looting Machine*. We are given only the supposed moral strivings of an individual European plagued by white guilt due to the immoral European imperialist machine. The African is once again a prop on the literary stage of European conquest and domination of Africa. Furthermore, there is something to be said about the white gaze implicit in the scholarship of those such as Hochschild, Stearns and Burgis. Juxtaposed to the scholarship of Africologists, there is no praxis of liberation for African people.[47]

---

43 Ibid, 4.
44 Du Bois, *World and Africa*, 26.
45 Thomas Burgis, *The Looting Machine: Warlords, Tycoons, Smugglers, and the Systematic Theft of Africa's Wealth* (New York, NY: PublicAffairs, 2015), X.
46 Du Bois, *World and Africa*, 26.
47 Mazama, *Afrocentric paradigm*, 31.

To be sure, Burgis mentions major players of African politics such as Robert Mugabe and Joseph Kabila. He even mentions that he personally interviewed President Alpha Condé of Guinea as well as a few other African heads of state.[48] However, what Burgis is attempting presents some of the same conceptual issues as Du Bois and the dignified gentlemen of the first Pan-African Congress. How did the men Burgis interviewed view the "native" and uneducated in their homeland? As alluded, many leaders of African nations received a Western education and, thus, were socialized by Western norms. Would they not by virtue of their European education and, more specifically, Eurocentric socialization, be problematic as it came to the centering of African culture and perhaps even the culture of their very own ethnic groups?

This line of questioning may seem disjointed from the realities of social, political, and economic oppression suffered by African people. But it is actually right at the heart of the issue. Du Bois asked his readers, "What in reality is the nature of the catastrophe? To what pattern of human culture does it apply?" I argue, just as Du Bois alludes, that the pattern is that of Eurocentric cultural ethos and that white supremacy is nothing more than an invitation to a war over cultural domination. Europe is the architect of this war, and it is a war on their terms and by their measurement of what a war should be. Afrocentric theorists have however sought to assail this war effort by demanding and forcing others to acknowledge and act by our own terms and rules of engagement. The Africologists wish to level the playing field so that no cultural norm is more or less universally accepted than others. Therefore, the Africologist "does not seek hegemony; [we] seek pluralism without hierarchy."[49]

However, our positioning of this aim does not make the facts of war and the power of our opponents any less daunting. As for the texts I have sighted by the white scholars Stearns, Burgis and Hochschild, I use these to exemplify the nature of this cultural war. *The Looting Machine* was praised by the *New York Times* and won the top awards by organizations such as the *Financial Times*. *Dancing in the Glory of Monsters* also received critical acclaim by the *New York Times*, *Foreign Affairs* magazine, the *Wall Street Journal* and others. As of latest tallies taken in 2013, *King Leopold's Ghost*, by far the most popular book, has sold more than 600,000 copies worldwide and has been printed in over a dozen languages. This has certainly benefited the West's literary market as well as expanded interest in such investigative journalism on the plights

---

48 Burgis, *Looting Machine*, 145–189.
49 Asante, *Afrocentric Manifesto*, 111.

of Africans. Though, again, Africans are simply props in the narrative, and the white perspective on their stories are but ample commodities for Western consumption.

This type of desensitization to the plight of African people is no different than the ambivalence and ignorance of white beneficiaries of African exploitation and atrocity that Du Bois described in his day. Further still, there are those of mind to be sympathetic to human rights causes and yet at the same time paradoxically care nothing for the livelihood of African people. Du Bois describes one such figure, Jan Smuts, who had "declared that every white man in South Africa believes in the suppression of the Negro," and yet stood before the United Nations and "pleaded for an article on 'human rights' in the United Nations Charter."[50] This too is no different than the followers of former United States President Donald Trump who lionized him when he declared African countries are "shit-holes" and yet prayed alongside his spiritual advisor, Paula White-Cain, that "angels be dispatched from Africa" in order to bring Trump an election victory.

Thus, today we see the nature of this continuing cultural war. It is a war of attrition. One that sees Eurocentric hegemonic ideals shield itself under a veil of supposed *normal* universal humanism while it continuously, and from a range of vantage points, assaults the character of African culture and cosmology by presenting it as the antithesis of *normal* human idealism. This effectively makes it so that any perspective on African phenomena must center Eurocentric needs. As alluded, meeting those needs requires a matrix of cultural apologetics. This is displayed within the most obvious of racist and contradictory Eurocentric opinions, such as that of Smuts, and within the seemingly solicitous and profoundly influential work of scholars such as Hochschild. With Hochschild in mind, it would seem that his influential perspectives on the plights of African people were not influential enough to cause the Western world to offer much substantial assistance to those who are suffering in Africa.

To be sure, each year billions of dollars in aid from the United States is handed over to African governments. However, such seemingly limitless humanitarian aid has done more harm than good, largely benefiting only the leaders of neocolonial and oligarchic governments. One must question why it benefits a government such as the United States to send such huge funding to "shit-hole" countries. Not only (at least on the surface) does it not appear to benefit the United States, there is no indication the funding is working to stabilize the countries. Could it be that the goal is not to assist in the eventual

---

50 Du Bois, *World and Africa*, 27.

independence of African countries but to maintain Africa's dependence on the West? Zambian economist Dambisa Moyo insists that the West's aid has only created more corruption and fosters dependency and poor governance. In her widely circulated book, *Dead Aid*, Moyo states:

> [...] much of Africa has received aid continually for at least fifty years. Aid has been constant and relentless, and with no time limit to work against. Without the inbuilt threat that aid might be cut, and without the sense that one day it could all be over, African governments view aid as a permanent, reliable, consistent source of income and have no reason to believe that the flows won't continue into the indefinite future. There is no incentive for long-term financial planning, no reason to seek alternatives to fund development, when all you have to do is sit back and bank the cheques.[51]

It is true that African countries suffer from oligarchic regimes. However, as alluded, it is also true that the European world benefits from Africa's condition. I argue that the European world is able to accomplish this primarily because it has stifled the African world within a cultural war. It has turned the conscious minds of Africans against their own conscious and unconscious cosmologies, and the paradoxes this creates have left African people vulnerable for exploitation. In a related manner, this is true among the leadership of African nations as well as among African American leaders in America. Even some of the most fierce and celebrated African American leaders have been unwitting pawns in maintaining such order in the United States.

African people contend with not just opponents on another side of a field but also with witting and unwitting Eurocentrists in our midst. It is fair to argue that Du Bois, Nkrumah, Mandela, Martin Luther King, Jr., and others have, even in their most righteous of causes, made mistakes paramount to ethnic betrayal due to the entrapment of Western cultural ethos. Some of them, such as Du Bois, have even critiqued the processes that allow for such betrayal. It is interesting to note that Martin Luther King, Jr., for example, was assassinated just hours after he gave a speech in which he delivered his closest rhetorical stance yet toward economic Black nationalism. Nevertheless, African leaders may not have at all been aware of their betrayal in this cultural war. It is, after all, a muted, invisible war against cultural pluralism.

---

51 Dambisa Moyo, *Dead Aid: Why Aid Is Not Working and How There Is a Better Way for Africa* (New York, NY: Farrar, Straus and Giroux, 2009), 45.

The Western world has done well in masking the demarcating lines behind a veil of universal assumptions. But how is this done? I argue that the primary culprit is Western education.

Socialization by Education

In his analysis, Burgis lambasts Robert Mugabe, the former president of Zimbabwe. Mugabe was fortunate (or, unfortunate) enough to be born into a situation where he received education from Jesuit priests. As such, he would remain Catholic his entire life. Mugabe was a brilliant and highly inquisitive scholar and by the time he became the president of Zimbabwe he used that intelligence at his whim, implementing both beneficial and disastrous policies for the Zimbabwean people. To be sure, Mugabe was an adamant African nationalist and Pan-Africanist who vehemently fought against both imperialism and colonialism.[52] His rise to power and ideological stances were celebrated by many in the African world.

But Mugabe would receive millions of dollars in foreign aid, and a great deal of it being American dollars.[53] Not only that, Mugabe's administration also allowed the continuation of Western forms of education to permeate throughout the country. Surely one could argue that receiving education isn't inherently wrong, and they would be correct. However, we know that education is fundamentally a socializing phenomenon.[54] Most schools in Zimbabwe teach their children in English, particularly in urban areas. Even in rural areas where students are initially taught in their native tongue, English eventually becomes standard.[55] Though Shona is rightfully spoken throughout the country, the lingua franca is English.

But this is not just in Zimbabwe. Of the 54 countries in the African continent, 24 use English as either an official or de facto language of their country. Furthermore, English isn't the only European language in Africa that is spoken pervasively. French, for example, is also an official or de facto language in yet another twenty or more African countries. These languages are taught to

---

52 Asante, *History of Africa*, 367–372.
53 "History: Zimbabwe," U.S. Agency for International Development, February 5, 2020, https://www.usaid.gov/zimbabwe/history.
54 Asante, *Afrocentric Manifesto*, 79.
55 Tyanai Charamba and Davie E. Mutasa, "Challenging the Hegemony of English in African Education and Literature: The Case of Zimbabwe," *South African Journal of African Languages* 34, no. 2 (March 2014): 213–224, https://doi.org/10.1080/02572117.2014.997058.

African youth during their primary education and are used to relay all forms of information within the educational fields of mathematics, science, literature and art. If we broaden our scope to the African world, we may include those in the Spanish, English, French and Portuguese-speaking Caribbean, those in the South and North American continents, as well as those Africans dotted throughout Europe and other countries.

The importance of pointing out the imposition of European languages in regard to education is that language can ultimately be considered the primary vehicle of a people's culture. Through the dutiful scholarship of Oyèrónkẹ́ Oyěwùmí we have learned the cultural baggage that language carries with it, and particularly when it is forcefully imposed on others. In *The Invention of Women*, Oyěwùmí charges us to consider that "a people's language reflects their patterns of social interactions, lines of status, interests, and obsessions."[56] In the text, Oyěwùmí is primarily concerned with exposing the imposition of the Western concept of gender into Yorùbá society and largely via the English language. According to Oyěwùmí, prior to European encroachment, the Yorùbá regarded age distinctions as the primary organizing principle of society juxtaposed to gender.[57] Being clear about the role of education in this process, Oyěwùmí summarizes this issue effectively by stating:

> Yorùbá and English have been in close contact over the last one hundred and fifty years. Because of colonization and the imposition of English as the lingua franca of Nigeria, many Yorùbás are now bilingual. The impact of English on Yorùbá continues to be felt through loanwords, translation of Yorùbá culture into English, and the adoption of Western values. The role of the educational establishment is crucial in this process. Schooling and academic scholarship represent the most systematic ways in which Yoruba society and discourse are being gendered.[58]

To the Western mind, the idea of gender may seem innocuous. But for the Yorùbá it has damaged the character of their unique culture and continues to sow discord in contemporary relationships between men and women in the society who exist within this ever-contradictory bilingual space. The imposition of Euromodernity continues to circumvent progress toward an

---

56 Oyěwùmí Oyèrónkẹ́, *The Invention of Women: Making an African Sense of Western Gender Discourses* (Minneapolis, MN: University of Minnesota Press, 1997), 158.
57 Ibid.
58 Ibid, 158–159.

Afromodernity—one in which African people arrive at their modern humanity via African cultural agency. It should be clear then that European languages and education has done the same for other modes and expressions of people activity such as religion.

Christianity as Tool of Socialization

Europe has utilized Christianity as both a sword and as a shield in their efforts to subdue and acculturate all who they subjugate. Both on the African continent and abroad, education was first administered via missionaries. Through this process, missionaries would socialize generations of African students into accepting European cultural norms while at the same time demonizing African cultural norms. This has left the African world in disarray, and we have seen how this contradiction has affected the thoughts and actions of even many of the brightest and boldest Africans.

One can only wonder, who would Robert Mugabe have been without the imposition of Catholicism? What, perhaps, may have been the character of the nation of Zimbabwe if ruled by a Mugabe that valued the traditional spiritual systems of Zimbabwe as paramount? There is no doubting the psychological affliction suffered by African people by way of Christian missionaries and their duplicitous offerings of the life-improving benefits of education for nothing in exchange but their soul. However, one could only speculate the implications of Mugabe who focused more on the Hunhu/Ubuntu philosophy of his native Shona juxtaposed to that of Christian doctrine. Would the African nationalist have also been an African culturalist? Would he have sought to instill within his country the pride of the Shona reflected in the building of thousands of monuments to Shona's supreme deity, Mwari, instead of the building of churches dedicated to the God of foreigners? The question is important because, if language is the vehicle of culture, then spirituality and philosophy are often the routes for which this vehicle transports the expression of culture. This includes epistemological and pedagogical expression, or education, which was often passed down orally in many precolonial African societies.

This, of course, cannot all be placed on the shoulders of one man. After all, there were plenty of Christians in Mugabe's administration. The same can be said for other African heads of state, even those very highly revered such as Kwame Nkrumah and Thomas Sankara. They too were born and socialized into this colonial condition. But it is important to remember that the religion of a country, or its most exalted spiritual practice, often dictates its national and cultural character and will always have implications for how education is administered. This is much the same for Africans in the diaspora. Most of the greatest African leaders in the United States were men of Christian faith. Men such as the charismatic preacher who believed in African repatriation, Henry Highland Garnett, the so-called Father of Black Nationalism, Martin R. Delany, the Pan-Africanist Marcus Garvey, as well as the Civil Rights leader Martin Luther King, Jr. All of them were molded by Christian education in some form or fashion. Because of such contradictions in their ideologies about themselves, their culture and their people would arise.

The first of these men, Garnett, had enough agency to suggest to the enslaved Africans, "[…] hereditary bondsman, if you wish to be free, ye must first strike the blow," but at the same time conditioned enough to be elated to see England colonize Yorubaland under the pretense of *civilizing the natives*.[59] According to African American historian John Blassingame, in Garnett's time there were about one million African Americans, or roughly a quarter of the population in the country, attending regular church service.[60] By the time of King, however, the African American Christian population was significant enough to allow him to lead mass movements and base the purpose around Christian creeds. However, something interesting would occur in 1962 that would create a paradox between education and the de facto national religion.

The decision by the United States Supreme Court to take prayer out of schools in 1962 was filled with irony. One must consider that students were still subjected to taking the pledge of allegiance, in which one proclaimed that the United States was "one nation under God." Of course, there are those of Muslim, Buddhist and other cultural faiths and national affiliation who are afforded the option to opt out. But that only makes the point clearer. What informs the cultural and national character which espouses the epistemology, "one nation under God" (or, more specifically, the Jewish deity YHWH)? Why is the wording not one nation under Eshu? Or one nation united by Mwari? Naturally, the answer is that the foundational cultural paradigm of the United States is Anglo-Saxon which, like most European nations, have

---

59 Richard K. MacMaster, "Henry Highland Garnet and the African Civilization Society," *Journal of Presbyterian History* 48, no. 2 (June 1970): 95–112.

60 John W. Blassingame, *The Slave Community: Plantation Life in the Antebellum South*, Revised. (New York, NY: Oxford University Press, 1979), 97–98. Du Bois also mentions a comparable number for Africans in the South, stating that some 468,000 were church members; 250,000 were Methodist and 175,000 Baptist. See: W. E.B. Du Bois, *The Negro Church* (Atlanta, GA: Atlanta Univ. Press, 1903). For a more recent analysis of these figures see also: Michael A. Gomez, *Exchanging Our Country Marks the Transformation of African Identities in the Colonial and Antebellum South* (Chapel Hill, NC: Univ. of North Carolina Press, 1998).

adopted Christianity as their de facto national religion. Furthermore, "God" is an English term with a very ancient cultural history yet stems from an unknown Germanic origin.

The emotions of the Anglo-Saxon toward the word "God," or even the concepts it invoked in their minds, were powerful enough that it survived even the 1066 francophonization period of England. In using the word "God," we understand this most powerful being via the unique perspective of Anglo-Saxon cultural ethnocentrism. Therefore, it is steeped with thousands of years of cultural conceptual baggage that others must adopt by their very use of the term. Africans in the francophone world suffer similar ethnocentric subjectivities operating under the term "Dieu." Religion is embedded into the very heart of cultures and the nations they run are sociologically molded by the cosmologies they embody.

Therefore, the irony in removing prayer or religion from schools is that the very character of education in the United States rests upon religion. Weeks begin with Sunday, a day in which schools are closed primarily because of church services. For the child, the fact that schools are closed on this day for the purpose of attending church is innately an educational experience. Thus, the days considered days of rest are dictated by a religious perspective that sees Sunday begin the week as the holiest day and Saturday end the week as arguably the most secular day. Schools are also run, and classes are taught, by people who are overwhelmingly Christian. The ways in which teachers impart knowledge from their perspectives onto their students has implications for how students interpret historical, scientific and sociological data. Further, there are the students themselves who come from predominantly Christian homes and carry with them the presupposition of Christian attitudes. This is the character of the nation and such character conditions the development of the nation's educational system.[61]

Du Bois, of course, was no stranger to education, and especially by way of Christian conditioning. In fact, Du Bois was an adamant churchgoer as a child.[62] But events would come about in his life that would by his 1940 autobiographical work, *Dusk of Dawn*, make him state that he was "critical of religion and resentful of its practice."[63] One of these events occurred while he was a student at Fisk. He had joined the congregational church at Fisk not long before he and several other younger members were "accused

---

61 Asante, *Afrocentric Manifesto*, 83.
62 W. E.B. Du Bois, *Dusk of Dawn: An Essay Toward an Autobiography of a Race Concept*, ed. Henry Louis Gates (New York, NY: Oxford University Press, 2007), 16–17.
63 Ibid, 17.

before the church for dancing."[64] Dancing, and dancing in spiritual and religious celebration, is a natural custom of those of African heritage. But many African American Christians of varying denominations had allowed the Eurocentric view of dancing being a gateway to "sin" to prevail over the African heritage of dance. Therefore, the contradiction they foresaw was solved by demonizing their inherent cultural practices.

To further this point on the Black Church and the demonization and suppression of their own Africanity, there is an early example of this contradiction that is quite obvious within the writings of Bishop Daniel Alexander Payne. Payne was an educator and devout Christian who helped shape the early African Methodist Episcopal Church. In 1878, ten years before Du Bois would graduate from Fisk, Payne visited Philadelphia to attend a church service that he would later describe as a "bush meeting." Payne would bemoan, "after the sermon they formed a ring, and with coats off sung, clapped their hands and stamped their feet in a most ridiculous and heathenish way."[65] Payne was so angered by the Africanity displayed in such a ritual that he immediately forced the people before him to stop before demanding that their leader encourage his congregation to worship "in a rational manner" as this was "a heathenish way to worship and disgraceful to themselves, the race, and the Christian name."[66] Payne's indictment is an interesting contradiction as he takes prideful membership in a denomination which bears first in its name the recognition that its congregants are African, yet he despises and demonizes any display of Africanity. Payne would also eventually become the first president of Wilberforce College, and during his tenure oversaw the education of many African Americans who attended this Historical Black College.[67] Payne exemplifies the paradox created by the interplay of Western religion and education in the socialization of African people.

Warring Cultures

The Eurocentric indoctrination both in Africa and the diaspora is so damning upon our psychology one would be made to think, like Payne, that to be an African who does not "disgrace" his race one must not behave like an African. Though, perhaps not consciously considered by Payne and others,

---

64 Du Bois, *Autobiography of W.E.B. Du Bois,* 110–111.
65 Gomez, *Exchanging Our Country Marks,* 269.
66 Ibid.
67 Ibid.

the natural antithesis of behaving as an African in their setting would be to behave as a European would. This unconscious adoption of Eurodominant behavior is accomplished primarily by creating a social atmosphere by which the Eurocentric standards of people activity in education, religion, art, science and industry are presented as the universal standards of humanity. But, as aforementioned several times, the truth of the matter is that these standards are simply an amalgam of European cultural subjectivity.[68] This, of course, can only be maintained as long as Europe remains in power. So long as the United States continues to maintain its status as the master of industry and militarism as well as the hypocritical voice of moral democracy, Europe shall remain in power. Though this too counts on the ability of Britain to maintain its regal status as progenitor of Westernity, and it, as well as the other colonial powers, such as France, Spain, Portugal and Germany, continue to hold on to the wealth they have plundered and continue to plunder from Africa and the rest of the world. Therefore, as alluded, the war over resources and the war of cultures are intricately linked.

But Du Bois predicted that the European world is in the midst of collapse. I argue that he is still correct and yet that the collapse is slow, but ongoing. What Du Bois did not live to see, but has remained a soothsayer in his arguments of a collapsing Europe, are the events leading up to the present day. Since his death there have been several significant events that prove a languishing European world and the loosening of its grip over the African world. This includes the continuation of African independence movements that had begun nearly a decade prior to Du Bois' death with the independence of modern Sudan and Ghana as well as the ongoing internal issues within the European world.

The ending of the so-called Cold War was significant. But the escalation of the political rivalry between Russia and the United States and the European Union has resulted in a similar so-called Second Cold War. In America, there is an education crisis arguably brought on by the measures set forth during Reagan's administration which limited funding to education. The recent Brexit ordeal was interesting, as dissenting views from Northern Ireland continue to grow, and an increasing pool of young adult voters who oppose the measure call for reentering the European Union. There is also the fact that another global pandemic, exactly one hundred years after the end of the last, has since March 2020 caused great discord. Finally, it appears, having

---

68 Asante, *Afrocentric Idea*, 1.

already just recently recovered from a recession, the West may well be on the eve of another global economic crisis.

However, perhaps the most glaring visual affront to the superiority of whiteness was the fact that for eight years the most powerful position in the world was held by a man of African heritage named Barack Hussein Obama. Naturally, one could make valid arguments that Obama, in his capacity as the United States President, piloted the very vessel that has for decades been the flagship of white supremacy. Nevertheless, it cannot be denied that no president and presidential family before him has received as much vitriol both within the United States and abroad.[69] I argue that the very image of an African man sitting at the helm of world politics placed fear in the faith of European civilization and exacerbated the type of xenophobic reactions we have seen, for example, in the Brexit affair or the efforts by the Trump administration to have a wall built along Mexico's border.

Trump also limited or outright restricted immigration from African nations like Nigeria, while supporting the flux of immigrants from European countries. These types of reactions will only continue as the population of European nations continues to see stifled numbers among whites and increasing birth numbers among other ethnicities. In the United States, we are already seeing that a majority of states are dealing with the reality of fewer births than deaths among white people.[70] This is also an increasing trend across most of Europe.[71]

Nevertheless, as the trend of Europe's collapse continues and Europe eventually falls, they may yet still win the cultural war. Again, this cultural war has been a war of attrition. Europe has used its arsenal of psychological warfare to whittle away at the Africanity of African people just as fervently as it has used physical warfare to whittle away at Africa's mineral resources. What if, for example, white people in the United States disappear tomorrow and African Americans magically find themselves controlling every aspect of governance? Would that version of the nation be any less different than the one Whites controlled? One can argue that African Americans would champion "Black issues" such as legalizing reparations or reforming the criminal justice

---

69 See: Molefi Kete Asante, *Lynching Barack Obama: How Whites Tried to String up the President* (Brooklyn, NY: Universal Write Publications, 2016).
70 Sabrina Tavernise, "Fewer Births Than Deaths Among Whites in Majority of U.S. States," *The New York Times*, June 20, 2018, https://www.nytimes.com/2018/06/20/us/white-minority-population.html.
71 Matt Broomfield, "The Research That Shows Europe Can't Be Getting 'Full'," The Independent (Independent Digital News and Media, January 16, 2016), https://www.independent.co.uk/news/world/europe/more-people-europe-are-dying-being-born-research-finds-a6816651.html.

system. Perhaps even the aesthetics of Blackness would be more visible at the federal level by way of art and music.

However, what would be the core ethos in which African Americans will operate? What will be the character of the nation? Will English still be considered the standard language and Ebonics inferior? Would the nation continue to exploit the African world for resources? Will the Englishman's suit still be considered the revered attire for doing business? Will European classical music still be considered the standard of music theory? I argue that to effectively create, as Frantz Fanon gave us the language to describe, black skins in white masks is the lasting legacy of the Eurocentric Masquerade on African people. Its final act would see that the absence of white people will not necessarily mean the absence of whiteness.

Furthermore, when America does fall, who then are African Americans without America? If that title is taken to mean that our ethnic identity is African and our national citizenship is American, then would we not at such a time simply be Africans? What then would it mean to be an African person in a world without the American plantation? I argue that the fundamental answers to these questions lie buried deep within the history of what occurred prior to the formation of the West at the expense of the African world. As alluded, the "rape of Africa," as Du Bois put it, was not simply the ravishing of Africa's resources, it also sowed within African people the seeds of Eurosupremacy and African inferiority. Du Bois bemoans this reality when he states:

> With all this went the fall and disruption of the family, the deliberate attack upon the ancient African clan by missionaries. The invading investors who wanted cheap labor at the gold mines, the diamond mines, the copper and tin mines, the oil forests and cocoa fields, followed the missionaries. The authority of the family was broken up; the authority and tradition of the clan disappeared; the power of the chief was transmuted into the rule of the white district commissioner. The old religion was held up to ridicule, the old culture and ethical standards were degraded or disappeared, and gradually all over Africa spread the inferiority complex, the fear of color, the worship of white skin, the imitation of white ways of doing and thinking, whether good, bad, or indifferent. By the end of the nineteenth century the degradation of Africa was as complete as organized human means could make it. Chieftains, representing a thousand years of striving human culture, were decked out in second-hand London top-hats, while Europe snickered.[72]

---

72 Du Bois, *World and Africa*, 49.

Du Bois was heading in the right direction when he thought the best course of action was to "appeal to the past in order to explain the present."[73] Though But Du Bois is missing something in his analysis. Something that is obvious enough that he mentions it himself yet neglects to fully delve into the implications. He mentions the disruption of the African family by missionaries, the plundering of Africa's mineral wealth that was so valued by the people, and the demonization of African religion, corporeal aesthetics and philosophy. He also gave us an anecdote which exemplifies the Eurocentric Masquerade when he states that the regal African chieftains, who represented thousands of years of African culture, were now wearing secondhand European clothing "while Europe snickered." This is the very essence of the cultural war. But what did Du Bois fail to provide? As aforementioned, he failed to provide a cultural-historical matrix in which to anchor his contentions. Providing a history of African achievements may provide pride in a bygone past, but it does little to connect the history in such a way that people of African descent, especially African Americans, realize an ontology and cosmology based on their Africanity.

Du Bois somewhat alludes to understanding this as he laments that African people "lost in modern thought their history and cultures."[74] He is essentially lamenting the loss of African paradigms that would have informed an Afromodernity. I contend that it is the Afrocentric reclamation of that history and culture which will provide the paradigms needed for our Afromodernity. It is through the rediscovery and reforming of African cosmology, being the history, philosophy, religion, motifs and aesthetics of African people, that we unmask and defeat the Eurocentric Masquerade and truly bring about a world of cultural pluralism. To be clear, it is not as if African culture is destroyed. An Afromodernity does exist in various fashions. However, it is often entrapped in the lowest rung of hierarchical cultural modernisms. Nevertheless, traditions, though often in vestige, do remain. It is only a matter of piecing together what Marimba Ani refers to as the *asili*, or "the germinating matrix," of African culture.[75] This is done by looking to the past for, according to Du Bois, "[…] the past is the present […] without what *was*, nothing *is*."[76]

Therefore, in the next three chapters I shall analyze Du Bois' *The World and Africa* and bring it into conversation with contemporary scholarship on

---

73 Ibid, 50.
74 Ibid.
75 Ani, *Yurugu*, 498.
76 Du Bois, *World and Africa*, 50.

African history and culture. In connecting past and present cultural ontology, people of African descent can today identify ourselves in modern speech patterns, art, religiosity and various other expressions of Africanity. Therefore, in my analysis of the various African societies and ethnic groups Du Bois covers in his *The World and Africa*, I utilize my own AWAM to compare various African cultural phenomena. In the next two chapters, I will apply this methodology in ways that exemplifies how scholars may build upon how we understand the African cultural-historical matrix. I will later in this text suggest the implications for functionalizing the data embedded in this historical-cultural matrix by actively positioning African cultural phenomena as paradigms for the purpose of cultural restoration and cultural maintenance.

Chapter 2

DU BOIS ON AFRICAN HISTORY AND CLASSICAL ANTECEDENTS

Du Bois and Africa

The fields of social science and humanities in the Western world developed with inherent biases about the hierarchical nature of civilizations, cultures, languages, and customs. Du Bois, though he was trained by the West, appears to have some appreciation of this fact as he writes *The World and Africa*. However, there are a number of things that Africologists recognize today as *Agency Reduction Formations* that Du Bois did not have the theoretical foundation necessary to pinpoint as such.[1] Nevertheless, his insight on the reduction of African agency was still profound. Recall, he once stated of an increasingly colonized Africa, "By the end of the nineteenth century the degradation of Africa was as complete as organized human means could make it."[2]

It is apparent that Du Bois understood that Europe, through power and force, had positioned itself as the superior culture between itself and Africa. Du Bois would state, "A system at first conscious and then unconscious of lying about history and distorting it to the disadvantage of the Negroids became so widespread that the history of Africa ceased to be taught," and that "every effort was made in archaeology, history, and biography, in biology, psychology, and sociology, to prove the all but universal assumption that the color line had a scientific basis."[3] This "color line" would be famously voiced by Du

---

1 Africologist Michael Tilltson defines Agency Reduction Formations as, "any system of thought that distracts, neutralizes, or reduces the need and desire for assertive collective agency for African Americans." Though Tillotson applied this specifically to African Americans, it is likewise applicable to all persons of African descent. For an in-depth explication of *Agency Reduction Formations* see: Michael Tillotson, *Invisible Jim Crow: Contemporary Ideological Threats to the Internal Security of African Americans* (Trenton, NJ: Africa World Press, 2011).
2 Du Bois, *World and Africa*, 49.
3 Ibid, 13–14.

Bois as the primary issue of the twentieth century. Many attribute the notion of the "color line" to arguments for social justice measures intended to bring about equal treatment and socioeconomic conditions among those of African and European descent.

However, Du Bois may have meant something a bit more than social justice. I argue that in this text, *The World and Africa*, Du Bois, despite his aforementioned ideological shortcomings, is actually advocating for cultural justice. Du Bois argues, and I agree, that the European world has distorted the facts of history in order to misattribute upon itself all notions of human technological advancement and intellectual heritage. As Du Bois put it, "Without the winking of an eye, printing, gunpowder, the smelting of iron, the beginnings of social organization, not to mention political life and democracy, were attributed exclusively to the white race and to Nordic Europe."[4]

This *eurocentric masquerade* has done its job at standardizing ways of knowing under a type of false universalism. This universalism, a set of Eurocentric subjectivity, always places Europe as hierarchically preeminent. But it is quite simply only by deception and force that such could be the case. Du Bois exhibited his understanding of this when he derided the British's disgraceful deeds against Ethiopia, particularly the acts of Herbert Kitchener, decrying, "Everywhere is this sordid tale of deception, force, murder, and final subjection."[5] This statement is quite poignant as it illuminates a very clear pattern. As shall be discussed in later chapters, European nations came to African shores first with the promise of friendship and mutual partnership. This, we know well today, to have been a bed of lies and deception that they persuaded African monarchs to lie in. As the Europeans slowly learned the geopolitics of the various African nations they encountered, they began to plot and implement forceful measures to bring various nations under their control. This would most often result in revolt and retaliation from African nations, leading to the mass murder of African people. I should be clear here that Africa may have been taken by force, but it was not at all easy for Europeans to do so. Du Bois would note that the Asante, for example, fought six wars with the British between 1803 and 1874, and were not officially defeated until 1894, after nearly a century of war.[6]

In fact, despite the use of early gunpowder weapons that Europeans may have thought would give them tactical advantage, many African nations held their own in war against European forces, some even well into the early

---

4 Ibid, 14.
5 Ibid, 21.
6 Ibid, 102.

twentieth century. The slow loading time of early gunpowder weapons, such as European muskets for example, which were though quite powerful at killing, many times proved largely ineffective at defeating the well-trained military units of various African nations. However, by the closing of the nineteenth century, more advanced weapons such as rapid-fire rifles and machine guns would give Europeans the edge.[7] Thus, by the late nineteenth and early twentieth century subjugation and colonization were well on their way to being the norm in Africa for decades to come.

When discussing African history, Du Bois' statement that the "old [African] religion was held up to ridicule" is one worth noting. It is understood that a society's religious or spiritual foundations prove essential for the national character of a people. Various epistemologies form around spirituality. The ways in which people develop their historical narratives and the systems in which they use to chronologize them are often dictated by spiritual foundations. In Kemet, for example, the new year, or *wepet renpet*, which occurred around June or July, was associated with the deity Ausar, as he represented, among other things, cycles of death and rebirth observed in nature. To be more specific, he represented the annual flooding and receding of the Nile which was signaled by the heliacal rising and reappearance of the star, Sepdet, known today as Sirius.[8] However, due to the influence of foreign religios, particularly the Abrahamic variety, New Year's in modern Egyptian society conforms to the honoring of non-African deities and religious figures. This is important to consider when placing forth a narrative of African history. It is something that Du Bois himself was seemingly on the precipice of understanding yet failed to execute in his analysis.

Chronology and Christendom

There is much work to be done in order to create a truly Afrocentric historiography. To begin a history on Africa from an Afrocentric perspective, several assumptions must be investigated. The first issue that must be examined is the paradigm of chronological dating that is used to write such history. Specifically, the most commonly used system of dating, the Gregorian calendar, revolves around the idea of European superiority that is maintained

---

7 See: Bruce Vandervort, *Wars of Imperial Conquest in Africa: 1830-1914* (London, UK: UCL Press, 1998). Also, a well-documented example of this is the massacre of the Herero by German troops. See: Timothy Joseph Stapleton, *A Military History of Africa*, vol. 2 (Santa Barbara, CA: Praeger, 2013), 108–111.
8 Asante, *History of Africa*, 36–37.

largely by perpetrating their religious values on others. For example, in the West, discussions about ancient civilizations are most often done within the calendarial framework which bifurcates historical events based on the alleged existence of the biblical figure, Jesus. Du Bois begins his chapter on Kemet by stating that human culture had "begun more than four thousand years before Christ."[9]

We must ask the question, historically, who is this Christ to the African world? Why is it that we center this mythological deity as the beginning and ending of an age above or juxtaposed to African deities such as Maat, Het-Heru, Ausar, Shango, Legba, Oshun and Oya? This is something perhaps Du Bois began to wrestle with near the end of his life. Just two years after the publication of *The World and Africa*, a correspondence with a Christian priest revealed that Du Bois did not believe in "a person of vast power who consciously rules the universe for the good of mankind," but perhaps rather "a vague force which, in some uncomprehensible way, dominates all life and change."[10] This theory of a "vague force" flies in the face of world chronology as developed by Christendom, which positions the absolute existence of a patriarchal God, Son, and Holy Ghost as the metaphorical hallmarks of Primordial, Classical and Modern time.

Du Bois would express that "a nation's religion is its life," and, "as such, white Christianity is a miserable failure."[11] To that end, the father of Afrocentricity, Molefi Kete Asante, expresses that "Europe spoke of itself as Christendom and when it did, Christendom was seen as being superior to all other religious communities."[12] This religious superiority complex, coupled with the history of colonialism, emboldened Europe to establish the nature of time for all people as they saw fit. Thus, we have come to accept notions such as "prehistoric" and "pre-civilization" in regard to the history of a people in which no written documents have been discovered. This has perpetuated the lie of racial inferiority. As it relates to African people, many African cultures use orature, which is a type of performance with oral narration that serves the purpose of recording and passing down historical events. The issues presented by Christendom as well as the importance of orature will be discussed in subsequent chapters.

However, I bring attention to this now because any history written by someone trained in the Western academy will be rife with these biases, rather

---

9 Du Bois, *World and Africa*, 63.
10 Phil Zuckerman, ed., *Du Bois on Religion* (Walnut Creek, CA: Altamira Press, 2000), 8.
11 Ibid, 11.
12 Asante, *Afrocentric Manifesto*, 59.

they be conscious or unconscious of them. Du Bois was, of course, no exception to this conditioning. However, an Afrocentric historiography must seek to either create or revive a system of chronology that centers African cultural-historical agency. A methodology for this operation is not currently within the scope of our frame of work. But, until one has been developed, it must nonetheless continue to be considered. Nevertheless, I do not in this text use the Western conventions of BC for "before Christ," or AD, meaning *anno Domini*, Latin for "year of our Lord," in which to discuss African history. I do, however, with a great deal of caution, use BCE, or "Before Common Era," and CE for "Common Era" as a measure of dating. This, of course, still in some ways adheres to the conventions of Christendom, but I prefer their secularity in usage juxtaposed to the invocation of a Eurasian deity. I also use the conventions *kya* and *ybp* for "thousands of years ago" and "years before present" respectively.

Du Bois on the Peopling of Africa

Du Bois begins his chapter on the peopling of Africa by referring to "seers," assuredly scientists of that time, who had measured the Earth to be billions of years old and had discovered that insects, reptiles, and mammals have been roaming the African continent for tens of millions of years.[13] He sides with Charles Darwin that the cradle of humankind is indeed the African continent, a fact that has in recent decades been borne by the consensus of scientific evidence.[14] Du Bois would have been 14 at the death of Darwin but his book, *On the Origin of Species by Means of Natural Selection, or the Preservation of Favoured Races in the Struggle for Life*, remained popular as well as sparked the Social Darwinism movement within the social sciences, which arguably could have influenced even some of Du Bois' earlier thinking.[15]

---

13 Du Bois, *World and Africa*, 52–54.
14 See: Asante, *History of Africa*, 1–12.
15 Unfortunately, Du Bois and Charles Darwin share another ideological link in eugenics. Those who subscribe to eugenics principally believe that one may improve the gene pool of humanity by excluding those thought to have adverse or undesirable genes. While Charles Darwin died before the eugenics movement took form, his works were a major influence on this movement. In fact, Darwin's son, Leonard Darwin, was once chair of the British Eugenics Society, now known as the Galton Institute, which in turn is named after Leonard and Charles' cousin, Francis Galton, the father of eugenics. However, by the writing of *The World and Africa*, Du Bois seems to have abandoned the ideas of eugenics and his own theory on the talented tenth. His 1948 essay, "The Guiding Hundredth," a deep revision of "The Talented Tenth," was a treatise on cultural solidarity with other groups and a focus less so on the intellectual

Though dubious, Du Bois accepted racial classification based on the shape and structure of skulls.[16] He makes several mentions of classifications such as *Negroids*, which he referred to as, "long-headed dark people with more or less crinkled hair." He also refers to *Mongoloids* as "broad-headed yellow people," and *Caucasoids* as a possible mixture of Negroids and Mongoloids, being "possibly formed by their union, with bleached skins and intermediate hair."[17] There is even mention of *Negrillos*, those of whom are today pejoratively referred to as pygmies. Du Bois describes this group as, "small men with reddish-brown hair or dark skin and brachiocephalic [small] heads."[18] These classifications, though, again, dubious, are however indicative of the times in which he lived and Du Bois himself seemed keenly aware of their dubiousness as he acknowledges that "no scientifically accurate definition of these races could be made which would leave most of mankind outside the limits."[19] Thus, with a great deal of caution, he continues to use these throughout the remainder of the chapters on African history.

As aforementioned, Du Bois' inclinations about Africa as the origin of humanity continue to hold truth. For 1946, he was ahead of many social and even natural scientists of his day. However, perhaps one could argue that Du Bois' bias toward African people could have pointed him toward this truth as much as his attempts at objectiveness. Regardless, he did not give in to the repetitive attacks of his day that would argue that anything the West considers indicative of civilization in Africa must have come from some foreign source. Though he used the classifications of Negroid, Mongoloid and Caucasoid, he denounced the idea that there was a "Negro" race that only achieved greatness when mixed with a mythical "Hamitic race."[20]

Du Bois argues, justifiably, that over five thousand years ago the people of the North African coast were identical with the early inhabitants of Kemet. He argues further that the people of East Africa offer a mostly tall and slender variety of people of African stock, some perhaps with admixtures of Asian

---

prowess of various group leaders, but more so on the moral character of those called to leadership (see: Reiland Rabaka, Against Epistemic Apartheid: W.E.B. Du Bois and the Disciplinary Decadence of Sociology (Lanham, MD: Lexington Books, 2010). I would argue that perhaps this evolution in thinking softened his views on the so-called African *natives* and at the same time enriched his Pan-African politics by allowing himself to appreciate the potential in various groups of African and African diaspora people.

16 Du Bois, *World and Africa*, 56.
17 Ibid, 54–55.
18 Ibid, 61.
19 Ibid, 74.
20 Ibid, 58.

blood. Those in West Africa he states are, again, tall, but darker in skin tone. He is curious about the Fulani, who he states are mixed "perhaps with Asiatic blood."[21] He states this of the Fulani because of their lighter skin and looser hair coils in comparison to other groups in the region. We know today that the Fulani are overwhelmingly African, but they may have however received some Eurasian admixture by way of their contact with the Tuareg and other Amazigh groups during their conversion to Islam in the seventeenth century.[22]

Nevertheless, he identifies the peoples in the Gulf of Guinea, immediately to the south of the Fulani, as distinguishable by their languages, particularly Twi, Ga, and Ewe. These belong to the "Ashanti, moderately tall men, long-headed with some broad heads; the Dahomey, tall, long-headed and black; the Yoruba, including the peoples of Benin and Ibo, dark brown or black, closely curled hair, moderate dolichocephaly [elongated-heads] and broad-nosed. Their lips are thick and sometimes everted, and there is a considerable amount of prognathism [protruding jaw]. The Kru, hereditary sailors, are typically Negroid with fine physiques. The Hausa of central Sudan are very black and long-headed but not prognathic and with thin noses."[23] There is a brief discussion of KhoiKhoi, of whom he refers to as the so-called Hottentot, as well as the San, who were known as Bushmen. I should note that these terms, Hottentot and Bushmen, are pejoratives that derive from the Dutch Boers.

Du Bois ends his description of the peoples of Africa with a short note on the Bantu. He identifies four major groups of the Bantu in South Africa: the Shona, the Zulu-Xhosa, the Suto-Chwana [Soto-Tswana] and the Herero-Ovambo. The Bantu, of course, are largely identified by their close linguistic similarities. However, in recent decades we have come to discover that both the Bantu and the Niger-Sudanic languages make up one phylum commonly referred to as Niger-Congo languages.[24] It is interesting that he begins his description of Bantu languages in the west with Cameroon as we have come to discover that it is from southern Cameroon that the Bantu expansion began as early as 3000 BCE.[25] He would then describe the Bantu of Equatorial Guinea, Gabon, Congo, Angola, Zambia and modern Zimbabwe (which at that time was Rhodesia).

---

21 Ibid, 60.
22 Shillington, *History of Africa*, 4th ed., 249.
23 Du Bois, *World and Africa*, 60.
24 Christopher Ehret, *History and the Testimony of Language* (Berkeley, CA: University of California Press, 2011), 121–122.
25 Ibid, 122, 151.

The reasoning behind the effort of Du Bois to list these principal groups in the African continent he makes clear by referring back to the notion of a single "Negro type." His intention is to show that the people of Africa are just as varied as those in Europe or Asia. This is an ideal goal as it is certainly important to show that the African people are not a phenotypically and socially monolithic people and what exists among them is a varied and dynamic culture. However, this analysis is also a bit incomplete. I argue that along with allotting these groups the agency of individual identities, Du Bois could have also just as easily stressed the close relationship between many of these groups using the same linguistic and ethnographic data. Some of which may come off as apparent in the general outline he provides, but there is no attentiveness on the part of Du Bois to make sure that this is clear to his readers.

The importance of such here is that Du Bois is, as aforementioned, attempting to pen a history of Africa that not only illustrates the complexity and humanity of African people, but also justifies his political motivations for Pan-Africanism. I continue to argue that Pan-Africanism cannot be based simply on African struggles against Western domination, though that is a major reality. In my estimation, Pan-Africanism should indeed be viewed as an imperative because of the current reality of struggle against Western domination, but also, and most importantly, considered a sacred charge for people of African descent based on historical-cultural ties and the collective will to continue the African cultural project. This collective will should not be based on the activities and will of outsiders. Just as Du Bois in his earlier chapter was clear, though perhaps unwittingly, about the Pan-European cultural connections involving various nations such as Germany, Russia, England, France and others, his basis for Pan-Africanism, I argue, must illustrate the cultural connections between African people. To be sure, as early as *The Negro*, Du Bois made brief mention of what he perceived as the phenomena of cultural continuity. However, without a theoretical paradigm to base this cultural continuity, Du Bois presents these cultural phenomena in sometimes troubling ways.

For example, continuing with *The Negro*, in the chapter "West Indies and Latin America," he quotes Hurbert Aime's "African Institutions in America," suggesting, quite Eurocentrically, that Dessalines supposedly inherited the "despotic" political systems of African chiefs.[26] Du Bois also makes mention of polygamy and postulates, again quite Eurocentrically, its supposed relationship with the rise of sexual promiscuity among the enslaved Africans in

---

26 W. E. B. Du Bois, *The Negro* (Philadelphia, PA: University of Pennsylvania Press, 2001), 174.

the Americas. He also argues that certain spiritual elements saw cultural continuity such as Obeah worship.[27] In later chapters of *The World and Africa* Du Bois describes war, peace, alliances and struggles of various African groups in relation to each other but fails to fully explore or extrapolate from the cultural matrices these types of relationships form. In both texts, Du Bois provides similar shallow attempts at historicizing social relationships between Africans and African Americans, but offers no analysis of how these interactions have, for example, shaped modern African civilization or formed the cultural foundations of African Americans in ways that could provide any solid cultural basis for Pan-African unity.

Du Bois on Kemet

Like many historians and social scientists of his day, as well as a great majority today, Du Bois refers to Kemet as ancient Egypt. However, I argue that these terms should always be distinguished by two eras of indigenous and then foreign governance. Kemet, or "the Black nation," as distinguished by the symbols "to darken/Black" and "nation" in the mdw ntr, is the land occupied and governed by the indigenous people of that region in north-east Africa. The term "Egypt" is Greek and should only refer to the time period of foreign Greco-Roman rule and perhaps as a symbol of their occupation thereafter. For the purposes of this text, I will use the term "Kemet" where Du Bois often applies the usage of Egypt. Similarly, I also refer to the so-called region of Ethiopia and to Ethiopians as Kush and Kushites, respectively.

In Du Bois' discussion on the racial identity of the people of Kemet, he insists that the European Trade of Enslaved Africans is the primary justification for the European world to label the people of Kemet as racially "white." In the words of Du Bois, "It was due to the fact that the rise and support of capitalism called for rationalization based upon degrading and discrediting the Negroid peoples."[28] Du Bois finds it of great interest that the field of Egyptology came to prominence at the height of American slavery. However, with evidence of their racialization to the contrary, Du Bois would submit, "We may then without further ado ignore this verdict of history, widespread as it is, and treat Egyptian history as an integral part of African history."[29]

Du Bois is very clear that the Kemetic people are members of the African race. Of course, we may understand the notion of race today to be unfitting,

---

27 Ibid, 189.
28 Du Bois, *World and Africa*, 64.
29 Ibid.

it is clear that the cultural foundations of the people of Kemet are indeed what we would call African. It is interesting that Du Bois states of the Kemetic people, "Probably they came up from Nubia."[30] He describes the modern-day Beja as "the modern representatives of the old predynastic Egyptian stock," and particularly the Hadendoa, who Du Bois explains were mocked as the "Fuzzy Wuzzy" by British soldiers during the late nineteenth-century Mahdist War. They were referred to as such because of their coarse and curly hair that was often grown out into a hairstyle known as *tiffa*. Du Bois would state that it is Kemet that "set the pace" for the human endeavors of government, defense, family, property, science, art and religion.

Kemetic religion, Du Bois would argue, "came naturally from the primitive animism of the African forest and progressed to the worship of Ra, the sun god, giver of life and beauty to the Nile valley which was the world." It is curious that Du Bois interprets cosmological developments based on the African forest as "primitive" and the spiritual interpretations of which as "animism." Certainly, one could argue that much of African culture, even before the formation of Kemet, came from inner Africa which would constitute the forest areas. However, Du Bois is perhaps also projecting his own biases toward the legitimacy of African religion and that of the "primitive" culture stemming from the *native* forests. The use of animism often denotes the belief that what is being practiced is uncivilized and occult; one in which those involved are unable to distinguish the supposed natural hierarchy between people, animals and inanimate objects. Africologists should be wary of such Eurocentric characterizations that reduce the agency of African people, particularly in this case African spirituality and cultural cosmology. This line of erroneous thinking helps legitimize in the minds of the West the aforementioned chronology issue; bifurcating what is old and new timelines and old and new realities based on the hierarchical positioning of the religion of the European world.

Du Bois is quick to point out that women in Kemet had from the earliest of times, "singular prominence and power" and refers to the Kemetic Goddess Auset, whom the Greeks refer to as Isis, as "the Black woman." Again, he is doubling down on the race issue, being clear that in his interpretation of the facts, the people of Kemet were African people and categorically Black people by contemporary racial standards. He makes this even clearer when he states, "They themselves were brown and black and so depicted themselves on their monuments."[31] Though he does also suggest that many Asiatic peo-

---

30 Ibid, 65.
31 Ibid, 66–67.

ple drifted in from the east and mixed with the populations both in Kemet as well as North Africa in general, Du Bois would contextualize the issue of race in Kemet as such:

> It would be interesting to know what the Egyptians, earliest of civilized men, thought of the matter of race and color. Of race in the modern sense, they seemed to have had no conception. On their monuments they depicted peoples by the color of their skin and their hair. The hair was treated in many ways: sometimes it was straight and Mongoloid; perhaps more often it was curled and Negroid. Now and then it was curly and hidden by wigs. The Egyptians painted themselves usually as brown, sometimes dark brown, sometimes reddish-brown. Other folk, both Egyptians and non-Egyptians, were painted as yellow. Often brown Egyptians were coupled with yellow women, either signifying less exposure to the sun or intermarriage with Mongoloids and whites. A few were painted as white, referring to some parts of North Africa and Europe.[32]

It is important that Du Bois notes that the Kemetic people had no conception of race in the modern sense. But he goes on to explain that if there be any sense of hierarchical separation in Kemet it would have been by cultural status. This is important because while there were cohesive cultural foundations in Kemet, which can be most readily exemplified by an interrogation of the spoken language, ciKam, there also existed cultural diversity between regions.[33] Those groups stemming from Upper Kemet, or what the Western world would consider Kemet's southern region, were perhaps the most important to consider in Kemetic history as much of Kemetic culture came from inner Africa. In fact, during times of turmoil it would often be the Upper Kemetic royal families living in or near Waset, or what the Greeks called Thebes, who expelled foreigners and reunited the nation. One of those times, and perhaps more may come to light when the material record allows, we even saw Kemet reunited and under the vassal-ship of Kush, the Nubian nation which existed outside of the borders of Upper Kemet. Du Bois would continue his description of the people of Kemet with this understanding in mind:

---

32 Ibid, 67.
33 Asante, *History of Africa*, 40–42.

The separation of human beings by color seemed to have had less importance among the Egyptians than the separation by cultural status: black Pharaohs and black women; brown and yellow Pharaohs and yellow women. Their attitude toward people, white or black, was based on cultural contact. Black people and yellow people were often depicted as conquered and yielding obeisance to their brown conquerors. Sometimes they appeared as equals, exchanged gifts and courtesies. Sometimes the Mongoloids and Negroids and whites were bound slaves; but in Egyptian monuments slavery was never attributed solely to black folk. We conclude, therefore, that the Egyptians were Negroids, and not only that, but by tradition they believed themselves descended not from the whites or the yellows, but from the black peoples of the south. Thence they traced their origin, and toward the south in earlier days they turned the faces of their buried corpses.[34]

"For five thousand years," posits Du Bois, "mankind evolved a *pattern of human culture* which became the goal of the rest of the world and was imitated everywhere." He argued that for this span of time Kemet was the one place where the world would look to in order to understand and study science, art, government and religion. It is interesting that he continues the use of the phrase "pattern of human culture." Earlier in the text he used this phrase to refer to Europe in which he perceives as the pattern of human culture that has led the world to ruin. I argue that Du Bois, though enamored with the wonders of the European world in his earlier days, was by this time beginning to understand the contemporary cultural war through the juxtapositions discovered in his continued study of African history.

Du Bois understood that, naturally, all history is human history but there were differing patterns of human culture that are unique to various groups and should hold no sense of hierarchy over one another. Nevertheless, Du Bois is also perhaps identifying a sense of envy on the part of Europe for the wonders of the African world, and particularly for Kemet with its ancient and masterful structures they described as pyramids, tombs, sphinxes and temples. This envy would, of course, cause them to attribute the greatness of Kemet and, for that matter, all they perceived great in Africa, to their likeness. However, even the earliest European social scientists in Africa could not disregard the facts. To that end, Du Bois would quote David Randall-MacIver in stating, "The more we learn of Nubia and the Sudan, the more evident does it appear that what was most characteristic in the predynastic culture

---

34 Du Bois, *World and Africa*, 67–68.

of Egypt is due to intercourse with the interior of Africa and the immediate influence of that permanent Negro element which has been present in the population of southern Egypt from remotest times to our own day."

As an aside, Randall-MacIver worked with Flinders Petrie, the famed "Father of Egyptology," before being called to examine the site at Great Zimbabwe located in modern-day Zimbabwe. A year before becoming the first professional Egyptian Curator of the University of Pennsylvania Museum, David Randal-MacIver spent a year in Zimbabwe dispelling false notions about ancient Semitic peoples founding Great Zimbabwe and properly attributing the founding of that civilization to the ancestors of the Shona. Prior to Randal-MacIver's sojourn to Great Zimbabwe, the site was drawing in a host of attention and funding from Europeans who believed it to be some product of *Hamitic* people, or "lesser Europeans." Needless to say, Randall-MacIver was not wanted at the site for long after giving his professional opinion.[35] Nevertheless, his story exemplifies the contention that Europeans went to great lengths in order to argue that African people had no history and everything arguably great to be discovered in Africa were created by those coming from the outside of the continent.

No exception to this type of characterization was that of the aforementioned "father" of the field of Egyptology, Flinders Petrie. No one can argue against the fact that Petrie was a brilliant individual as his development of seriation as an early dating method for material culture is still widely used in the field today over a century later. Petrie is still cited to this day as it relates to Egyptological matters. He added much to Du Bois' work, and in fact they shared a few years of correspondence. However, Petrie's racist, and perhaps even racial-religious ideological proclivities, would see him invent a theory known today as *dynastic race theory*.

This theory suggested, based on the erroneous notion that greater intelligence can be attributed to skulls possessing greater cranial capacity, that the larger skulls found in Kemet must have been foreign and thus these presumably more intelligent invaders from Eurasia formed the first dynasty and ruled over the less intelligent indigenous populations. Contrarily, what we know today is that studies of crania show Kemetic people to be more similar to that of Nubians, particularly the Kushites to the south. Historian Robert Harms points this out in his text, *Africa in Global History*, in which he states:

---

35 Saul Dubow, *Scientific Racism in Modern South Africa* (Cambridge, UK: Cambridge Univ. Press, 1995), 88–89.

Studies of crania from southern Egypt dating between 4000 and 3100 BCE show them to be more similar to the crania of ancient Nubians and Kushites (Egypt's African neighbors to the south) than to those of ancient southern Europeans. In a similar way, studies of the limb proportions of skeletons, which vary between tropical and colder climates, show tropical proportions, even though Egypt itself was not in the tropics. The conclusion is that the southern Egyptians, who created the Egyptian state, were Africans with measurable biological affinities to their African neighbors.[36]

Nevertheless, Du Bois would point out that even Petrie had to admit how remarkable it was that seemingly renewed vitality would come to Kemet always from the South.[37] This southerly origin serving as the continued source of Kemetic vitality should have led Petrie, as brilliant as he may have been, to the most likely conclusion for the cultural origin of Kemetic state formation. I argue that, especially being raised a Catholic during the latter half of the nineteenth century, racist and socioreligious impulses would inform Petrie's obtuseness toward these observations. Du Bois went one step further to suggest that of all the, at that time, recent data being put out about the ethnicity of the people of Kemet and their supposed racial makeup "in the United States," Du Bois notes, "all these would be legally Negroes."[38]

Du Bois' historical survey of Kemet is a standard overview of the various dynasties of Kemet. By this time the conventions of Old, Middle and New Kingdom were already well established in order to describe the great periods or so-called "Golden Ages" of Kemetic history. Du Bois postulates that "before the First Dynasty there must have been a long series of rulers who came out of the south, conquered the people, and consolidated their powers. Upper Egypt historically always had precedence over Lower Egypt, and the First Dynasty came from the direction of the heart of Africa."[39] Clearly Du Bois studied the various analysis of the material record with prophetic insight as much of modern evidence continues to bore this out as truth.[40]

Of the Third Dynasty Du Bois notes that this was the period of the building of the great *Mir*, known to the Greeks as the great Pyramid. Du Bois refers to it as "the greatest monument that any man ever had." He notes the decline

---

36 Robert W. Harms, *Africa in Global History: With Sources* (New York, NY: W. W. Norton & Company, 2018), 57–58.
37 Du Bois, *World and Africa*, 68.
38 Ibid.
39 Ibid, 69.
40 See: Asante, *History of Africa*, 15–38.

during the Seventh Dynasty known as the first intermediate period and subsequent reunification in the Twelfth dynasty under Senusret III, whom Du Bois refers to as Usertesen III.[41] This period of reunification did not last long as the invasion of the western Asiatic hordes known as the Hyksos in the Thirteenth Dynasty, as well as the low inundation of the Nile, brought chaos once again to the nation and fragmented it into several concurrent dynasties.

Naturally, however, it would be Wasetian royals in Upper Kemet who would set out to restore the nation beginning in the Seventeenth Dynasty, culminating in the complete reunification of Kemet by the start of the Eighteenth Dynasty. With this, Du Bois closes his chapter on Kemet with Ahmose I and his "Black Queen" Nefertari. He contends that the remainder of Kemetic history from this point cannot be discussed in earnest without the intertwining of the history of the Kushites, whom the Greeks referred to as Ethiopians.

Du Bois on Kush

Du Bois entitled his chapter on Kush, "Land of the Burnt Faces," as this was the English translation of the Greek term for this area, Ethiopia. It is important to note that this Ethiopia, much like ancient Wagadu (Ghana), does not coincide with the modern country named Ethiopia. In fact, at various times the Greek use of the word "Ethiopia" could mean the regions below Kemet (also known as Nubia), Africa in general or even what they considered a region of "burnt-faced" peoples extending from Africa to modern India. Nevertheless, Du Bois is applying the term "Ethiopia" to those regions below Kemet, and primarily to the territory of Kush. However, this is more so a continuation of his earlier discussion on Kemet, perhaps largely because at this time much of Nubian archaeology, or Nubiology, was geared primarily toward the discovery of Kemetic authority in the area.

This chapter begins with Du Bois reasserting his earlier arguments about the Western world's insistence on characterizing those of African descent as inferior beings in justification of the European Trade of Enslaved Africans and the continued inhumane treatment of those of African descent in his day. He argues that the facts about Kemetic and Kushite history have been altered in order to corroborate this false notion of African inferiority. "When Asia overwhelmed Egypt, Egypt sought refuge in Ethiopia as a child returns to its mother," Du Bois states, adding that, "Neither Greece, Rome, nor Islam succeeded in conquering Ethiopia." Du Bois would argue that this interpretation

---

41 Du Bois, *World and Africa*, 72.

of African history exhibits the falsehoods of the theory of a "natural and eternal inferiority" of African people, "which rendered them natural slaves and a cheap labor force for nineteenth-century industry."[42]

Du Bois argued further that "the mixture of blood among the three races is always referred to as an explanation of the advance among Negroes and the retrogression among whites," yet, "nothing is ever said of the influence of Negro blood in Europe and Asia."[43] This argument by Du Bois is an appeal for readers to understand the contradictions in the claims of the Western world that Africans are inherently inferior for clearly there were many examples in his day (and before) of profound men and women of Europe and Asia who were mixed with African blood. However, the understanding of the difference between mild genetic mixing and what is to be considered cultural identity is often applied to Asians and Europeans, but not to African people, particularly the people of Kemet. Du Bois explains:

> There was and is wide mingling of the blood of all races in Africa, but this is consistent with the general thesis that Africa is predominantly the land of Negroes and Negroid peoples, just as Europe is a land of Caucasoids and Asia of Mongoloids. We may give up entirely, if we wish, the whole attempt to delimit races, but we cannot, if we are sane, divide the world into whites, yellows, and blacks, and then call blacks white.[44]

Du Bois continues his argument by submitting that the Greeks viewed African people as equals in their own literature such as the *Iliad*. "In the dawn of Greek literature," he begins, "in the *Iliad*, we hear of the gods feasting among the 'blameless Ethiopians.'"[45] Du Bois would then go on to note many examples of the Greek's reverence for Kush either by way of mythology or historical accounts. In so doing, he expands upon an argument that racism toward African people is a modern invention and those whom the European world identifies as their ideological and cultural forefathers, the Greeks, had no racial prejudices against African people that can be indistinguishable from the system of racism which exists today.

Regardless, while this may be a good argument to present in the humanizing of African people by Western standards, I find it to be a regressive argument in

---

42 Ibid, 75.
43 Ibid.
44 Ibid, 76.
45 Ibid, 78.

advancing Pan-African ideals. Firstly, though undoubtedly not operating on the very same racial attitudes as today, the history clearly shows that Greece and Rome were imperial and prejudicial nations just as their presumed cultural and intellectual contemporary progenies, the nations of Europe, remain today. I argue that the primary difference that existed between the Greco-Roman powers' relationship with Africa and that of today's Western nations is that Greece and Rome were never able to truly conquer inner Africa. Despite any superficial prejudices they may have had, their respect for African nations was due to the African's ability to remain autonomous and fend off European encroachment. Secondly, though undoubtedly many sources to be used in the writing of African history exists in readily accessible Greek texts and translations, and thus becomes useful to Du Bois' penning a narrative on Africa, the emphasis on Greek, and, by extension, Eurocentric standards of what and who is regarded as respectable is agency-reducing.

The better, more agency-affirming argument would involve a survey of how precolonial African people thought of themselves and others. As this applies to his discussion on Kush, it would be wonderful if the Meroitic script, the official script of Kush while the capital of the nation was centered at Meroë, was fully deciphered. We know that Kemetic writings about the Mediterranean world are abundant and many were certainly available to Du Bois. Perhaps through his relationship with Flinders Petrie, Du Bois may have been able to use some primary sources. However, literature written in Ge'ez, the official script of the Kingdom of Aksum, which also remains the current liturgical language of the Ethiopian and Eritrean Orthodox Tewahedo Church, could also serve as a potential resource for African perspectives during the time of the Roman conquest of North Africa and after. In serious Afrocentric scholarship, we must do away with relying on the opinions of Europeans and their standards of humanity, and particularly how such standards regard African people. Though historical resources from other cultures may be necessary for historical contextualization, it is imperative to position African perspectives as primary in any analysis on African phenomena.

To be sure, Du Bois uses the writings of the Greek, Diodorus Siculus, to suggest, "The Ethiopians looked upon themselves as the source of Egypt and declared [...] that Egyptian laws and customs were of Ethiopian origin." He would continue, "The Egyptians themselves in later days affirmed that their civilization came out of the south, and modern research confirms this in many ways."[46] Du Bois would make it clear many times that much of Kemetic society was continuously enriched from culture flowing up the Nile

---

46 Ibid, 79.

from inner Africa and that one should look toward Kush for the predynastic cultural foundations of Kemet.

However, Du Bois would, contradictorily, muddle the issue surrounding the supposed "Negroid" phenotypes of both the Kemetic people and the people of Kush. He argued that the people of Kush were "more purely Negroid," perhaps in continuation of the erroneous notion that the darker the skin color the more the terms *negroid* or African can be attributed. This isn't true regarding the San people of southern Africa, of whom the great majority are completely genetically African yet range in colors from dark brown to yellow. This is also phenotypically and culturally untrue for the Swahili of the eastern African coast, and the Amazigh of northern Africa. With this type of erroneous description however, Du Bois, though perhaps unintentionally, is perpetuating the lie of a standard Negro type, which, as aforementioned, is something he desperately argued against in earlier chapters.

Nevertheless, Du Bois' historical survey on Kush would cause him to revisit Kemet and their earlier contacts with Kush. He quickly focuses on the Eighteenth Dynasty and their expelling of the Hyksos with the assured assistance of Kushite peoples in Upper Kemet. He posits that noble families intermarrying with the people of Kush formed the bases of the Eighteenth Dynasty rulers. He notes the Kemetic Queen of Kushite origin, Ahmose-Nefertari and, returning to the racial issue, states that "naturally the legend of this black queen has caused heart-searching among white Egyptologists; they have called her 'Libyan'; and Libya was certainly partly Negroid in race; but since the Libyans have usually been counted 'white,' why was the Libyan Nofritari black?"[47] In the next few passages Du Bois continues the argument that Kemet is constantly saved and revitalized by peoples stemming from the south, and in this case Waset and its extended influence beyond the Nubian border.

It is from this Wasetian orientation Du Bois begins his focus on the remainder of the history of Kemetic civilization and particularly as it relates to Kush. He writes of Thutmose I and the short reign of his son Thutmose II. For the reign of Thutmose' sister, Hatshepsut, he describes the circumstances surrounding her commissioning an expedition to the land of Punt. Undoubtedly relaying the opinions of various Egyptologists on the description of the Queen of Punt as depicted on the walls of the temple of Deir el Bahri, he describes her as representative of "the modern Hottentot type [...] with the characteristic steatopygia."[48] I should note here that steatopygia is a

---

47 Ibid, 81.
48 Ibid.

Western medical term that often refers to someone who Europeans believe to have an unnaturally large buttocks. This is an offensively Eurocentric remark but is in line with Europeans' history of oversexualization women of African descent. Of course, it would seem that Du Bois was ideologically unequipped to address the Eurocentric and agency-reducing nature of this description.[49]

Du Bois mentions Amenhotep III and his association with the Greek mythological character, Memnon. This association is also due to the fact that during their reign over Egypt the Greeks renamed the two extant statues of Amenhotep III's likeness, "the Colossi of Memnon," a name that has remained ever since their occupation of Kemet. Du Bois also points out that Amenhotep's wife, Tiye, is very obviously of Nubian ancestry. He would briefly mention their son, Amenhotep IV, later known as Akhenaten, and his introduction of what Du Bois describes as an "imperial monotheism" by way of Aten worship. In fact, after an even briefer mention of Akhenaten's son, the so-called "boy King," Tutankhamen, Du Bois spends a few pages on the Hebrews and their introduction into Kemetic history during this time period. He begins this introduction with Rameses I, arguing that perhaps the Hebrew myth of being enslaved in Kemet occurred under his reign. There have before and since this time been many arguments over this very topic, and many modern scholars consider this mythological event to be a reference to the political circumstances that actually occurred during the reign of his grandson, Ramses II.[50]

Du Bois analyzes certain biblical passages, and the interpretations thereof, that seemingly relate to race, and generally via the description of their skin color. One passage describes that "Moses married a Black woman," whose name was Miriam from Ethiopia. Another example comes from the words of Solomon: "I am Black, but comely." He even highlights the Hebrew's views on Kush in passages describing their nervousness about the rising power of Kush, the hopes Kush would adopt the Jewish faith, as well as threats that

---

49 A famous example of this is Sarah Bartman, a Khoisan woman who, during the Maafa, or the era of African enslavement by Europeans, was paraded around as an exhibit known as "The Hottentot Venus" because of her so-called abnormally large buttocks. Notably, many African American women also have Khoisan DNA, as upward of 30 percent of African American DNA derive from Southern Bantu and Khoisan areas. This is not an abnormal feature in African people but is fetishized by the West. Nevertheless, the example of Ati, Queen of Punt, is a prime example of Western scholars' dehumanization of African corporeal. For more detail on Ati of Punt, see: Tristan Samuels, "Undoing the Hottentoting of 'the Queen of Punt' A Jamaican Afronography on the Kemetiu Depiction of Ati of Punt," *Journal of Black Studies* 52, no. 1 (2020): 3–23, https://doi.org/10.1177/0021934720945360.
50 Du Bois, *World and Africa*, 83–85.

their God would soon subdue Kush if they do not yield to their faith.[51] I should note here that Du Bois' discussion of these passages also represent common ideologies among African Americans surrounding the relationship between Africans and Hebrews.

There is no doubt that relationships existed and continue to exist between east Africa and the Levant. However, primarily due to the rise of the Trade of Enslaved Africans, there have been a number of erroneous notions on the identity of African Americans based on anecdotal parallels between enslaved Africans and the biblical Hebrews. A movement in Du Bois' day that many retroactively call Ethiopianism saw many African intellectuals around the world who were moved by the Hebrew story in relation to their own circumstances develop a myriad of ideologies on identity revolving around the Hebrew and Christian myths.[52]

To that end, another ideology that existed around the time of Du Bois but today still boasts small hubs of followers in major cities in the United States (and some abroad) are the so-called Black Hebrew Israelites. They are divided into many different sects with varying ideologies, but their principle collective belief is that African Americans are the ancestors of the Hebrews of biblical times. Some believe that both the people of Kemet and the Hebrews are within their ancestral line. Others consider it undesirable to be associated with any form of African history and culture or to even be described as Black. A bible, of sorts, for the propagation of their beliefs has been Rudolph R. Windsor's *From Babylon to Timbuktu*, in which Windsor used incredulous sources and false interpretations in order to paint a picture of Hebrew supremacy and large population dispersal in Africa. This false narrative falls along the lines of the Hamitic myths that would see only Eurasians be credited with the development of civilization in Africa.

Digressing, Du Bois next gives a good deal of consideration to the Kushites who formed the Twenty-fifth Dynasty of Kemet. The Kushites at this time had both their own unique culture but had also adopted much of Kemetic religious and cultural customs. Perhaps, however, what we will discover is that Kemet initially absorbed a lot of Kushite culture to the degree that the level of influence on one another can at times not appear clear to modern scholars. Regardless, Du Bois was right to point out just how closely associated the people of Kemet and Kush were as he recounts that during the time of the Hyksos invasion, "Ethiopia became a refuge for the conquered Egyptians

---

51 Ibid, 84–85.
52 John Cullen Gruesser, *Black on Black Twentieth-Century African American Writing about Africa* (Lexington, KY: The University Press of Kentucky, 2015), 20–49.

both physically and culturally."⁵³ In fact, Du Bois would once again turn Petrie's words on himself and the theory of a dynastic race when he quotes him stating: "This shows how southern was the center of thought when the whole of Egypt is reckoned as the north. Some writers say that Taharqa led expeditions as far as the Strait of Gibraltar."⁵⁴

Du Bois begins his discussion of the Twenty-fifth Dynasty with the Kushite patriarch, Piye, known at that time as Piankhi, and briefly mentions a line of other rulers before dealing with perhaps the most popular of them all, Taharka. He notes Taharka's reign to be one of "prosperity and cultural advancement." Indeed, Taharka would restore much of the arts as well as reintroduce customs that had not been seen since the Old Kingdom. But shortly after Taharka's reign the Kemetic empire would fall one final time, never again able to reach the great heights of authority it enjoyed for three millennia.

Du Bois briefly mentions the Kandakes of Kush who ruled from Meroë. He relates to his readers the legend of a Kandake who held at bay the armies of the Greco-Macedonian ruler, Alexander, not permitting them to enter her lands.⁵⁵ The veracity of this tale has yet to be confirmed, however one narrative of a Kandake described in Roman literature as "a masculine woman with one eye" is with great certainty a description of Amanirenas. Du Bois does not mention Amanirenas by name but suggests that she ruled sometime near the death of Cleopatra VII, and the historical record of today clearly pins Amanirenas as the one-eyed warrior who ruled over Kush at that time. Du Bois begins the conclusion of this chapter with a small passage about the neighboring Axumite Empire and their political history in the Arabian peninsula and Mediterranean world. Then he ends with a small note on the rise of Islam and the crumbling of various parts of Christian Nubia.⁵⁶

African World Antecedent Methodology

Many of the various African groups Du Bois covers in these chapters prove to be worthy candidates to investigate as classical antecedents for African American culture. Even in Du Bois' time he could have capitalized on various similarities in cultural phenomena that, while he may have not known the exact origins, would have allowed him to present a more powerful case

---

53 Du Bois, *World and Africa*, 80.
54 Ibid, 87.
55 Ibid, 91.
56 Ibid, 93.

for Pan-African unity based on cultural foundations. One may ask, why are cultural foundations important in building unity among African groups? For that answer, one would only need to look at the type of political organizing Europeans and Asians have been able to achieve by exploiting their own cultural-historical connections. As aforementioned, Du Bois is very clear about the cultural connections in Europe:

> The rebirth of Europe began in the fifteenth century [...] in Europe during the thirteenth and fourteenth centuries there began to appear national integration of culture patterns, with no little inspiration from the East and from Africa. There followed in the fifteenth and sixteenth centuries increased freedom of thought and impatience with dogma; and in the seventeenth, came scientific inquiry and the beginning of a demand for democratic control of government.[57]

This would involve the continuous cultural relationship between European nations. For Du Bois to begin that passage by stating that this era was the "rebirth" of European civilization, it represents a clear acknowledgment of modern Europe's somewhat manufactured narrative of an intellectual heritage stemming back to ancient Greece and Rome, or what Europe considers their classical civilizations. In that line of thinking, Du Bois does not shy away from the position that Kemet and Kush represent the classical civilizations of African people. In fact, he is very adamant about their Africanity. This is something he would share with the Senegalese scholar Cheikh Anta Diop, who not only interpreted the written evidence but set out to prove the Africanity of Kemet by way of scientific and linguistic evidence.[58]

However, harkening back to my discussion in the first chapter, if one wishes to draw inspiration from an idealized African antiquity, cultural connections must be made. Simply penning a history of these ancient African nations isn't enough to justify political unity based on some historical notion of *blackness*. One must demonstrate how the people of these nations and their descendants relate to each other transgenerationally and, due to modern circumstances, transcontinentally. This is an easy task for the people who exist on the isolated archipelago of Japan, for example, but for people of African descent, spread across not only the vast African continent but also across the globe, this is a monumental task. But I believe this task can be accomplished

---

57 Ibid, 28.
58 Mario H. Beatty, "W.E.B. Du Bois and Cheikh Anta Diop on the Origins and Race of the Ancient Egyptians."

if tackled properly. One must utilize the shared idealization of the ancient African past and the cultural connections that past has afforded its contemporary inheritors in order to bring about a political unity based not on shared oppression but shared ethos. An ethos I term the *African-World Cultural Project*.

The Western world often seeks both to emulate and find themselves within their purported classical history for the sake of sustaining their cultural and political power. Naturally, this involved a shared idealization of ancient Greece and Rome between European powers which has manifested cultural and political unity. This has come in several forms such as adopting Roman democracy and colonial aspirations, dynamically re-creating the Greek Olympic Games, adopting Roman architecture and naming their sciences and professions after Greco-Roman figures such as Plato, Hippocrates and Pythagoras. But such is due only to the history and myths surrounding a supposed relationship between the European world and those so-called classical civilizations. Du Bois mentions, for example, the rise and fall of Kemet and Kush, but does not make cultural and, by extension, intellectual heritage connections between those classical African civilizations and the modern African world. Therefore, below I have used AWAM to chart out some cultural phenomena that should be considered.

Kanna

First, to establish *kanna* (samenes) between these classical civilizations and African Americans would be difficult because of the expanse of time and the great many complications that have resulted from the Maafa. To be clear, culture is a dynamic phenomenon that changes over time whether or not the culture remains in the region in which it originated or has become transregional or even transcontinental. Cultural phenomena does not have to remain exactly the same to be considered *kanna*. However, for the sake of cautious categorization, direct antecedents that are considered *kanna* would show that certain cultural phenomena were passed down from the presumptive parent culture in either an unbroken or organic chain of historical events.

For example, we know that the last of Kemetic religious culture diffused into Kush before being snuffed out around the fourth century CE. The Kush capital at Meroë experienced economic decline and political instability before eventually facing defeat at the hands of the burgeoning Axumite empire. However, it appears that the Axumites were in some way influenced by the Kemetic and Kushitic tekenu (which the Greeks refer to as obelisks) as stele barring much similarity to these structures were erected to denote the final resting place of early Axumite kings. The continuation of religious culture between Kemet and Kush bears clear signs of *kanna* as much evidence exists to establish a direct connection. However, despite how clear it may be to us from an historical standpoint, the relationship between the tekenu of Kemet and Kush and the stele in Axum may fit more comfortably in *fanna* due to a lack of physical evidence. Therefore, even between civilizations that overlap temporally and spatially, evidence may not warrant the classification of *kanna* in comparing certain phenomena. To that end, there are a number of aspects we may categorize as *fanna* that are viewed first among these early civilizations and can be witnessed today among other African groups. These include circumcision rituals, libation and various spiritual aspects.

Fanna

The presence of similarity in cultural phenomena between Nile Valley cultures and the rest of the African world is quite clear. There are examples in art, music and even naming that we may draw evidence from. Importantly, we can infer some manner of diffusion from Nile Valley culture to various areas of the African continent though we have no clear way of establishing direct links in most cases. As alluded, circumcision existed in Kemet and possibly even in Kush.[59] In fact, some Kemetic writings have suggested that the practice originated in Kush.[60] There is also sufficient evidence for the ritualistic circumcision of both males and females in Kemetic society.[61] Through linguistic analysis and ethnographic observation it has been determined that a common ancestral group brought male circumcision from areas in the Sudan to other major areas in the African continent via the Bantu expansion.[62] This however leaves us curious as to the possibility of the diffusion of this cultural phenomenon from the Nile Valley into the Sudan or perhaps an independent development of such among Sudanic and West African groups that eventually spread to the more central and southerly Bantu areas.

---

59 Gerry Mackie, "Female Genital Cutting: The Beginning of the End," in *Female "Circumcision" in Africa: Culture, Controversy, and Change*, ed. Bettina Shell-Duncan and Ylva Hernlund (Boulder, CO: Lynne Rienner Publishers, 2000), 253–281.

60 Mary Ann Watson, "Female Circumcision from Africa to the Americas: Slavery to the Present," *The Social Science Journal* 42, no. 3 (January 2005): 421–437, https://doi.org/10.1016/j.soscij.2005.06.006.

61 Mary Knight, "Curing Cut or Ritual Mutilation?: Some Remarks on the Practice of Female and Male Circumcision in Graeco-Roman Egypt," *Isis* 92, no. 2 (2001): 317–338, https://doi.org/10.1086/385184.

62 Jeff Mark, "Aspects of Male Circumcision in Subequatorial African Culture History," *Health Transition Review* 7 (1997): 337–360.

While many ancestors of African Americans were brought from areas in Africa where circumcision was well practiced, it is important to state that there is no evidence to suggest their descendants continued this practice among males and particularly no evidence to suggest the practice persisted among females.[63] Nevertheless, it is important to mention this practice as it is one that was surely brought over in the minds of the enslaved and perhaps evidence of its continuance in some capacity will someday be discovered. Furthermore, as one of the principal ritualistic acts of Bantu populations, it is sure to relate to other vestiges of African culture among African Americans.

There is evidence of spiritual similarity that could provide a basis for investigating cultural diffusion from the Nile Valley. For example, in Akan spirituality, there is a distinction between a person's *ntoro* (spirit) and their *kra* (soul) which also bears similarities with the Bambara's position of *ni* (soul) and *dya* (double).[64] These are strikingly similar to the Kemetic cosmological juxtaposition of *Ba* (spiritual person) and *Ka* (interpretably, soul).[65] Both the Akan and Bambara are groups from which African people were kidnapped from and taken to the Americas, and much of their cosmology still remains in vestige. Africologist Kimani S. K. Nehusi argues in his text, *Libation: An Afrikan Ritual of Heritage in the Circle of Life*, that, "the *ka* of Kemet, the *kra* of the Akan in Ghana and Ivory Coast and most Afrikans in Suriname, [are] also the same as the *asé* (pronounced ashay) of the Orisas (Orishas) that are propitiated by Afrikans (and sometimes by non-Afrikans) in Yorubaland."[66]

Another interesting similarity comes in the form of something that the Western world describes as *fetishes*. Fetishes (or sometimes appearing in literature as fetishism) are a range of items that the ancients cherished and usually served some manner of sentimental and mystical application.[67] These came in the form of wrapped staffs, amulets bearing ankhs, beetles or even *shabtis*.[68] The term fetish was first coined by a Frenchman named Charles de Brosses who in his seminal work, *Du culte des dieux fétiches ou Parallèle de l'ancienne religion de l'Egypte avec la religion actuelle de Nigritie*, elaborates on his theories which

---

63 Mary Ann Watson, "Female Circumcision from Africa to the Americas."
64 Gomez. *Exchanging Our Country Marks*, 271.
65 In some works the Ka is related as "double."
66 Kimani S. K. Nehusi, *Libation: an Afrikan Ritual of Heritage in the Circle of Life* (Lanham, MD: University Press of America, Inc, 2016).
67 Rosalie David. *Religion and Magic in Ancient Egypt* (London: Penguin Books, 2002), 51.
68 Shabtis are ethereal servants in the form of wooden or stone dolls that are given specific tasks. They were often buried with the deceased.

linked Kemetic spirituality to west African spiritual systems.[69] As recent as the emergence of the African American, we find so-called fetishes in the form of objects used in voodoo and hoodoo spiritual systems.[70]

For example, the *minkisi* of modern-day Angola were among such amulets discussed by de Brosses and others. They are objects that house spirits or spiritual energy and are sometimes represented as humanoid figurines but can also be other various objects. In fact, their derivative, *nkondi*, which was a series of minkisi often activated by inserting a sharp object such as a nail into the spiritual figures, are widely used among the Bakongo of Angola, but also in the Caribbean, southern United States and South America. This is found particularly in places like Louisiana, Alabama, Haiti and Brazil, where Bakongo faith contributed to the development of new African faiths and practices such as Vodou,[71] Hoodoo, Santeria and Candomblé. I should note also that by the late nineteenth and early twentieth century, and perhaps facilitated by their interpretation of the Haitian revolution and the spirituality that guided the warriors of said revolution, the Western world's imagination and interpretation of minkisi created and perpetuated the idea that they were demonic figures, often referred to as *voodoo dolls*. Voodoo dolls, however, are not based in reality, and are in large measure a construction of Hollywood. I argue that they are based on a projection of Eurocentric tales of cultural mystics such as witches and their push-pin effigies used purportedly in order to harm others with their magic.[72]

Digressing, what we also find significant is the ease of several African ethnic groups, although supposedly linguistically unintelligible to one another, to bond with each other under apparent universal spiritual activities. Known today as "ring shouts," Africans from west and west-central Africa bonded over this spiritual dance, each bringing to it their own unique cosmological interpretations.[5] Dancing and music was also spiritually significant to the ancient people of Kemet. Often music and dance are described to accompany

---

69 Rosalind C. Morris and Daniel H. Leonard, *The Returns of Fetishism: Charles De Brosses and the Afterlives of an Idea* (Chicago, IL: The University of Chicago Press, 2017).
70 Michael Gomez, *Exchanging Our Country Marks,* 283.
71 I use the spelling Vodou here to exemplify a more correct dialect as pronounced by practitioners as well as to differentiate from the Voodoo of Hollywood, which is demonization and misrepresentation of the spiritual system in American popular culture.
72 Natalie Armitage. "European and African Figural Ritual Magic: The Beginnings of the Voodoo Doll Myth," in *The Materiality of Magic: An Artifactual Investigation into Ritual Practices and Popular Beliefs*, ed. Ceri Houlbrook and Natalie Armitage (Oxford: Oxbow, 2015), 85–101.

Kemetic ceremonies accompanied by an array of instruments. Depicted often in Kemetic iconography was the use of the sistrum, described in Kemetic works such as *The Instruction of Amenemope*.[73] The Mande people of West Africa, known well for the Griot tradition, are known to use *sistrums* and *djabara* (an apparent sistrum relative) as instruments for ritualistic proposes.

Further parallels can be drawn from burials and the placement of personal effects of the deceased, as well as items symbolic with the person being commemorated, in or around the burial site. Again, we understand this as the continuation of west-African customs brought over to America. Michael Gomez, professor of history, and author of *Exchanging Our Country Marks: The Transformation of African Identities in the Colonial and Antebellum South*, explains the use of items "such as personal effects last handled by the deceased, plates, cups, broken glassware, seashells, white pebbles, trees newly planted to mark the occasion [among other] [...] *minkisi*, or sacred medicines, deployed to properly guide the deceased's spirit to the ancestral realm." He states further that "the establishment of such an ethnically specific continuity is a major contribution to our understanding of African American culture and is consistent with the demographic evidence concerning the prominence of immigrants from West Central Africa in South Carolina, Georgia, and Louisiana."[74] However, we also see a very ancient form of this type of commemoration in Kemet and Nubia where personal effects used in life as well as numerous shabti have been discovered in excavated tombs of Kemetic royalty, noblemen and even many commoners. Such is also clearly displayed in images from reliefs found in various tombs.

Finally, I would be remiss to not single out the practice of libation. Libation is a cultural tradition that is well documented in Kemetic iconography but also seen throughout the African world. African Americans especially have continued this tradition and it is even displayed in culturally specific media such as movies, television shows and music. One famous example comes from the film *Cooley High* (1975), in which the main character pours out a bottle of liquor and proclaims, "This is for the brothers who ain't here." Further, Nehusi has singled out hip-hop artists such as Nas and Tupac for the perpetuation of the cultural practice of libation in their music and videos.[75]

---

73 Miriam Lichtheim, *Ancient Egyptian Literature*, Vol. 2 (1976), 91, 149.
74 Gomes, *Exchanging Our Country Marks*, 275.
75 Nehusi, *Libation*, 144.

Naani

The act of presenting Kemetic and Kushite culture that could be categorized as original and static presents issues counter to the issue of tracing aspects of *kanna*. I cannot think of one aspect of Nile Valley culture that in some form or vestige has not been displayed in the African world. There are certainly some things that may be hypothesized to be unique, however there is so much yet to be discovered about the spread of Nile Valley culture, and the protocultures thereof, that any guess at *Naani* at this moment would prove a futile exercise.

Chapter 3

DU BOIS AND THE FORMATION OF CONTEMPORARY AFRICAN HISTORY

Du Bois and the Conundrum of White Scholarship

In the preceding chapters on Africa's classical antecedents, Kemet and Kush, Du Bois was highly critical of the way the Western academy has presented the racial question in regard to the people of the Nile Valley. However, in the chapters in which Du Bois surveys what we may call the generators of contemporary African civilization, his critique is much less about the question of their race but instead the ways in which the West has attempted to reduce the agency of African groups based on their race. But before delving back into Du Bois' historical survey, I find it proper here to address the issues facing Du Bois on his path toward both writing this history and the shaping of his perspective along the way.

Du Bois borrows significantly from certain European scholars to write his histories on African people. But perhaps this would not be his choice if he had a better choice to make. For example, he leaves a footnote in his chapter on Kush explaining, "For the history of Ethiopia I have leaned heavily on [miscellaneous] material furnished me by Professor Leo Hansberry of Howard University."[1] In the foreword he expressed "regret that [Hansberry] has not published more of his work."[2] He also regrets that he could not use the works of Frank Snowden and that "classical journals in America have hitherto declined to publish his paper because it favored the Negro too much [...] I tried to get Dr. Snowden to let me see his manuscript, but he refused."[3]

Both Hansberry and Snowden were African American historians whose scholarship Du Bois apparently trusted and perhaps wished for their work to make up the bulk of chapters IV, V, and VI in *The World and Africa*, covering the peopling of Africa, and the histories of Kemet and Kush, respectively.

---

1 Du Bois, *World and Africa*, 94.
2 Ibid, xxxiii.
3 Ibid.

Interestingly, Du Bois does not at all mention Carter G. Woodson, whose works at the time could have contributed greatly to a number of chapters in the text. Perhaps this was due to their personal differences which occurred a decade before the book was published. This incident shall soon be covered but first we digress to Du Bois' conundrum with white scholars. Du Bois chose the name "Atlantis" as the title of the seventh chapter of *The World and Africa*, which he states is "the story of the West Coast of Africa and its relation to the development of the world from A.D. 500 to 1500."[4] Du Bois borrows the term *Atlantis* as a name for the West Coast of Africa from German archaeologist and ethnographer, Leo Frobenius, whose works he admittedly relied on when writing chapter VII.

Most know Atlantis to be the mythical city in the works of Plato. It has for centuries held the imagination of the Western world, considered to be a place of technological and aesthetic wonder. In the sixteenth century, European explorers began to consider that perhaps the *natives* of North America were some remnants of the people of Atlantis who were forced to emigrate after its destruction.[5] Frobenius' use of the term "Atlantis" to describe what he was witnessing in West Africa had a similar but perhaps even more racist connotation. Frobenius would surmise that an ancient and highly advanced European civilization, perhaps the remnants of the mythical Atlantis, emigrated to that region and established the beginnings of African civilization and that all that existed in West Africa that could be suggestible as civilization by European standards can be attributed to those ancient Europeans.[6] According to Frobenius, by the time of modern European colonization, any traces of that first white civilization must have vanished long ago and all that is left is a *heavily diluted* form represented by the Africans he encountered.[7] This supposed process Frobenius appallingly referred to as "negrification."[8]

Du Bois perhaps came across the works of Frobenius during his sojourn in Germany, studying abroad during the early portion of his graduate years at Harvard—from which institution he was the first African American to receive a PhD. Du Bois relies on Frobenius for a good deal of African ethnography

---

4 Ibid, 95.
5 Kenneth L. Feder, *Frauds, Myths, and Mysteries: Science and Pseudoscience in Archaeology*, 10th ed. (New York, NY: Oxford University Press, 2019), 203–212.
6 Joseph C. Miller, "History and Africa/Africa and History," *The American Historical Review* (1999), https://doi.org/10.1086/ahr/104.1.1.
7 Ibid.
8 Leo Frobenius, *Voice of Africa: Being an Account of the Travels of the German Inner African Exploration Expedition in the Years 1910-1912*, vol. 1 (London: Hutchinson & CO., 1913), 317.

and cultural history and has done so since his very first text on African history, *The Negro*. He and Frobenius also shared many years of correspondence with each other and Du Bois even invited Frobenius to participate in the creation of the *Encyclopedia of the Negro*.[9] Du Bois told American educator and historian, Anson Phelps Stokes, that Frobenius' letter to him expressing interest in the project was one that he "prize[d] very much."[10] Clearly, Du Bois held Frobenius in great reverence and yet Frobenius' theories on African civilization were no different from the others racists who argued Hamitic origins or that of Flinders Petrie's dynastic race theory.

Interestingly, Du Bois also had a long exchange of correspondence with Petrie. Some of which he would publish in *The Crisis* under the banner, "Self-Righteous Europe and the World: Correspondence with W. M. Flinders Petrie."[11] In those letters he was generally cordial with Petrie but also highly reproachful on the matter of race and the poor regard in which Petrie viewed the intellectual capability of his Egyptian workers. Nevertheless, Du Bois would also secure Petrie to collaborate as an advisor on the *Encyclopedia Africana*.[12] It is questionable as to why Du Bois would rely on those with racist theories he finds objectionable in order to complete this project. Naturally, one may consider the issue of needing the backing of well-respected scholars to secure financing for the encyclopedia. It should not be lost on us that the times in which Du Bois lived, and the activities in which he was engaged, was wrought with politics that would force him to at times rely on the favor of whites that even he found personally or even professionally unfavorable.

This nonetheless did not prevent Carter G. Woodson, the second African American to receive a PhD from Harvard, from criticizing Du Bois' dependency on white scholars and philanthropists. The first iteration of *Encyclopedia Africana* was instead called *The Encyclopedia of the Negro*. This version, to which Du Bois beseeched Woodson to assist with, was being funded by the Phelps-Stokes fund, under the direction of the aforementioned Anson Phelps Stokes, a wealthy philanthropist and educator, but also someone whom Woodson

---

9 W. E. B. Du Bois, *1868-1963. Letter from W. E. B. Du Bois to Leo Frobenius, February 9, 1937. W. E. B. Du Bois Papers (MS 312). Special Collections and University Archives, University of Massachusetts Amherst Libraries.*
10 W. E. B. Du Bois, *1868-1963. Letter from W. E. B. Du Bois to Anson Phelps Stokes, March 10, 1937. W. E. B. Du Bois Papers (MS 312). Special Collections and University Archives, University of Massachusetts Amherst Libraries.*
11 W.E.B. Du Bois, "Self-Righteous Europe and the World: Correspondence with W. M. Flinders Petrie," *Crisis*, 4, no. 1 (May 1912): 36–37 (New York, NY: Crisis Publishing Co., 1912), 1–6.
12 Du Bois, *Dusk of Dawn*, 161.

despised and held in lowest regard. When Du Bois asked Woodson to join the project, he responded, "I have nothing to say, however, that I am not interested. *I never accept the gifts of the Greeks*" (emphasis mine).[13] This letter was addressed to Du Bois in the spring of 1932, but by 1936 Woodson was approaching the topic of the Stokes-funded encyclopedia with a bit more hostility. On May 30, 1936 the *Baltimore Afro-American* published an article by Woodson lambasting Du Bois and the project:

> Any man who will join a crowd led by Anson Phelps Stokes and Thomas Jesse Jones, (both white) to put in permanent form what they and their co-workers think of the colored man, is a traitor to his race. For three centuries we have had the sort of literature flooding the markets with the thought of the white man who exalts the Hebrew, the Greek, the Latin and the Teuton, and despises the colored race as inferior. What the colored man needs is not to aid this misrepresentation of the race by those who view it from without, but to resort to scientific methods to study his race from within and thus enable him to unfold himself to the world. This is a task which only the colored man himself can do. *The white man, even when he is honest and sincere, cannot at his best write the history of colored people and portray their present status, when he does not live and move among them.* (emphasis mine).[14]

At the time, Woodson was arguably second to none other than Du Bois as an authority on African and African American history, as well as the social conditions of African Americans in particular. Woodson was also untrusting of white people and their philanthropy, especially as it came to any interest they may have in scholarship surrounding people of African descent. Perhaps he learned this lesson after working under Methodist funding for several years during his early career. Clearly, Du Bois too held some hostility for having to rely on the sponsorship of whites. He and Woodson both were omitted from the first meeting to organize the *Encyclopedia of the Negro*, and Du Bois and Woodson both seem of mutual mind as to why they were not invited. After accepting the invitation to the second meeting, and eventually being made Editor-in-Chief of the project, he would write his letter to Woodson

---

13 W. E. B. Du Bois and Herbert Aptheker, *The Correspondence of W. E. B. Du Bois*, vol. 1 (Amherst, MA: University of Massachusetts Press, 1973), 449.

14 Calls, DuBois a traitor if he accepts post. *Afro-American (1893-1988)*, May 30, 1936. http://libproxy.temple.edu/login?url=https://www-proquest-com.libproxy.temple.edu/historical-newspapers/calls-dubois-traitor-if-he-accepts-post/docview/531127178/se-2?accountid=14270.

encouraging his cooperation. In regard to Du Bois's mistrust of white scholars and white philanthropy, he would state to Woodson:

> I do not doubt but what you have made up your mind on this matter and that nothing I can say will change it. However, perhaps I ought to bring to your attention the motives that influenced me. I was omitted from the first call, as you were, and for similar reasons. My first impulse on receiving the invitation to attend the second meeting was to refuse, as you did. Then I learned that this invitation did not come from the Phelps-Stokes fund, but was the unanimous wish of the conferees, and that if I refused to heed it, I would be affronting them, even more than Stokes and Jones. Then, in the second place, I had to remember as both of us from time to time are compelled to, *that the enemy has the money and they are going to use it*. Our choice then is not how that money could be used best from our point of view but how far without great sacrifice of principle, we can keep it from being misused. (emphasis mine).[15]

Du Bois' thinking here is quite interesting. He expressed similar sentiment as Woodson on who the enemy of African Americans are, but his view is that he cannot procure proper funding without dancing with devils. Du Bois may have in fact prophesied this outcome for himself. In January of 1910 educator and first African American president of Morehouse and Atlanta University, John Hope, wrote Du Bois a letter expressing concern about the possible waning nature of their friendship amid Du Bois and others' critiques and teasing of Hope for receiving funding for Morehouse from Andrew Carnegie by way of his relationship with Booker T. Washington. Du Bois was evidently touched by Hope's concern that their friendship was in jeopardy. "You must not think that I have not known and appreciated your friendship for me," Du Bois begins in his reply, "or that I ever have doubted or doubt now your loyalty to the principles which we both so sincerely believe." He would go on to state however, "Of course I am sorry to see you or anyone in Washington's net. It's a dangerous place, old man, and you must keep your eyes open."[16] Du Bois was referring to the net of being indebted to white philanthropists and was apparently viewing Washington as some sort of Negro overseer. Nevertheless, his letter continues:

---

15 Du Bois, *Correspondence of W. E. B. Du Bois*, vol. 1, 448–449.
16 Ibid, 165–167.

Washington stands for Negro submission and slavery. Representing that, with unlimited funds, he can afford to be broad and generous and most of us must accept the generosity or starve. Having accepted it we are peculiarly placed and in a sense tongue-tied and bound. *I may have to place myself in that position yet, but, by God, I'll fight hard before I do it* [...] As I have said, so far, you have done what you had to do under the circumstances. I only trust that the pound of flesh demanded in return will not be vital. (emphasis mine).[17]

Du Bois wrote this response to Hope while in his early forties. But, by the time he comes to work on the encyclopedia in his midsixties, he must certainly had to have considered the position of his dear friend, Hope, and perhaps even Washington, for, as he mentions in his letter to Woodson, "The enemy has the money and they are going to use it." Perhaps this too may explain Du Bois' perplexing position toward Leo Frobenius and a number of white scholars he appears, at least in writing, to hold in high regard. Again, Du Bois had been quoting Frobenius in his works since at least his publication of *The Negro* in 1915.

But if we consider that by 1946, despite Du Bois' heavy critique of Western civilization as one of decadence and heading for collapse, he still somewhat relied on the charity of white scholars and philanthropy. Returning to the issue of the *Encyclopedia Africana*, recall that in 1937 Du Bois had written a letter to Stokes about Frobenius' interest in the project, a letter in which he "prize[d] very much." But it would be nearly another decade before this first iteration of the project was to be completed, as noted in a letter from Du Bois to Anson Stokes on May 10, 1946.[18] Interestingly, this would also be the same year as the publication of *The World and Africa*.

Frobenius died in the fall of 1938, so Du Bois could in no way be attempting to ingratiate himself any further to Frobenius for the sake of this or any future projects. But perhaps we must consider the concerns of Woodson regarding white scholars and the control over how African history is presented. Du Bois explains that no publications would at the time accept the works of Frank Snowden, whose works, in my estimation, represent no radical treatise, but, as Du Bois explained, "favored the Negro too much." So, if Du Bois wished for his works to be published and considered respectable scholarship by a

---

17 Ibid, 167.
18 W. E. B. Du Bois, *1868-1963. Letter from W. E. B. Du Bois to Phelps-Stokes Fund, May 10, 1946. W. E. B. Du Bois Papers (MS 312). Special Collections and University Archives, University of Massachusetts Amherst Libraries.*

wide audience, perhaps he felt he must use the popularity of some white scholars. Further, who better for him to use than those in which he shared a relationship with, if only on the account of academic interest. Nevertheless, given Frobenius' ideologies, for Du Bois to state that "he looked upon Africa with unprejudiced eyes and has been more valuable for his interpretation of the Negro than any other man I know,"[19] is quite startling.

To be sure, Frobenius had challenged some measure of racist thinking about Africans and colonial intrigue on the African continent, but he himself was still very much an imperialist, and though somewhat pessimistic of what colonialism was doing to distort genuine African culture, he was not at all oppositional to colonialism. Further, though again arguably less racist than many of his white contemporaries on the nature of African culture, he still regarded African culture as a degenerate version of the high culture of this mythical ancient Atlantis.[20]

To utilize the ideology of Petrie metaphorically, Frobenius essentially saw the mythological people of Atlantis as the dynastic race of Western Africa. Had it simply escaped Du Bois that Frobenius' theory on the mythological Atlanteans in West Africa was but another racist theory which sought to remove Africans from their historical agency? He had read Frobenius' volumes entitled *Atlantis* and stated clearly that Frobenius regards civilization along the Gulf of Guinea in West Africa "as possibly a development of the culture of that fabled island in the Atlantic."[21] But perhaps Du Bois simply decided to ignore or give little regard to the implications of such theory, deciding it to be simply, as he stated, "fanciful."[22] Nevertheless, this to some degree is representative of the ideology among the cadre of white scholars in which Du Bois was in communication with. We cannot rule out their possible influences on his thinking as he penned his histories of Africa. With that said, let us now return to the analysis of his historical survey of African history.

Du Bois on West Africa

Du Bois begins his chapter on West Africa, "Atlantis," with a critique that seems to be almost an affront to the very ideology behind its naming, though he does not mention Frobenius in this regard. He argues, "It has long been

---

19 Du Bois, *World and Africa*, xxxiii.
20 Suzanne Marchand, "Leo Frobenius and the Revolt against the West," *Journal of Contemporary History* 32, no. 2 (1997): 153–170, https://doi.org/10.1177/00220 0949703200202.
21 Du Bois, *World and Africa*, 96.
22 Ibid.

the belief of modern man that the history of Europe covers the essential history of civilization."²³ He challenges this ideology by stating the fact that the history of Europe is not a long one, and particularly when compared to the antiquity of Kemet and Kush, Europe is quite young. Du Bois even challenges the notion that history only occurs when there is written record to verify it. This notion, particularly in Du Bois' day, was the Western standard for determining which societies were to be labeled a civilization. Du Bois challenged this notion by stating:

> Let us turn to West Africa, where man tried a different way for a thousand years. First we face the query: how do we know what man did in West Africa, since black Africa has no written history? This brings the curious assumption that lack of written record means lack of matter and deed worth recording. The deeds of men that have been clearly and accurately written down are as pinpoints to the oceans of human experience. To recall that experience we must rely on written record, varying from direct narrative to indirect allusion and confirmation; we must rely also on memory-the memory of contemporary on-lookers, of those who heard their word, of those who over a lapse of years interpreted it and handed it on; we must rely on the mute but powerful testimony of habits, customs, and ideals, which echo and reflect vast stretches of past time. Finally, we agree upon as true history and actual fact any interpretation of past action which we today believe and want to believe is true. The relation of this last historical truth to real truth may vary from fact to falsehood.²⁴

Du Bois' thinking here suggests that a mere written account is insufficient in order to gain a holistic perspective of past events. He regards the memory, customs, habits and ideals of any group of which history is being recorded to be equally valuable. In this regard, Du Bois may have praised the works of Jan Vansina, an Africanist scholar who wrote extensively on the concept he referred to as "oral tradition" and its use as history. However, Vansina often failed to understand the African cosmological factors that shape *orature*. Oral literature and oral tradition must be more accurately described as orature. *Orature* is a term developed in the sixties by Ugandan linguist Pio Zirimu to

---

23 Ibid, 95.
24 Ibid, 96.

combat the stagnate condition being placed upon oral tradition by limiting it to simply a form of literature.[25]

Unfortunately, due to Zirimu's murder by agents of Idi Amin in the late seventies, he was never able to fully develop the concept.[26] However, Zirimu's contemporary, prolific scholar Ngũgĩ wa Thiong'o, directs us to South African scholar Pitika Ntuli as a legitimate source for a sophisticated, contemporary definition, being that orature is "a fusion of all artforms," or more descriptively, "orature is more than the fusion of all art forms. It is the conception and reality of a total view of life. It is the capsule of feeling, thinking, imagination, taste and hearing. It is the flow of a creative spirit."[27]

I must acknowledge that Vansina, Zirimu, Thiong'o and others were quite young on the scholarly stage, or not on the stage at all, at a time when Du Bois was quite old and perhaps would have considered some of their scholarship fringe and unscientific due to a lack of a well-established methodology at the time. Perhaps if Du Bois had lived long enough to see the maturation of such scholarship, he would have found it of great use. Nevertheless, I argue that this passage from Du Bois concerning memories, habits, customs and ideals, was quite close to their line of thinking in regard to orature, and perhaps the text, *The World and Africa*, itself represents in some small measure the spirit of the political motivations of authors such as Zirimu and Thiong'o.

Digressing, Du Bois' argues that the more arid temperatures in Europe perhaps allowed for the preservation and persistence of writing in those regions whereas, "heat and rain made written record in West Africa almost impossible and forced that land to rely on the memories of men." Du Bois also astutely observed that Africans "developed over the centuries a marvelous system of folklore and tradition." He would finish this argument with an assertion on the tradition of orature: "Back of both methods lay real human history recorded in cultural patterns, industry, religion and art."[28]

Du Bois mentions the Asante, referring to their art and textiles as something that was of great beauty and required a great deal of skill. He then spends a number of passages on the importance of art, tools and textiles to West African society in general. Moving away from the Asante, he focuses on the bronzes of Benin. He mentions, "When the state was seized by the British in 1897, they found carved elephant tusks, bronzes cast by the *cire-perdue*

---

25 Micere G. Mugo, *African Orature and Human Rights* (Roma, Lesotho, South Africa: Institute of Southern African Studies, National University of Lesotho, 1991), 40.
26 Ngũgĩ Wa Thiong'o, "Notes towards a Performance Theory of Orature," *Performance Research* 12, no. 3 (2007): pp. 4–7, https://doi.org/10.1080/13528160701771253.
27 Ibid.
28 Du Bois, *World and Africa*, 96.

process, including the well-known bronze head of a Negress, now in the British Museum, a masterpiece of art."[29] Interestingly, he neglects to mention that Benin was not merely seized but was burned to the ground during a raid and its arts and wares thus looted by British soldiers.

Du Bois mentions that Frobenius was led to discover a bronze statue in Nigeria sometime between 1910 and 1912. According to Du Bois, Frobenius suggested that the bronze statues as well as the discovery of terracotta sculptures were artifacts that belonged to an ancient Central African protoculture which existed some 4000 yBP. Frobenius may have been on to something, but only partially so. While not Central Africa exactly, we know today that the terracotta was created by the so-called Nok culture of modern Nigeria and dates back to at least 500 BCE. Further, the bronze castings from the town of Igbo-Ukwu in Nigeria have however only been dated to as early as 900 CE.[30] But both sets of artifacts require people to be proficient in iron smelting and we know that the earliest signs of iron smelting in Africa have been discovered around the Lake Chad area and date to as early as 1000 BCE. Although, given the nature of archaeology in Africa, it would be unsurprising that in some time in the near future more evidence would wield earlier dates.[31] Interestingly, we also see iron smelting emerge in Kemet, though much later than Lake Chad, sometime after 670 BCE.[32] Further, the Kush capital of Meroë became an iron-producing industry around 300 BCE.[33]

With that in mind, Du Bois also discusses Frobenius' suggestion that there is some link between these protocultures of West and Central African civilizations to those "which flourished along the banks of the Nile and in the Mediterranean Basin in the Classical and pre-Classical Ages."[34] There have been scholars in recent times who have made similar suggestions. Notably, the Senegalese scholar Aboubacry Moussa Lam and his text, *De l'origine égyptienne des Peuls*, translatable as *The Egyptian Origin of the Fulani*, in which he uses egyptological, linguistic and historical data to provide an analysis of the migration of certain groups of African people and flow of culture from the Nile Valley region to West Africa.

Works such as Lam's, according to Molefi Kete Asante, "serve to show that the continent was much more interactive than originally thought by

---

29 Ibid, 97.
30 Shillington, *History of Africa*, 102.
31 Ibid, 51.
32 Ibid, 53.
33 Ibid, 59.
34 Du Bois, *World and Africa*, 97.

the European historians who first encountered African people."³⁵ However, Lam's scholarship is meant to be a constructive analysis of unifying cultural foundations inherent within African societies. But given Frobenius' inclusion of the Mediterranean into his analysis, this suggestion was possibly a continuation of his Atlantean version of dynastic race theory. Further, given his use of the terms "Classical" and "pre-Classical ages," one can only ponder if the era of the ancient Mediterranean that Frobenius is referring to is one dominated largely by Greco-Roman influence.

Du Bois continued to quote Frobenius at-length concerning his ethnographic travels throughout West Africa. In an area known as Kassai-Sankuru, Frobenius witnessed what he assuredly thought of as oddities, such as, "villages of which the principal streets were bordered on each side, for leagues, with rows of palm trees, and of which the houses, decorated each one in charming fashion, were works of art as well."³⁶ This area named for the Sankuru river, is in the southwest of the Democratic Republic of the Congo, formerly known as the Kasaï-Oriental region. Frobenius speaks of a seemingly utopian area that when unaffected by European civilization existed as such:

> No man who did not carry sumptuous arms of iron or of copper, with inlaid blades and handles covered with serpent skin. Everywhere velvets and silken stuffs. Each cup, each pipe, each spoon was an object of art perfectly worthy to be compared to the creations of the Roman European style. But all this was only the particularly tender and iridescent bloom which adorns a ripe and marvelous fruit; the gestures, the manners, the moral code of the entire people, from the little child to the old man, although they remained within absolutely natural limits, were imprinted with dignity and grace, in the families of the princes and the rich as in the vassals and slaves. I know of no northern people who can be compared with these primitives for unity of civilization. Alas these last 'Happy Isles'! They, also, were submerged by the tidal wave of European civilization. And the peaceful beauty was carried away by the floods.³⁷

This passage perhaps exemplifies the aforementioned words of Carter G. Woodson when he suggested that "the white man, even when he is honest

---

35 Asante, *History of Africa*, 103.
36 Du Bois, *World and Africa*, 100.
37 Ibid.

and sincere, cannot at his best write the history of colored people and portray their present status, when he does not live and move among them." Frobenius cannot help but suggest what is "worthy" of being compared to the "Roman European style." Why is it that Romanesque stylings must be considered the standard by which to measure the stylings of a central African civilization? Do these African people have the same standards of beauty, functionality or even durability of product as that of Europe? Could Frobenius not have simply compared what he saw in this area to other regions in Africa in which he visited? To be sure, one could certainly argue that Frobenius is writing for a Western audience and thus must make comparisons with phenomena that Europeans are more familiar with. However, for the purposes of the overall message Du Bois wishes to convey in *The World and Africa*, I find it essential to challenge these comparisons with European culture. Of course, these are questions that Du Bois may not be entirely equipped to ask of Frobenius' descriptions, but they are worthy questions to ask all the same.

After all, Du Bois himself was the one to suggest that Europeans had forced Africans to view themselves and their culture as inferior. Is that not the meaning of his words, "the old culture and ethical standards were degraded or disappeared, and gradually all over Africa spread the inferiority complex, the fear of color, the worship of white skin, the imitation of white ways of doing and thinking, whether good, bad, or indifferent"?[38] How else would Europeans impose a sense of cultural inferiority on the African if not by stating that their cultural ideology, aesthetics, motifs and products may or may not be "worthy" of the standards of their own?

It is of great certainty that the people Frobenius described living in Kassai-Sankuru viewed themselves as standard and, at least until the coming of colonization, were unconcerned by the standards and morals of Europe. Frobenius himself seems to allude to this in some crude and still comparative way when referring to their sense of unity, but yet still refers to these people he encountered as "primitives." The casual application of such language was perhaps something Du Bois at the time elected to ignore, or he himself saw no issue. After all, as covered in the first chapter, Du Bois' use of the term *native* bared much similarity in condescension and assured superiority.

On religion, Du Bois states, "All this industry in West Africa was developed around the Africans' ideas of religion: the worship of souls of trees and plants of animals; the use of the fetish; the belief in fairies and monsters. Along with this went training for medicine men and chiefs, and careful rules for birth,

---

38 Ibid, 49.

marriages, and funerals."[39] If only Du Bois had lived to see another decade of life, he could have perhaps gained much insight on the nature of African religion from John Mbiti and his text, *African Religion and Philosophy*. There is much to find in praise and criticism concerning the scholarship of Mbiti, but his works are still considered authoritative. Mbiti would state within: "According to African peoples, man lives in a religious universe, so that natural phenomena and objects are intimately associated with God." Mbiti would follow this by stating, "Many concepts are reported which associate God with natural objects and phenomena. We have already mentioned that African peoples regard this as a religious universe, and this attitude is fully illustrated by the way they 'read' God into various objects and phenomena."[40]

What Mbiti challenges in this passage is the false notion that traditional African spirituality sees African people doltishly worshiping animals and inanimate objects. Instead, Africans understand that they too are a part of nature and are simply another creation of whatever name they reserve for the creator. They believe that they must respect as well as be in harmony with nature. This would have been a useful analysis for Du Bois to utilize in his discussion of African religion. Alas, Du Bois died roughly six years before Mbiti published the first edition of this text. Further, just as with the likes of Thiong'o and Zirimu, even if Du Bois had lived long enough to assess his work, he may have considered Mbiti simply another young scholar just finding his way to the academic stage and not worthy of much attention.

Digressing, Du Bois again called upon the opinions of Frobenius in order to discuss Yoruba religion. Frobenius was apparently awestruck by the tales of Shango, but again is, as Woodson would put it, limited in his capacity to understand African people and their cultural phenomena due most certainly to his foreign disposition:

> There is, *among the deities possessed by all the other dark-skinned African nations combined, not one who can equal Shango*, the [West African] Yoruban God of Thunder, in significance. This country's first royal ruler sprang, as its people believe, from his loins. His posterity still have the right to give the country its kings [...] Myth relates that Shango was born of the All-Mother, Yemaya. Powerful, warlike, and mighty, *he was as great*

---

39 Ibid, 100.
40 John S. Mbiti, *African Religions & Philosophy*, 2nd ed. (Oxford, UK: Heinemann, 1990), 62.

a God as was ever created in the minds of a nation striving for self-expression. (emphasis mine).[41]

In the remaining pages on West Africa Du Bois focuses a bit on architecture and, obviously impressed, he refers to it as being "strikingly integrated with climate, physiography, and culture."[42] Due to the damp climate in this part of Africa, Du Bois once again stresses the importance of "the art of memory recording, of tradition handed down," and, again obviously impressed, he states, "Here [that tradition] was developed to an astonishing extent."[43] But he also mentions there being evidence in his day of systems of writings existing in modern-day Guinea-Coast and Cameroon, and opines that there were "probably others."

Du Bois found particular interest in the Mossi people. Relying on the work of French ethnographer Maurice Delafosse, Du Bois would posit that "the Mossi state did not make territorial conquests and always constituted a rampart against the extension of Mohammedanism. In its integrity it represented a civilization uniquely and really Negro."[44] He ends the chapter with a brief on the history of The European Trade of Enslaved Africans in West Africa and the beginnings of colonialism, and how such affected the various African nations involved. With great certainty, Du Bois concludes that the level of culture among West Africans in the fifteenth century was beyond that of Europe. He argues further that the so-called slave trade is what "stopped and degraded this development."[45] Du Bois would elaborate:

> The character of culture on the slave coasts slowly changed; an element of cruelty crept into states like Benin and Dahomey, although other states, like that of the Yoruba, seem to have resisted to some extent. But the ancient culture of the Atlantic coast was ruined by the trade in slaves, by the importation of gin, and by the European trade; European goods drove out native art and artistic industry.[46]

---

41 Du Bois, *World and Africa*, 100.
42 Ibid, 101.
43 Ibid.
44 Ibid.
45 Ibid, 103.
46 Ibid.

Du Bois on the Bantu

The eighth chapter of *The World and Africa* focuses on the Bantu migration. *Bantu* is a phrase extracted by German philologist, Wilhelm Bleck, from a collection of African languages spoken by the descendants of the people that participated in this migration.[47] It is used both linguistically and historically to describe the collection of peoples to whom the language belongs. The word "Bantu" is a mixture of the stem *ntu*, meaning "person," and the prefix *ba-*, meaning "plural," to form the term, "people." However, the term "Bantu" itself does not refer to any one language or group of people.[48]

Du Bois would say of the Bantu, "The migration and formation of the Bantu peoples was a long slow movement beginning a thousand years or more before Christ and extending to the nineteenth century of our era with periods of stoppage and acceleration."[49] This would place Du Bois' estimate of Bantu migration at approximately 1000 BCE, or roughly 3000 yBP. Du Bois would also suggest that the earliest Bantu languages formed around the headwaters of the Nile near the so-called Great Lakes region. It is uncertain how Du Bois received this estimation. Perhaps it was from the scholarship of British linguist Harry H. Johnson, of which he cites in his footnotes, but not specifically for this particular bit of information.

Recent scholarship has however discovered that the proto-Bantu language actually developed in southwestern Cameroon, either at or before 3000 BCE.[50] This would place the beginnings of the migration at around 5000 yBP, which aligns with the time of the first dynasty of Kemet. Perhaps the migration of Bantu speakers both east and south was sparked by some of the same motivations that drove Saharan Africans to the Nile Valley. We know that around 6000 yBP, which would date to around 4000 BCE, a rapid event of aridification in the once lush Sahara region must have stood as a primary motivator for the Saharan groups to migrate to the Nile Valley due to waning resources and population pressures.[51] Interestingly, very early signs of complex societies in West Africa begin at around the same time, c. 4000 BCE.[52] Perhaps we may soon find that to be a valid motivator for the

---

47 Dubow, *Scientific Racism in Modern South Africa*, 78.
48 For a detailed treatment on the Bantu language see: Christopher Ehret, *History and the Testimony of Language* (Berkeley, CA: University of California Press, 2011).
49 Du Bois, *World and Africa*, 107.
50 Ehret, *History and the Testimony of Language*, 122.
51 Asante, *History of Africa*, 10.
52 Graham Connah, *African Civilization: an Archaeological Perspective*, 3rd ed. (New York, NY: Cambridge University, 2016), 157.

Bantu as well. After all, the Bantu language, though spoken across one-third of Africa, is but a branch of the larger Niger-Congo language family,[53] which extends into the Sahara border.

Nevertheless, next Du Bois mentions the "Hamitic race" theory, of which he quickly, and without any other thought to this regard, submits is "an entirely unnecessary hypothesis." As aforementioned in previous chapters, Du Bois is quite certain the hypothesis of foreign origins for African civilization is racist and an attempt to reduce the agency of African people. Next, Du Bois categorizes the types of Bantu cultures his study has exposed, being agriculturalists, herdsmen and those knowledgeable of iron and copper metallurgy. He would even state that it is possible that the so-called "invasion" of Bantu speakers was facilitated by their use of iron weapons.[54]

This note on iron weapons may hold some weight, but it is important that we reconsider the use of "invasion" to describe their migration. An "invasion" would imply that the Bantu were an entirely foreign force to the regions that they came to occupy. As of now, we do not have a complete picture on the nature of the Bantu expansion into various parts of Africa. There is the possibility that migrations to-and-fro also occurred which would blur the lines between who is to be considered foreign to a region. Thus, such language paradoxically fails to consider that these movements took place over the course of thousands of years which would include much time for cross-cultural exchange such as trade, intermarriage and other culturally unifying factors that would stymie the argument of a purely invasive force. Certainly, minor historical events that would amount to an invasion between certain groups most likely occurred, but this would not account for the whole of Bantu migration history.

Continuing with his survey, Du Bois would argue that the Kingdom of Monomotapa, also known as Mutapa, a kingdom which expanded well beyond the borders of modern-day Zimbabwe, as well as other minor kingdoms such as Kitwara, perhaps pre-dated the Bantu migration. On this note, he could not have been more wrong as the Bantu populations had already migrated to those regions long before the founding of those kingdoms. The founders of Great Zimbabwe, for example, were ancestors of the Shona people, who in every form are Bantu in origin. Their language, chiShona, is one of the most widely spoken Bantu languages.[55]

---

53 Ehret, *History and the Testimony of Language*, 10.
54 Du Bois, *World and Africa*, 108.
55 Ehret, *History and the Testimony of Language*, 110.

Du Bois ends his chapter on the Bantu migration with an extensive note on Zimbabwe and the remains there known today as Great Zimbabwe. Of which he states, "The ruins of Zimbabwe show today an extraordinary cultural past, presenting certain phenomenal remains not to be found anywhere else in Africa south of the Great Lakes."[56] He mentions extensive gold mines, tons of colossal stone buildings and, interestingly, "forms of ceremonial not common among present Bantu people." He also suggested that there were "impressions of some Asiatic influence."[57]

To be sure, there has been evidence of wares in Great Zimbabwe that were imported from China;[58] however, this played no significant influence on their civilization. We also know that the rise of inland trade with the Swahili coast (consisting of some Arab and Indian merchants) did not pick up significantly until the eighteenth century, though with a few small waves of trade activity dating back to before 1500 CE.[59] Du Bois attempts to make clear in one of the concluding passages:

> That Asiatic and even Chinese influences were present at times in this remarkable cultural development, with its irrigation and fortresses, is not improbable. The trade between Asia and Africa by way of the East Coast dates back to pre-history and was especially rife when Mohammedans took refuge there in the seventh, eighth, and ninth centuries. But just as neither Arabs, Persians, nor Portuguese ever dominated the blacks here in historic times, *so the culture of Zimbabwe was without doubt always dominantly Negro*, with that cultural inspiration that everywhere comes with foreign contacts. (emphasis mine).[60]

Du Bois on Asia in Africa

Du Bois ends the previous chapter, "March of the Bantu," somewhat alluding to the Asian influence in Africa. Once again, he reaches back in ancient history to present what he specifies as "the story of the outpouring of Asia into Africa from A.D. 500 to 1500, and the effect which the interaction of these two continents had on the world."[61] Du Bois' initial passages on this history

---

56 Du Bois, *World and Africa*, 110.
57 Ibid.
58 Asante, *History of Africa*, 153.
59 Basil Davidson, *A History of East and Central Africa: to the Late Nineteenth Century* (New York, NY: Doubleday, 1969), 191.
60 Du Bois, *World and Africa*, 111.
61 Ibid, 113.

suggest a number of erroneous things. First, though he correctly guessed the origins of humanity to be Africa in earlier chapters, he doubles back here to suggest that it is "doubtful which continent is the point of origin."[62] Though this is an honest enough position given the information available to him at the time, it is a regression in his thinking.

Du Bois also displays confusion as he deals with the differences between phenotype and cultural identity. It is important to distinguish between phenotype and cultural identity. I state this because this is something Du Bois should have considered given his own unique circumstance as an African in America who was not of darker skin. While it is true that much of the population of Africa is dark skinned, this is not the case for all Africans. Some, such as the San, are quite light skinned and required no outside genetics for this to be the case. It is simply a matter of geographical and climatic circumstances. For Du Bois to suppose that Melanesians and Dravidians are African or "Negro" simply because of their darker color removes their cultural agency. Indeed, both Dravidians and Melanesians migrated from the African continent tens of thousands of years ago. However, so did the Europeans, who did so at a much later date even.

Du Bois' suggestion of "pre-Dravidian negrillos" and "Dravidian negros" could just as equally apply to Europe in a form that would suggest "pre-European negros." Such a suggestion would, just in the case of Du Bois, form some legitimacy based on purely color basis, but holds no weight as it comes to cultural foundations. To be sure, we know that the Indus Valley traded with East Africa, particularly Kemet and Kush, for many centuries. There too perhaps was a trade in various cultural aspects as well as goods and wares. For example, the worship of Het-heru, who is represented as a cow and is arguably the most ancient known deity of Kemet, shares many similarities with the Kush civilization's deification of cows which in India exists today even after the cultural disruption and confusion known as Vedic period. However, the Greeks and Romans appropriated and reappropriated a whole pantheon of Kemetic deities, but that in no way makes them African people, or "negroes" for that matter.

However, for what it is worth, recent scholarship indicates Du Bois may have been correct to suggest that Krishna was the indigenous deity of the Dravidian ancestors, that was eventually, yet paradoxically, incorporated into the Vedic pantheon during the Indo-Aryan migration into India.[63] Once

---

62 Ibid.
63 Scholars during Du Bois' day had already been suggesting a Dravidian origin for Krishna, see: Paul Masson-Oursel, Philippe Stern, and Helena de

referred to as the Indo-Aryan invasion, this description is no longer favorable. There is still much debate over the true origins of Hindu culture. Much of the debate stems from political motivations by Indian nationalist who disregard the Indo-Aryan migration analysis in favor of a completely indigenous origin for the peoples of the Indian subcontinent. There is however far too much linguistic and archaeological evidence that suggests otherwise, and that the true origins of indigenous Indian culture and mythology lies with the Indus Valley civilization and their descendants, the Dravidians. Nevertheless, neither the people who formed the culture of the Indus Valley nor the Indo-Aryan who miscegenated with them during the Vedic period can be classified as culturally African.

Du Bois spends a great deal of time in this chapter focusing on what he perceives to be the African presence in various parts of Asia such as India, China and even Japan.[64] He then switches to a discussion on the apparent Blackness of many Arab groups. Naturally, there is some validity to the apparent Africanity of certain Arabic phenotypes by way of miscegenation, such as Tippu Tip, the east-African slave trader. However, while Tippu appeared African in phenotype, as well as partially African in blood, he was culturally and politically an Arab, who had little regard for the African lives he both stole and massacred in the Congo basin.[65] Again, Du Bois is reaching for connections that bear no cultural significance. We can argue that this was simply a product of racial attitudes in his time, which regarded color as a symbol of being either African or Asian, and the apparent lack of "color" a measurement of whiteness.

There is little mention of the Bantu populations surrounding Kilwa and other areas of the Swahili coast, of which Du Bois references Portuguese sources who describe the miscegenation of Bantu Africans and Arabs. Next, Du Bois turns our attention to the Ottomans. He first reminds us that the Persians and then the Turks would come to rule Kemet, now known as مصر, or Maṣr, in the contemporary local Arabic language. The remainder of the chapter focuses on either Ottoman or general Islamic influences in the African interior. Perhaps Du Bois found it significant to acknowledge what was known at the time of Africa's relationship with the Asian world as this chapter is more about the African presence in Asiatic cultural and

---

Willman-Grabowska, *Ancient India and Indian Civilization*, trans. M. R. Dobie (London, UK: Routledge, 2013). For a more updated treatment on this theory see: Andrée F. Sjoberg, *Dravidian Language and Culture: Selected Essays* (Kuppam, India: Dravidian University, 2009).
64 Du Bois, *World and Africa*, 113–115.
65 Asante, *History of Africa*, 223–224.

sociopolitical history, and particularly when some of that history occurred on the African continent.

I would argue today that any such discussion would be better served with sources that engage with language. We know today that the Semitic language family is but one of the six branches of Afrasian languages that all share their beginnings in the African continent. Of the six, the others being Cushitic, Omotic, Chadic, Tamazight and Kemetic, the Semitic branch is the only one to branch outside of Africa into the southwestern extremities of Asia.[66] This is significant to mention because it helps bolster Du Bois' point that while Asiatic cultures certainly had cultural exchange with Africa, the linguistic data seems to suggest that the bulk of influence has historically stemmed out of Africa into Asia. Digressing, Du Bois closes his chapter with a note on the "mutual fertilization of cultures" between Africa and Asia, before preparing readers for a history on the so-called Black Sudan and how the people in those lands brought civilization to Europe.

Du Bois on the Sudan

Chapter 5, which serves as the penultimate chapter in Du Bois' text on Africa, is titled "The Black Sudan." This chapter begins with a brief on the so-called Moorish conquest of Spain. Once again, Du Bois relies on the works of Frobenius, this time to inform his readers that the eleventh-century civilizations south of the Sahara, or "negro Africa" as Frobenius refers to it, were in full bloom and, though many were Muslim, the beautiful turbans and clothes of the Sudanese were well in use before the birth of Mohammed.[67] Du Bois too makes this distinction between "Berbers," who I respectfully refer to as Amazigh, and "Negroes." Perhaps this is his reasoning for the erroneous term "Black Sudan."

To be sure, Du Bois acknowledges that the Amazigh are not Arabs, but this distinction between the so-called "Black Sudan" and other African groups is a consistent sign of a prioritization of skin color in which to designate the difference between Africans and other groups. The *bilād as-sūdān*, or "Black Sudan," is a geographic and racial characterization grounded by the false assumption that the Sahara served as a barrier that made the cultural bifurcation of the whole of North Africa and the "bilād as-sūdān" a social, cultural

---

66 Ehret, *History and the Testimony of Language*, 136–137.
67 Du Bois, *World and Africa*, 128.

and demographic reality.⁶⁸ Many today still operate on this false assumption, but the reality of the situation is that Africans have for millennia traversed the Saharan desert region for a variety of purposes and the resulting cultural exchange continues to this very day.

Nevertheless, Du Bois speaks of the Amazigh who formed the Almoravid dynasty as, "Berbers with Negro blood, and hosts of pure Negro adherents."⁶⁹ The Amazigh are culturally African people and have been in the northern regions of Africa for several thousands of years. Furthermore, according to Molefi Kete Asante, "The Amazigh have not been interested in the racial politics of Europeans who claim that the Amazigh, because of skin color, are Europeans."⁷⁰ Recall also, their language, Tamazight, is one of the six branches of Afrasian languages.

Next, Du Bois' historical survey branches into the ancient Sudanic empires of Wagadu (Ghana), Mali and Songhai. He briefly mentions Sundiata and his capture of the old Wagadu's capital, Kumbi Saleh, in 1240. Naturally, Du Bois also gives a bit of attention to the most famous king of Mali, Mansa Musa and his pilgrimage to Mecca. He seemingly takes delight in reporting what he knows of Mansa Musa's exploits along his journey, such as the fact that he brought with him a large entourage who managed the transport of the Mansa's eighty camel loads of gold dust.

Du Bois then brings the readers' attention to the fact that Europe was still suffering their "Dark Ages" during this golden period of empire in the Sudan. Du Bois states of this era that "the Mandingan empire of Melle [*sic*] occupied nearly the whole of what is now French Africa and part of British West Africa."⁷¹ He then quotes at great length the words of Ibn Battuta, who Molefi Kete Asante designates as one of the four historians whose writings are responsible for what we know of, and I venture to say as well as how we may somewhat interpret, the history of the Sudanic empires.⁷² Du Bois quotes

---

68 For a detailed analysis of the concept of the *bilād as-sūdān*; see: Michael A. Gomez, *African Dominion: A New History of Empire in Early and Medieval West Africa* (Princeton University Press, 2019).
69 Ibid, 129.
70 Asante further illustrates the issue: "The question of race in Africa is not the same question as in America or in Europe. A person whose ancestors have been in Africa for several thousand years is clearly African in behavior, attitude, and response to environment. Blackness is a color, but it is also an experience: that is, a cultural and historical experience related to social practice, language, and cultural expressions." See: Molefi Kete Asante, *The History of Africa: the Quest for Eternal Harmony* (New York, NY: Routledge, 2019), 20–21.
71 Du Bois, *World and Africa*, 131.
72 Asante, History of Africa, 120–121.

Ibn Battuta as stating, "One has the impression that Mandingo was a real state whose organization and civilization could be compared with those of the [Muslim] kingdoms or indeed the Christian kingdoms of the same epoch."[73] We see again in this statement the desire to compare African civilization with that of European, and now Arab. Du Bois, as I mentioned before, is perhaps attempting to help his readers understand the extent of the greatness of African civilization by providing a reference for which they are familiar. Battuta perhaps the same. However, therein lies the supposition that primitiveness and savagery should exist here instead of civilization. Take the words of Ibn Battuta for example:

> The state of affairs amongst these people is indeed extraordinary. Their men show no signs of jealousy whatever; no one claims descent from his father, but on the contrary from his mother's brother. A person's heirs are his sister's sons, not his own sons. This is a thing which I have seen nowhere in the world except among the Indians of Malabar. *But those are heathens*; these people are Muslims, punctilious in observing the hours of prayer, studying books of law, and memorizing the Koran.[74]

Battuta, struck dumb by the cultural customs of Mali, immediately wants to compare the men and women to the supposed heathenism he perceives in similar cultural structures in India. However, for Battuta, what saves the Mandingo from the rank of savagery is their adherence to Islam. Just as Du Bois dismissed the agency of the *natives* of his day, it is curious as to how Battuta, and Du Bois in turn, would describe the people of Mali if not for their practice of the Muslim faith. This is important to consider because Batutta is relying on the idea that those without Abrahamic religion are savage heathens. Du Bois too once utilized the term "savage." In *The Negro* he used the term more than a few times and not only to describe ancient groups but also to describe people who lived in the same century as he did. Most notably he describes how during the Haitian Revolution mulattoes began to turn against Dessalines by stating, "The educated mulattoes especially objected to submission to the savage African *mores*."[75] However, by the publishing of *The World and Africa*, except for when quoting others, he uses the word "savage" descriptively in relation to Africans only once to describe a period in Kemetic

---

73 Du Bois, *World and Africa*, 132.
74 Ibid.
75 Du Bois, The Negro, 175.

history.[76] Nevertheless, as he clearly lacks an agency-affirming cultural analysis such as Afrocentricity, it is imperative to continuously tease out the subtle nuances of cultural hierarchy Du Bois presents.

Digressing, later in the chapter Du Bois recounts the story of *Parsifal*, written by German poet Wolfram von Eschenbach. This is the story of a European knight who meets an African queen and supposedly falls in love with her because, according to Du Bois, "her noble and pure character seems to him quite equal to that of a Christian."[77] The knight then marries, impregnates, and, not long after, abandons the African woman, being supposedly "disturbed" by their religious differences. Given the circumstances in this brief summary, it should be more appropriate that his contradictory socioreligious beliefs left him with such weak resolve that the one who should be "disturbed" is the queen. Nevertheless, years later the knight married another woman who bore him a son, Parsifal.

Following the knight's death, Parsifal supposedly becomes an even greater knight than his father, and is charged with leading the search for the mythical Holy Grail. Along his journey he meets a man named Feirefiz, or "colored man," who is revealed to be, unbeknownst to Parsifal, his older brother by way of the African queen his father abandoned. They do battle and, upon breaking his sword, Parsifal thought for sure he had met his end. However, Feirefiz honorably spares his life. After some friendly discourse they discover that the two of them are indeed brothers. The story ends with Feirefiz, after falling in love with a European woman, agreeing to be baptized and before he "carries Christianity to the East."

Du Bois relays this story as an apparent example of the attempts of Western writers' to soften the tensions of race relations. "It points toward the bridging of the gaps between creeds and races," begins Du Bois, "and is of great significance in revealing the thought of enlightened and civilized society in Europe in the thirteenth century."[78] This is an irresponsible statement. Tales like these only serve to propagate the Christian faith and the apparent superiority of European culture. This tale is similar to others at the time such as that of *The Adventures of Esplandián*, written by Spanish romance novelist Garci Rodríguez de Montalvo. In which, he relates the story of a mythical Queen, Califia, who supposedly falls in love with a Spanish prince and challenges him to battle for a chance to marry him.

---

76 Du Bois, *World and Africa*, 85.
77 Ibid, 137.
78 Ibid, 138.

Califia fails in battle and is forced to admit the prince's betrothed, a European woman, is more beautiful than she and that the Christian religion must be the one true religion as opposed to her *pagan* one.[79] The name Califia, though in the tale she was "pagan," was actually a reference to the term "caliph," a Muslim term for ruler, as Califia was the queen of an all-woman nation of warriors. The parallels in von Eschenbach's tale, *Parsifal*, as reported by Du Bois, and that of Califia, both written during the era of the Crusades, is clear that Europe regarded itself as superior to other cultures and did so with religious justification.

I argue that Du Bois suffered from what Ama Mazama refers to as *cognitive hiatus*.[80] There is a lapse in Du Bois' thinking for him to suggest that fables about African monarchs being smitten by the supposed beauty and righteousness of European people, culture and religion to the degree that they readily turn on their own culture and religion is somehow an example of "bridging the gap between creed and races." These stories instead represent assimilationist propaganda that forces upon the consciousness of those who imbibe these stories a perpetual hierarchical imposition of Eurocentric norms.

For the great remainder of the chapter, Du Bois, drawing upon the works of J.A. Rodgers and Stanley E. Lane-Poole, tackles the question of race as it involves the so-called Moors. He centers on Shakespeare and his use of African or "Moorish" characters in plays such as *The Merchant of Venice* and *Othello*. Of which he suggests, "Despite this there are critics who have almost had hysterics in seeking to deny that Shakespeare meant to paint a Negro as a noble warrior and successful suitor of a beautiful white woman."[81] One can only question here why should Du Bois want his target audience, especially if the audience is principally meant to be of African descent, to care about this circumstance? Perhaps he himself is still at this time affected by his *double consciousness* of 40 years before, being "two unreconciled strivings; two warring ideals in one dark body." For, as aforementioned, Du Bois recognizes in one instance that "all over Africa spread the inferiority complex, the fear of color, the worship of white skin, the imitation of white ways of doing and thinking, whether good, bad, or indifferent," and yet he himself is concerned about the ways in which Europeans interpret the intentions of other Europeans in the midst of using Africans as literary plot devices and propaganda tools.

---

79 As a side note, Califia was the mythical queen of California, which is how the US state received its name. For a detailed account of this tale see: Edward Everett Hale, *The Queen of California: the Origin of the Name of California*, ed. Eric Jones (Eric M. Jones; Kindle Edition, 2014).
80 Mazama, "Cognitive Hiatus and White Validation Syndrome," 25–38.
81 Du Bois, *World and Africa*, 138.

African World Antecedent Methodology

In chapters IX and X, Du Bois capitalized on a range of sources that were available to him. As aforementioned, Du Bois heavily relied on Leo Frobenius and his accounts of West and West-Central Africa. While the notes of Frobenius that Du Bois employs merely imply some notions of cultural continuity, it is not something that at all becomes a focus. Du Bois quotes the French ethnographer, Maurice Delafosse on the nature of individualism versus collectivism in West Africa:

> West Africans are still today in the period of integral collectivism, known to our ancestors before the Middle Ages, while we have arrived at individualism. The question which presents itself is to know whether indeed we have made definitive progress in this line, since many of our thinkers, of the so called advance guard, demand, as a benefit, the return to collectivism, although of a somewhat different form. This proves that the peoples of Negro Africa have not marched at the same rate of speed as the peoples of Europe, but in nowise proves that the former are inferior to the latter. Who knows, indeed, whether the latter have not gone too fast?[82]

Du Bois offers no analysis of this passage, but it is quite a curious one. I argue that perhaps the issue is not that West Africans have not "marched at the same rate of speed" or that Europeans have "gone too fast" but yet different and unique cultural circumstances have yielded different and unique cultural ethoses. But the culture of collectivism is not found singularly in West Africa. It can be argued that throughout the whole of the African continent indigenous African cultures primarily see collectivism, rather than individualism, as the norm rather than the exception. This collectivism is a primary aspect of the African cultural matrix, or *asili*. Which, according to Marimba Ani, "must be identified in order to make sense of the collective creations of its members."[83] I will opine more on this in the final chapter.

Du Bois' relatively short chapter on the Bantu leans heavily on the works of the British colonialist and explorer Harry Johnston and to a smaller degree on the scholarship of Ghanaian doctor and historian Raphael Armattoe. Du Bois uses their works to suggest patterns of civilization accountable only because of the Bantu migration and resulting cultural influence. However, it

---

82 Ibid, 102.
83 Ani, *Yurugu*, XXV.

is the words of German explorer and ethnologist, Georg Schweinfurth, that bears the most interest. Du Bois quotes him as stating:

> Not a custom, not a superstition is found in one part which is not more or less accurately repeated in another; not one contrivance of design, not one weapon of war exists of which it can be declared that it is exclusive property of any one race. From north to south, and from sea to sea, in some form or other, every invention is sure to be repeated; it is "the thing that has been." If we could at once grasp and set before our minds facts that are known (whether as regards language, race, culture, history, or development) of that vast region of the world which is comprehended in the name of Africa, we should have before us the witness of an intermingling of races which is beyond all precedent. And yet, bewildering as the prospect would appear, it remains a fact not to be gainsaid, that it is impossible for any one to survey the country as a whole without perceiving that high above the multitude of individual differences there is throned a principle of unity which embraces well-nigh all the population.[84]

For Du Bois' survey on the Asiatic presence in Africa, he relies a bit on African American historian, J. A. Rodgers, whom Du Bois himself admits is with faults in his theory and historicism. To that end, he also uses other authors such as Stanley Lane-Pool and Reginald Coupland. Travelogues such as those of the Portuguese explorer Duarte Barbosa and Moroccan scholar and explorer Ibn Battuta were also employed. Both Lane-Pool and Barbosa speak on the apparent cultural unity of Moorish populations, while Coupland and Battuta speak on East Africa and their relationship with the Middle East and India by way of either warfare or enslavement. Perhaps some of these groups became the modern-day Sidi people in India who, while having adopted a good portion of Indian culture, in many respects are still very culturally and linguistically Bantu.[85]

Du Bois' notes on the Sudan are likewise suggestive of cultural cohesiveness and continuity between the various Sudanic empires of Wagadu, Mali and Songhai. He even notes the relationship between these well-known civilizations and that of the less acknowledged kingdoms of Kanem and Bornu.

---

84 Ibid, 111.
85 Helene Basu, "Music and the Formation of Sidi Identity in Western India," *History Workshop Journal* 65, no. 1 (January 2008): 161–178, https://doi.org/10.1093/hwj/dbm069.

Naturally, Du Bois had to deal with the encroachment of Islam and the effects Asiatic Muslim groups such as the Turks had on African culture. Islam, just as Christianity, drastically affected African life and culture. Du Bois seemingly focused on the aspects of Islam which may have been unifying. However, as aforementioned, he then began to focus a great deal on the parallels he foresees between African culture and European mythology and folklore.

As you read through the brief AWAM analysis, notice that I continuously make a triangular connection between African Americans, the Afro-Caribbean and Africa. If the reason is not apparent, it is imperative to understand that while various dynamic nouveau-African cultures have developed in the Americas with their own unique and rich histories, those histories have been, and continue to be, constantly intertwined. In fact, modern African, African American and African Caribbean culture would not at all be what they are today without this history of constant exchange.

Obviously, this also includes nouveau-African cultures in South America; however, though I am very general about the areas covered, this current analysis does not include South America for the sake of brevity. This is by no means an attempt at exclusion, as there is much to gain from an analysis which includes the African populations of countries such as Mexico, Guyana, Suriname, Colombia, and, of course, Brazil. Furthermore, this is not an exhaustive or even extensive list of cultural continuity. However, it provides an example of the type of framework that should be considered for anyone willing to develop a comparative analysis of specific African cultural groups.

Kanna

There are a number of direct cultural antecedents that link African Americans to this time period. Cultural phenomena such as food, aesthetics, music, dance, motif and language extant among African Americans can all be traced back to various groups on the African continent. One very apparent bit of cultural phenomena deals primarily with the corporeal and corporeal aesthetics. African people from coast to coast tend to wear clothes of bright colors and many patterns. This is something seen quite evident in African American culture as well and has been documented as a cultural element that derived from the various ethnic groups African Americans were stolen from.

Zora Neale Hurston once stated, "The will to adorn is the second most notable characteristic in Negro expression."[86] Hurston was a famed African

---

86 Helen Bradley Foster, *New Raiments of Self: African American Clothing in the Antebellum South* (Oxford, UK: Berg, 1997), 71.

American novelist and anthropologist who studied African American and Afro-Caribbean culture with both earnestness and a passion that signifies her personal connection to the history and culture of her people. Art historian Helen Foster, in her text, "*New Raiments of Self*," has this to say about her words:

> [Hurston's] remarks about twentieth-century African Americans mirror what others had noted about the West Africans whom they had encountered in earlier centuries. The West Africans who were brought to the New World filtered new ideas about bodily raiments through much older ideas about self-presentation.[87]

In the text, Foster notes a number of African cultural phenomena as it relates to clothing as aesthetics. She mentions topics ranging from the need during the antebellum era to use bones and wood to make West-African style combs,[88] the need to be fashionable for all religious gatherings,[89] as well as contemporary arguments about wearing braids in corporate America.[90] Perhaps the most interesting person she quotes is Charles Ball. Assuredly, Charles Ball was not his original name as he was captured in West Africa before being transported to the southern United States. Likely as a matter of comparison to the phenotypic aesthetics of his own people Ball would exclaim, "I had never seen white people before; and they appeared to me the ugliest creatures in the world."[91] With that statement, it is with great certainty Ball had not been afflicted with an inferiority complex. Though such sadly became the fate of many African descendants in the so-called Americas.

In the last chapter I mentioned Akan spirituality, particularly I addressed the distinction between a person's *ntoro* (spirit) and their kra (soul). I also mentioned that this bears similarities with the Bambara's position of *ni* (soul) and *dya* (double). Michael Gomez believes that these elements were merged along with other West and Central African cultures during the formation of what's known as the *ring shout*. Gomez noted:

> The embrace of the shout allowed the Igbo, the Akan, and the Mende to understand just how much they had in common with respect to their

---

87 Ibid.
88 Ibid, 250.
89 Ibid, 188–189.
90 Ibid, 269.
91 Ibid, 23.

veneration of the ancestors and their connection to the land. The Akan distinction between the *ntoro* (spirit) and the *kra* (soul) would have found resonance in the Bambara division of *ni* (soul) and *dya* (double). Lesser deities, such as the *agbara* of the Igbo and the *abosom* of the Akan would have found reciprocity, while these same two groups merged with the Bambara and Sierra Leonians in their belief in reincarnation. The shout brought them together, transcending cultural barriers and hastening the creation of a pan-African cultural matrix with numerous points of intersection.[92]

Interestingly, not only do we find that the word "Vodou" (Voodoo) comes from the West-African Dahomean terms *vodu* or *vodun* for a loas (deity or god),[93] but in both Haitian and New Orleans Vodou also exists a duality of spirits known as the *gwobonanj* and the *tibonanj*. This passage from Molefi Kete Asante and Ama Mazama's, *The Encyclopedia of African Religion,* informs us the difference between these two Vodou terms:

> The [*tibonanj*] ti-bon-age is responsible for one's personal character, and it is this aspect of the soul that stands in judgment to account for the life one has lived. The ti-bon-age is related to the Egyptians' Ka or one's double, which is responsible for bestowing personality; it possesses an independent existence [...] The gwobonanj, in contrast, is the primal substance that gives life to a human being. It is the divine essence of an individual, and it derives its force directly from Bondyé, the Supreme Being, whose presence permeates the cosmos. Unlike the tibonanj, the gwobonanj is recycled and given a new life to continue its eternal mission, which is to carry out the will of the Creator.[94]

In music, we can make clear arguments for the African influence in the African American creations of jazz, blues and hip-hop (as well as a host of other American music genres); however, we know for certain that the Banjo, a stringed instrument that shares a relationship with the West-African *kora, xalam* and *goje* instruments, arrived in the United States by way of the Caribbean.[95]

---

92 Gomez, *Exchanging Our Country Marks*, 271.
93 Ibid, 55–56.
94 Molefi Kete Asante and Ama Mazama, eds., *Encyclopedia of African Religion* (Thousand Oaks, CA: Sage, 2009), 196.
95 For a detailed analysis on the African antecedents of African American music, dance and associated art, see: Samuel A. Floyd, *The Power of Black Music: Interpreting Its History from Africa to the United States* (New York, NY: Oxford University Press, 1997). For

In folklore, we know that tales throughout the African American South and Afro-Caribbean such as that of Brer Rabbit, Signifying Monkey and Anansi share origins in Africa in either fixed, dynamically reincarnated or otherwise similar forms.[96] This, of course, is the nature of folklore, as even on the African continent such tales remain increasingly dynamic. This is naturally a general treatment of these aspects of Kanna. Certain antecedents can be traced quite clearly based on spatial and temporal circumstances, but the brevity of this treatment will not allow for such specificity.

Fanna

There are, of course, many similarities between African and African American culture. Some of which can be gleaned from the aspects discussed above in the *kanna* category. The possibilities are much too vast for an extensive treatment, but I will list one very interesting phenomenon that may be classified as *fanna*. This cultural phenomenon involves the creation of two rice dishes in both Senegal and in southern Louisiana known as Jollof and Jambalaya, respectively. Recently, African American journalist Kayla Stewart, after combing through files in the national archives and making several trips to West Africa, has detailed her findings on the origins of Jambalaya. What perhaps many suspected would produce an origin story of Jambalaya from Jollof actually turned out to be a story of how these two dishes developed at the very same time by way of similar colonial circumstances.[97]

According to Stewart, West Africans who had been taken to the southern United States from areas such as Senegambia and Akan country were introduced to the tomato by way of the French and went on to create what we now know as Jambalaya. This was around the same time that a Senegalese woman, also a victim of French colonial terrorism, after being introduced to the tomato, created the first Jollof dish in West Africa.[98] This would be

---

religion, see: Joel E. Tishken, Tóyìn Fálọlá and Akíntúndé Akínyẹmí, eds., *Sàngó in Africa and the African Diaspora* (Bloomington, IN: Indiana University Press, 2009). For art see two of Robert Farris Thompson's works: Robert Farris Thompson, *Flash of the Spirit: African and Afro-American Art and Philosophy* (New York, NY: Random House, 1983) and Robert Farris Thompson, *Aesthetic of the Cool Afro-Atlantic Art and Music* (Pittsburgh, PA: Periscope, 2011).

96 Floyd, *Power of Black Music*, 48.
97 Kayla Stewart, "Tracing Jambalaya," ART19, 2019, https://art19.com/shows/proof/episodes/31b81374-a953-47cd-9fba-2bccfdadbf2f.
98 Ibid.

classified as *fanna* because, while one dish may not have developed from the other, they both share heavy similarity in formation.

Naani

When it comes to African Americans, and for that matter any other African diasporic group, *Naani* presents a host of issues. One could attempt to argue, for example, that Jazz, Blues, Soul and Hip-Hop, are solely African American cultural properties as they were created by Africans in America under specific circumstances. However, how then would one explain the African cultural elements present within all of these musical art forms? Perhaps someone could challenge that certain lexical creations such as *fleek* are uniquely African American, but they would then have to contend with the fact that these are dynamic historical recreations of terms such as *cool* which symbolize a particular type of West-African cosmology. In dance, one could attempt a similar argument for *twerk-ing* but would likewise have to contend with the history of African dances such as the predecessors to the modern *ndombolo* in the Kongo which exists in many forms throughout the African-populated Americas. Further, even if there were cosmological uniqueness in the lexicon, there is a preponderance of grammatical similarities with African languages that exists throughout the African diaspora.[99]

One further note to consider is that African Americans have developed their versions of American art forms unique to the African American experience. Let us use film for example. African American film directors such as Spike Lee and Robert Townsend have led the genre of Black film which focus solely on the socioeconomic and cultural experiences of African Americans. Certainly, African Americans didn't create the art that is cinema, but what they have created is space for African ontology on screen.

I mention this because it is unique in the fact that since the time of arguably the most famous of the first African American filmmakers, Oscar Michaux, the African American community has attempted to create images of themselves that combat the racist caricatures perpetuated by white society. This is important to this analysis because here is a form of art created from the need to contend with a particularly unique experience of racial subjugation of being a minority population in a majority white society. Nevertheless,

---

99 For a general treatment of the presence of both African grammar and lexicon from ancient times to present diaspora populations see: Kimani S.K. Nehusi, "From Medew Netjer to Ebonics," in *Ebonics and Language Education of African Ancestry Students*, ed. Clinton Crawford (New York, NY: Sankofa World Publishers, 2001), 56–122.

portrayed in many of these films are a host of diasporic cultural phenomena. Thus, this would need further consideration in order to be considered a truly unique phenomenon.

For African American phenomena to be placed soundly within the category of *Naani* such would have to live up to the scrutiny of overlapping evidence of African cultural influence. While African Americans are certainly a unique, independent and dynamically varied cultural group in their own right, it is quite difficult to pinpoint an aspect of their culture that does not more soundly exist within the category of *kanna* or *fanna*, and particularly as it pertains to their relationship to the West, Central and South African cultures covered by Du Bois and analyzed by me in this chapter. Nevertheless, I do not rule out the possibility that more detailed examinations could perhaps identify some cultural phenomena that could soundly be categorized as *naani*.

Chapter 4

LOCATING DU BOIS

Du Bois' Andromeda Complex

The year was 1911; W. E. B. Du Bois' *Souls of Black Folk* had apparently found itself on the international scene and drew a response from J. E. Casely Hayford, one of coastal Africa's most prominent theorists of Ethiopianism—a social-cultural movement that was partly religious and centered Ethiopia as the redeemer of the African race. Hayford wrote in his manifesto, *Ethiopia Unbound*, a critical response to Du Bois' theory of *double consciousness*, and regarded the theory as "one of the most pathetic passages in the history of human thought."[1] Du Bois perceived "a world which wields him no true self-consciousness […] this sense of always looking at one's self through the eyes of others, of measuring one's soul by the tape of a world that looks on in amused contempt and pity. One ever feels his twoness—an American and Negro; two souls, two thoughts, two unreconciled strivings; two warring ideals in one dark body."[2] This thinking apparently sat in sharp contrast with Hayford's self-conscious Ethiopianism. Hayford's retort was piercing:

> It is apparent that Mr. Du Bois writes from an American standpoint, surrounded by an American atmosphere. And, of course, it is not his fault, for he knows of no other. To be born an African in America, in that great commonwealth of dollars and the merciless aggrandizement of the individual, where the weak must look out for himself, and the cry of the innocent appeals not to whom who rides triumphantly to fortune, is to be entangled in conditions which give no room for the assertion of the highest manhood. *African manhood demands that the Ethiopian should seek*

---

1 Casely Hayford, *Ethiopia Unbound: Studies in Race Emancipation*, ed. Molefi Kete Asante (Baltimore, MD: Black Classic's Press, 2011), 179.
2 W. E. B. Du Bois., *The Souls of Black Folk*, ed. Brent Hayes Edwards (Oxford, UK: Oxford University Press, 2008), 2.

not his opportunity, or ask for elbow room, from the white man, but that he should create the one or the other for himself. (emphasis mine).[3]

Hayford's critique of Du Bois at this time differs very little from Carter G. Woodson's indictment decades later in which he proclaimed that, ostensibly unlike Du Bois, he didn't "accept the gifts of the Greeks." This, of course, was in response to Du Bois' position that he must make use of the money, and, subsequently, the opinions that came from with that money, being offered by whites in order to create the *Encyclopedia of the Negro*. To be fair, Du Bois too was quite critical about the project and viewed the whites who headed it as "the enemy." Nevertheless, he was eventually persuaded to join and then developed a lifelong correspondence with the primary investor, Anson Stokes. Could this circumstance simply be, as Hayford's critique suggests, Du Bois' way of "seeking opportunity" or "elbow room" at the table of his oppressors?

It is curious that Du Bois chose "Andromeda" as the title of the very last chapter of *The World and Africa*. He described the general contents of this chapter to be about "the future of the darker races and their relation to the white peoples."[4] The chapter largely deals with issues in colonialism and Du Bois' early history of Pan-African struggle. However, before we delve into that survey, there are some points that prove pertinent to make. It is quite interesting that near the very same time Du Bois was writing a very early version of *The World and Africa*, entitled *Africa, Its Geography, People and Products*, Carter G. Woodson published his, *African Myths and Folktales*.[5] Always a fierce critic of those who elevate Eurocentric cultural phenomena at the expense of or even in relation to African culture, Woodson appeared to be looking for solutions to counter African Americans' needs to relate their experiences to Greco-Roman myths. I mention this because although Du Bois himself was a fierce critic of the Western world, he was clearly still very much enthralled with European cultural history.

If we consider Du Bois' experiences in education, this may help us to understand why he remained so enthralled. To be sure, the educational institutions then, as it is today, as Molefi Kete Asante pointed out, are "conditioned by the character of the nation."[6] Unfortunately, this would mean the same for Historically Black Colleges and Universities (HBCUs). Du Bois' alma mater

---

3 Hayford, *Ethiopia Unbound*, 182.
4 Du Bois, *World and Africa*, 143.
5 As a side note; this would also be around the time Woodson developed Negro History Week, which is now Black History Month.
6 Asante, *Afrocentric Manifesto*, 83.

is Fisk University, a private HBCU located in Nashville, Tennessee. In Du Bois' day, it was one of the premier Black educational institutions in the country. However, like most others, Fisk suffered structural problems in its pedagogy, particularly in regard to its centering European culture as the standard that should aspire. Carter G. Woodson, in his *Miseducation of the Negro*, stated this issue quite plainly:

> Negro colleges offer courses bearing on the European colonists prior to their coming to America, their settlement on these shores, and their development here toward independence. Why are they not equally generous with the Negroes in treating their status in Africa prior to enslavement, their first transplantation to the West Indies, the Latinization of certain Negroes in contradistinction to the development of others under the influence of the Teuton, and the effort of the race toward self-expression? A further examination of their curricula shows, too, that invariably these Negro colleges offer courses in Greek philosophy and in that of modern European thought, but they direct no attention to the philosophy of the African. Negroes of Africa have and always have had their own ideas about the nature of the universe, time, and space, about appearance and reality, and about freedom and necessity. The effort of the Negro to interpret man's relation to the universe shows just as much intelligence as we find in the philosophy of the Greeks. There were many Africans who were just as wise as Socrates.[7]

Perhaps Du Bois, try as he might, could not escape such conditioning as all of his professors at Fisk but one was white, and it is also where his love for European music and art was first kindled before his experiences in Germany continued it further.[8] Du Bois would also learn the German language while at Fisk. Therefore, Fisk was intermedial in centering European culture in the mind of Du Bois while his stint at the University of Berlin among the Germans, or *Teutons* as Woodson would describe them, cemented his affinity for Europe. But Du Bois suffered a conundrum. Though he was clearly a student of Europe, he too desperately wished to be both a student and champion of Africa. However, this *twoness* oftentimes resulted in Du Bois' life and work being filled with much contradiction.

As we covered in the previous chapter, Woodson argued that Du Bois' work on *The Encyclopedia of the Negro* would, in his view, perpetuate a historiography

---

7 Woodson, *Miseducation of the Negro*, 136–137.
8 Du Bois, *Autobiography of W. E. B. Du Bois*, 108, 169.

that describes African people from the perspective of Europeans. Not only that, but Woodson perhaps also saw that such an encyclopedia funded by Anson Stokes and his ilk would again center European standards while the so-called Negroes would remain mere props in their own historical settings and backgrounds. After all, if we use the Greeks as a literal example, many of the gifts of myth and historiography left behind by the actual Greeks have been discovered to be the result of appropriation. In such way, Auset, Ausar, and Heru of Kemet become Isis, Osiris, and Horus of Egypt, respectively. Not only did their names change, they influenced the formation of new divine identities such as Zeus and Athena, but their phenotype and color would also be altered so that the Greeks could center their own likeness. Clearly, the Greeks do not bestow gifts but instead plunders the gifts of others. However, the Western world has presented the Greeks (and Romans) as the classical standard by which the rest of the world should admire.

This leads me to the issue of Du Bois choosing to identify African people with the Greek mythical figure, Andromeda. Let us consider the facts that in the Greek myth Andromeda is the daughter of Cepheus, ruler of Aethiopia. We know that Aethiopia, or Ethiopia (Kush), is how the Greeks referred to the lands and people below Kemet, as the term "Ethiopia" means "lands of the burnt faces." However, though we do know that the Roman poet Ovid emphasized that Andromeda had dark skin for she was born in Kush,[9] mysteriously, there is no known Greek art that depicts Cepheus nor Andromeda as African. In fact, in various art, while the attendants of Andromeda were depicted as African, she remained quite white in appearance. If we consider this "gift" the Greeks have left us, one can only ponder as to why Du Bois did not address such contradictions. Perhaps he was not all too familiar with the collection of Greek artworks concerning Andromeda, or he was more familiar with the works of Ovid or other authors who cite him. Du Bois leaves us with no indication of either case as he does not cite where he received his version of the story.

Nevertheless, most versions of the story generally depict Andromeda as the child of Cepheus and his morbidly vain wife, Cassiopeia. The latter, who is apparently just as vain about her offspring, gloats about the beauty of Andromeda and suggests to all who will listen that she is more beautiful than the *nereids*, which are sea nymphs and daughters of the sea god Nereus. Poseidon, being married to one of these sea nymphs, was apparently offended by the suggestion and sent both a deadly wave and a sea monster, Cetus, to

---

9 Elizabeth McGrath, "The Black Andromeda," *Journal of the Warburg and Courtauld Institutes* 55 (1992): 1–18.

destroy their nation. Upon consulting the oracle, Ammon (associated with Amun of Kemet), Andromeda's parents are informed that they must sacrifice Andromeda to the monster in order to bring an end to the catastrophe. Cepheus then chained Andromeda to a cliff by the shoreline, offering her up for sacrifice. Meanwhile, the demi-god Perseus, returning from slaying Medusa, just so happens to fly overhead and witness the helpless Andromeda and the sea monster approaching her. He slayed the monster and afterward fell in love and married Andromeda.

Du Bois found this myth endearing. Throughout the chapter he applies the phrase, "releasing black Andromeda," in order to address a number of social and racial challenges. First, he states that the recognition of "world democracy" could free Andromeda.[10] Next, he insists that the Western world has degraded Africa and the correction of which is likewise allegorical to the releasing of Andromeda.[11] Finally, in somewhat reiteration, Du Bois points out many deeds African people have done that are valued by the Western world. He describes those deeds as such:

> Few people realize what Africa and her children have done to win the World Wars. In the first, the Senegalese saved France at the first onslaught of the Germans; black soldiers of Africa conquered the German colonies; American Negroes rushed the critical supplies to Europe which turned the tide of victory. In World War II thousands of Africans fought in Europe, Burma, India, and Africa; they formed a large part of Montgomery's Eighth Army in the decisive North African campaign; an American Negro physician contrived the banks of blood plasma which saved tens of thousands of lives; Negroes built thousands of miles of strategic road under direct enemy fire; Negroes handled three-fourths of the ammunition in the European Theatre of Operations and fired much of it. Negro fighting troops took part in the invasion of Normandy, in the invasion of Italy, and as flight squadrons and hospital corps. In America eight Negro scientists were engaged in the research on the atomic bomb.[12]

Apparently satisfied with the impressiveness of this description of African accomplishment, Du Bois then declares, "The stars of dark Andromeda

---

10 Du Bois, *World and Africa*, 162.
11 Ibid, 163.
12 Ibid, 164.

belong up there in the great heaven that hangs above this tortured world."[13] These sentiments from Du Bois once again display his cognitive hiatus. It is interesting that he advances the notion of "world democracy," particularly given the Athenian origins of such governance. To be sure, there is nothing wrong with a government by which people have equal say in their governing representatives and thereby have choice over the social, political, and economic decisions which will impact their lives. But in these passages Du Bois seems to believe that American democracy is only in need of repair. That if only we can stemmy prejudices, dissolve "the color line," and evolve capitalism into a more transparent system then the world will know true democracy. To be sure, before his death and the publication of his posthumous biography Du Bois had evolved in his thinking:

> First, I would emphasize the fact that today Africa has no choice between private Capitalism and Socialism. The whole world, including Capitalist countries, is moving toward Socialism, inevitably, inexorably. You can choose between blocs of military alliance, you can choose between groups of political union, you cannot choose between Socialism and Private Capitalism, because Private ownership of capital is doomed.[14]

Alas, though Du Bois had pulled away from the capitalist camp, his embracing of Western socialism, from an Afrocentric standpoint, is still problematic. Marxism was in Du Bois' day considered a popular political philosophy—albeit a dangerous one to publicly espouse considering the politics of the "red scare." By the 1950s, Du Bois and many other African intellectuals had taken a liking to socialist and Marxist thoughts. Marx's bases for his economic and social theories were, naturally, the historical events surrounding the European Agrarian Revolution and the subsequent European Industrial Revolution.[15] It in no way incorporated African cultural-historical paradigms nor was it of any character to promote Afrocentric unity among African nations. However, as Molefi Kete Asante points out, one of Du Bois' protégés, Kwame Nkrumah, would eventually develop both a parallel and contesting ideology known as *consciencism*. Using this form of African socialism, or

---

13 Ibid.
14 Du Bois, *Autobiography of W. E. B. Du Bois*, 402.
15 Ana Monteiro-Ferreira, *The Demise of the Inhuman: Afrocentricity, Modernism, and Postmodernism* (Albany, NY: State University of New York Press, 2015), 55.

Nkrumahism, Asante would note that Nkrumah wished for Africans to make Africa "the center of their ambitions":

> Nkrumah wanted to see a new African evolve who would practice the philosophy of consciencism and make Africa the center of their ambitions. But to do this, the African has to revise Marxism, which Nkrumah believed to be the most combative ideology for challenging colonialism, and demonstrate that African communalism could move through its traditions to African socialism.[16]

Digressing, Du Bois' insistence that the Western world, or "this pattern of human culture," has degraded Africa is complicated by his reliance on the Western cultural norms that he believes can save Africa. Du Bois' call to release Andromeda is ultimately metaphorical for freeing a Europeanized Africa, an Africa remade in an image that Europe regards as most beautiful and civilized, and saved only from the monstrosities Europe itself has released upon the world. This would presumably place the burden on *civilized* Africans to slay the evils of the color line and free Andromeda. Imagine if in Du Bois' mind Perseus represents the *civilized* intellectuals of the African world, born of the circumstances between Europeans, a self-deified race, and their raping Africa of her human resources. Therefore, in the mind of Du Bois, the demi-god-like more civilized African world would use the power of their god-half, albeit culturally antithetical, in order to free Andromeda; to free up the image and dignity of Africa and do so by Western standards. Du Bois may have recognized that Europe successfully demonized African religion, denigrated the original African culture and distorted their ethical standards,[17] but he lacked the theoretical framework necessary to not fall prey to perpetuating the Eurocentric masquerade.

Du Bois' understanding of the war between cultures was largely limited to the historical contributions to world civilization which Europe had deprived of African people. Certainly, Du Bois understood that cultures possess unique characters displayed through their religion, philosophy and art, but he had failed to grasp the very nature of the Eurocentric Masquerade, which isn't simply a hierarchical placement of European norms but an establishment of those norms as universal cultural standards humanity. Thus, the harmonic style of eighteenth-century European musicians, which Du Bois apparently cherished, became "Music Theory," and Greco-Roman classical history

---

16 Asante, *Afrocentric Manifesto*, 34.
17 Du Bois, *World and Africa*, 49.

became "Classics." This becomes so normalized in the minds of colonized people that Du Bois, for example, does not consider it an issue to compare Africans to the European caricatures of African people found in *Andromeda*, *Parsifal* or *Othello*, because he has been socially engineered to understand such as *universal standards*.

Du Bois on the Early Twentieth Century

Du Bois begins his survey of contemporary African history with a series of inquiries. He questions whether or not the world needs Africa and if, in turn, does Africa need the world. Du Bois describes a number of African products the world of his day is dependent on such as cotton, gold, coffee, cocoa, various oils and rubber.[18] He then speaks on the large reserves of human labor Africa has to offer, as well as the agricultural potential of the continent. Du Bois also hints at the early stages of industrialization on the African continent. He mentions how much of it is unencumbered by laws to limit labor and that profits are lightly taxed.[19]

Next, Du Bois mentions a number of, in his day, contemporary surveys of Africa and African peoples, such as Malcolm Hailey's *African Survey* which, Du Bois argues, "Omits consistently the point of view of the native and any body of fact which weighs against European aggression." To that end, Du Bois also mentions W. Walton Claridge's *History of Ashanti*, which he states, "Frank criticism of Great Britain creeps in [...] but the story is heavily weighted on the side of the imperialists."[20] It is not surprising that Du Bois is able to pinpoint such reductions of African agency, but I argue it is primarily because this is a largely contemporary critique. Du Bois is naturally sympathetic to the plight of so-called *natives* in his lifetime even though, as aforementioned, he too had in his younger days been guilty of not considering the needs and wants of indigenous African people.

Du Bois continues his discussion on the wealth of Africa's resources and just how much the European world has pillaged those resources with little regard for the negative effects such actions have had on the lives of African people. Further, he charges that writers who favor imperialism have attempted to downplay just how much Europe has benefited from the gross exploitation of African labor as well as the lack of regulation on the exportation of goods.

---

18 Ibid, 144–145.
19 Ibid, 145.
20 Ibid.

Du Bois accuses Malcolm Hailey, English Baron and president of the Royal Asiatic society, specifically of this as he states:

> The actual value of capital goods at the time of their investment in Africa, as compared with the realized value of the labor and material taken from Africa by investors and other claimants, legal and illegal, would if known, without shadow of doubt prove the enormous theft which Europe has perpetrated on peoples deliberately made helpless before greed and aggression. In the face of fact, statements like that of Lord Hailey as to the meager profits of African exploitation must be reinterpreted.[21]

This downplay of the wealth in material and human resources Europeans have stolen from Africa is a common trend that persists even within the twenty-first century. Sure, recent texts such as Martin Meredith's *The Fortunes of Africa* and Edward Baptist's *The Half Has Never Been Told* has elucidated a great deal of the facts to contemporary society; however, such literature has very little of the impact today than it may have had in Du Bois time, especially within a society which reading books is increasingly less of an interest. Instead, many in the Western world turn to television for their understanding of local, national, and international affairs. They want the "facts" interpreted for them by the seasoned reporters available on twenty-four-hour news stations. Undoubtedly, this is one of the results of the social conditioning that Du Bois mentions in the earlier chapters of *The World and Africa* where he states, "Every effort was made to keep women and children and the more sensitive men deceived as to what was going on [...]" and that, "elaborate writing, disguised as interpretation, and the testimony of so-called 'experts,' made it impossible for charming people in Europe to realize what their comforts and luxuries cost in sweat, blood, death and despair."[22]

Nevertheless, what Du Bois highlights about the actual value of capital goods and the manufacturing of the interpretation of how those goods and services are made accessible to Europeans at the expense of African people is a continued reality in the face of Pan-African struggle. To help his readers understand the frustrations of African people which led to Pan-African struggle, Du Bois quotes the words of J. E. Casley Hayford, the Ghanaian barrister who critiqued his idea of double consciousness some decades prior.

---

21 Ibid, 146.
22 Ibid, 22.

Hayford spoke of a type of African democratic system in which the African chiefs of the Gold Coast were more or less the mere representatives of the people in which they governed. However, Britain, during their colonial aspirations in the land which would become modern-day Ghana, would disrupt this system in favor of British industry. "[Britain] gave Negroes partial elective representation in the 'Legislative Councils,'" says Du Bois before continuing, "but the councils still 'advised' the governor, who retained large power of legislation. British industry sat directly on the Council and in England continued to name West African governors and dictate colonial policies."[23] This, Du Bois contends, brewed early sentiments for modern Pan-African politics.

Du Bois and Pan-Africanism

Having covered much of this subject in earlier chapters of *The World and Africa*, Du Bois gives a more truncated summary of his experiences within the early history of Pan-Africanism. He argued that the Pan-African movement represented a growing sentiment on the part of continental and diaspora communities to be self-governing and "to unite in mutual exchange of culture and co-operation for social betterment."[24] This push toward self-governance was of course in response to the harsh history of colonial control over Africa which had left the African people largely destitute and their nations underdeveloped; done so for the purpose of exploiting human and material resources for European benefit.[25] However, Du Bois then singled out what he referred to as simply "another movement, stemming from the West Indies," which was the Pan-African and Black Nationalist politics of Marcus Garvey. Du Bois would state of this movement:

> It was led by Marcus Garvey and *it represented a poorly conceived but intensely earnest determination to unite the Negroes of the world*, especially in commercial enterprise. It used all of the nationalist and racial paraphernalia of popular agitation, and its strength lay in its backing by the masses of West Indians and by increasing numbers of American Negroes. Its weakness lay in its demagogic leadership, poor finance, intemperate propaganda,

---

23 Ibid, 149.
24 Ibid.
25 For a proper treatise on this subject consult Walter Rodney's *How Europe Underdeveloped Africa*. Particular attention should be given to the chapter entitled "Colonialism as a System for Underdeveloping Africa," in which he briefly outlines the circumstances, both on the African continent and abroad, that led to the rise of Pan-Africanism.

and the natural apprehension it aroused among the colonial powers. (emphasis mine).[26]

To consider Garvey's movement "poorly conceived" yet "intensely earnest" is perhaps partly a sign of the resentment Du Bois felt toward Garvey himself. After all, the correspondence between the two does not reveal the kindest of words and sentiments for each other. But Garvey was perhaps the quintessential Black Nationalist and Pan-Africanist to arise in the early twentieth century. He was a culmination of the most fervent aspects of the movement. He epitomized the philosophy of an African renaissance, the profound love and thirst for knowledge of African people and history, a philosophy of strict independence, and ambitions of Pan-African advancement.

Garvey and first wife Amy Ashwood founded the Universal Negro Improvement Association (UNIA) in Jamaica in 1914 before relocating to the United States. By 1918 membership had extraordinarily flourished as thousands of membership certificates brandishing the greeting, "To the Beloved and Scattered Millions of the Negro Race," were issued. By June of 1919 Garvey calculated that the UNIA had a membership of over two million while the ever watchful Du Bois gave a conservative estimate of just under 300,000 who were actual paying members. Membership was of course restricted to only those of African ancestry and the requirement to donate 25 cents a month (2017 value of $4.03 monthly, accounting for inflation)[27] of disposable income greatly benefited the organization's treasury.[28]

What Garvey's movement did reaffirm was that while after three centuries of Africans being displaced in the Americas had brought on an ambivalence of returning to their ancestral home, whether by knowledge of history or nature of condition, they still saw themselves as somehow connected to the African world. However, Garvey's movement began to crumble under the weight of what some scholars perceive to be his heedless arrogance and poor management of certain divisions of UNIA operations such as the Black Star Line. Through his own investigations, Du Bois himself outlined in his article "Back to Africa" that Garvey lost around $800,000 on the Black Star Line enterprise due largely to the fact that many of the ships that were purchased were often abandoned because they were old and in constant need of

---

26 Ibid.
27 "CPI Inflation Calculator." U.S. Bureau of Labor Statistics. Accessed March 29, 2021. https://data.bls.gov/cgi-bin/cpicalc.pl?cost1=.25&year1=1918&year2=2017.
28 Colin Grant, *Negro with a Hat: The Rise and Fall of Marcus Garvey* (New York, NY: Oxford University Press, 2008), 117, 164.

expensive repairs.²⁹ Certainly this could be at the heart of the "poorly conceived" sentiments of Du Bois, but the fact of the matter is that Garvey had developed a movement which stood significantly larger than anything Du Bois would ever accomplish.

Further, the entirety of this movement was built on the sole contributions of Black men and women, something that Du Bois could only dream of accomplishing. In 1920, at arguably the height of the UNIA, Garvey organized the first UNIA Convention preceded by a huge parade beginning at the UNIA offices on 135th street in New York City.³⁰ The Jamaican historian Colin Grant, author of the extensive narrative, *Negro with a Hat: The Rise and Fall of Marcus Garvey,* lends his insight into the parade's proceedings:

> [...] the UNIA-sponsored event international convention would culminate in the crowning of a provisional president of Africa. His majesty would be elected by the delegates, and would be charged with governing an as yet undelineated African Empire constituting the 400 million Negroes of the world. The system of honours that Garvey proposed and the conferencing of titles on an imagined African government-in-exile was the one aspect of the convention that would receive the most unflattering rebukes from Garvey's critics. He thought his proposal no more absurd than Eamon de Valera's appointment that year as the provisional president of Ireland.³¹

Assuredly, what Garvey's first job as print worker, and eventually manager, at a large printing establishment in Jamaica had taught him was the power of propaganda. As most of the African continent was at the time colonized by Europeans, Garvey needed to appeal to his base not only in America but also the grassroots in his organization spread all over the African world, especially on the African continent itself. The need for the inclusion of prominent continental Africans in the organization he sought at best to meet. Thus, for outstanding appeal, Garvey included at the convention George O. Marke, who he had placed as the official representative of the Freetown division of the UNIA in Sierra Leone. Even more distinguished was the high-profiled Liberian Gabriel Johnson, soon duly installed as "Potentate Leader of the Negro Peoples of the World." Johnson's family was among the most powerful

---

29 W. E. B. Du Bois, *1868-1963. Back to Africa. W. E. B. Du Bois Papers (MS 312).* Special Collections and University Archives, University of Massachusetts Amherst Libraries.
30 Ibid, 242.
31 Ibid, 243.

Americo-Liberian ruling elite in Liberia. Johnson's father was once elected the Liberian president in 1884 and his niece was married to then president, C.D. King.[32]

Nevertheless, all of this W. E. B. Du Bois would however be considered to be a bit of a circus. Du Bois, then in his early fifties, had begun showing signs of evolving beyond the "double conscious" prognosis of his youthful thirties. Through much effort in diplomacy, cunning and plotting, Du Bois had begun to establish his own Pan-African front. He had engineered the congress in Paris and was hoping to capitalize on the accomplishment if he could keep the post-war powers from hindering him with any due resistance. Thus, he grew increasingly concerned with the actions of Garvey and, as Du Bois perceived it, his absurd claims to an African empire.

Garvey had already infuriated him a short while before as Du Bois had received a letter from the UNIA leader to inform him that at the convention a leader of the American Negro people would be elected by popular vote and Du Bois was, of course, an obvious candidate. On request that Du Bois submit his name for nomination, Du Bois retorted, "I beg to say that I thank you for the suggestion, but under no circumstances can I allow my name to be presented."[33] Was the letter some type of joke on the part of Garvey or perhaps some curious way to show some manner of respect toward the highly respected public intellectual? Regardless, Du Bois was well within character to turn down such an invitation given his politics at the time. What would his white pen-pals and philanthropists think of such a promotion or even just the simple association with such a group?

Nevertheless, Marcus Garvey should be considered among the most ambitious and passionate leaders in the struggle for African freedom and autonomy. Many during his day, even those who were once considered close to him, turned away from the leader. In examining the record of witnesses, faults in Garvey's character, particularly his pomposity and obstinacy, hindered his activities and added to the growing number of detractors. However, many also failed to see the great possibilities of Garvey's visions and his unfettered dedication to the advancement of African people knew no equal. Even Du Bois had to admit his sincerity as he once wrote, "[Garvey] has been charged with dishonesty and graft, but he seems to me essentially an honest

---

32 Ibid, 244.
33 Ibid, 244–245.

and sincere man with a tremendous vision, great dynamic force, stubborn determination and unselfish desire to serve."[34]

Early on Du Bois was indeed concerned that his "Pan-African movement" was being confused with what he dubbed "the Garvey agitation." But after the Paris meeting he felt that the Western world was beginning to differentiate between the two. It is a shame that Du Bois wished not to be associated with a movement that expressed self-determination and autonomy on the part of African people, but perhaps he prophesied early on that the Western powers were too fearful, envious and petty to allow such a movement to flourish while they held power. Perhaps the indictments Du Bois has developed of the West in the late 1940s are part of a long-standing perception that he elected to remain mute until he was sure that the Western world was absolutely "heading for collapse." We can only speculate for in the next few decades Du Bois would slowly turn toward Marxist and socialist ideas before relocating to the newly independent nation of Ghana at the twilight of his life.

Interestingly, a primary motivation for Du Bois' move to Ghana was Nkrumah's invitation and support of him using Ghanaian resources to edit the *Encyclopedia Africana*. Prolific scholars Charisse Burden-Stelly and Gerald Horne offer their opinion of this event in their text, *W.E.B. Du Bois: A Life in American History;* though the subtitle may misguide, as this treatment of Du Bois' life is comprehensive and extends into his activities abroad, including his final years living in Ghana. Burden-Stelly and Horne note:

> Thus, becoming a national of an African nation while supervising an encyclopedia important to its future development was like a dream come true for Du Bois […] underlining the importance of liberating Africa from colonialism, it was Ghanaian independence that reanimated the idea to bring this laudable idea to fruition. Du Bois was not sufficiently spindly to be kept from drawing up an ambitious scheme to bring this project to completion. His proposed encyclopedia was focused on Africans because, at this juncture, knowledge of them and their accomplishments were either shrouded or distorted, whereas virtually all European explorers, missionaries, colonial officials, and so on were to be excluded, simply because this information could be found in abundance elsewhere.[35]

---

34 Edmund David Cronon and John Hope Franklin. *Black Moses; The story of Marcus Garvey and the Universal Negro Improvement Association* (Madison: University of Wisconsin Press, 1969), 208.

35 Charisse Burden-Stelly and Gerald Horne, *W.E.B. Du Bois: A Life in American History* (Santa Barbara, CA: ABC-CLIO, An imprint of ABC-CLIO, LLC, 2019), 191–192.

This is the interesting thing about Du Bois' long life. Harkening back to his troubles with Booker T. Washington, Carter G. Woodson and even Marcus Garvey, we come to find that his life and experiences would prove many of their contentions to be the most correct. Here is Du Bois, now living in an independent African nation, working on an independent African publication at the exclusion of European experiences and opinions, and also being funded exclusively by African dollars. More interestingly, there appears in his last autobiography no metaphors or parallels to be had between the plight of African people with Greek myths. Du Bois' devotion to Pan-African struggle near the end of his life appeared to take on a more fiercely independent and autonomous attitude. In fact, on March 11, 1957, just five days after Ghana gained its initial independence, Du Bois had this to say:

> Ghana must on the contrary be the representative of Africa, and not only that, but of Black Africa below the Sahara desert. As such, her first duty should be to come into close acquaintanceship and cooperation with her fellow areas of British West Africa and Liberia; with the great areas of black folk in French West and Equatorial Africa; with the Sudan, Ethiopia, and Somaliland; with Uganda, Kenya and Tanganyika; with the Belgian Congo and all Portuguese Africa; with the Rhodesias and Bechuanaland; with Southwest Africa, the Union of South Africa and Madagascar; and with all other parts of Africa and with peoples who want to cooperate. All the former barriers of language, culture, religion and political control should bow before the essential unity of race and descent, the common suffering of slavery and the slave trade and the modern color bar.[36]

One can only wonder what another decade of the evolution of DuBoisian thought and practice may have produced. With the looming Black Power and African independence movements on the horizon, Du Bois would have certainly kept tabs on these political happenings and allowed such to continue to develop him as an intellectual. If the vessel of human flesh weren't so fleeting, would Du Bois' continued growth had developed him into a more revolutionary Pan-African, and perhaps an all the more Afrocentric individual? These are, of course, questions for which an answer will never exist. However, they are important questions for the evolution of DuBoisian thought as well for the future of Afrocentric scholarship.

---

36 Du Bois, *World and Africa*, 188.

Chapter 5

"PAN-AFRICA"

My great-grandfather was carried away in chains from the Gulf of Guinea. I have returned that my dust shall mingle with the dust of my fathers.
—W. E. B. Du Bois[1]

Coining "Afrocentric"

What I have offered in this analysis is a clearer lens for examining Du Bois' scholarship, particularly as it pertains to notions of cultural-political centeredness. As aforementioned, *The World and Africa* is an important text when considering the time in which it was written and the issues that it raises. However, Du Bois' scholarship was often seriously limited by Eurocentric ideals of civilization and progress. In his early years, such shortcomings were clearly displayed in the lexicon he chose to describe African people and their social, political, and economic conditions. Further, he was not able to produce within the text a cultural-historical matrix and, without such, his arguments for political unity became somewhat superficial. To base an argument for unity purely based on the circumstances of a common oppressor limits the range of agency for African people.

To be sure, it is certain that unity in the face of shared oppression can occur between even the most antithetical of groups. However, Du Bois, to the best of his ability, penned a history of the African world. He intended to use this history as the basis of his argument for what it meant historically to be an African person and how African people have contributed to world history. Thus, Du Bois was acknowledging some notion of a composite African ontology comprised of various historical and contemporary African groups. His analysis displayed some understanding of historical cross-cultural relationships within the African continent, particularly as it related to his discussion of the Bantu migration. Du Bois would attempt in the last chapter,

---

1 Meyer Weinberg, *The World of W.E.B. Du Bois: A Quotation Sourcebook* (Westport, CT: Greenwood Press, 1992), 46–47.

and in several works following this text, to use this historical argument of the achievement and character of the composite African identity in order to argue for Pan-African unity.

This argument involves a useful cultural composite illustration that is no different from the historical-cultural connections, and modern sociopolitical unity, Du Bois mentions in the earlier chapters of *The World and Africa* regarding Europeans. Nevertheless, Du Bois failed to capitalize on the cultural argument regarding African people and instead focused more so on arguments that could valorize Africa to the Western world. This effectively weakened his contention that African people should seek to "save" Africa. An Afrocentric approach to saving Africa is an approach that values revitalizing African cultural and social norms. However, instead of Afrocentric norms, and although Du Bois seemed to be advocating for the right of Africans to govern their own affairs, Du Bois' argument for saving Africa would see further imposition of Eurocentric norms.

Du Bois would perhaps have better understood his folly if he had delved deeper into precolonial African cultural cosmology. Certainly, an examination of African history can lead people to further understand African cultural cosmology, but such understanding will only be cursory if one doesn't delve into the myths, customs, orature and other such cultural phenomena. But such a deep examination did not seem to be an interest of Du Bois during the writing of this text. An examination of African cultural phenomena with an Afrocentric lens would produce more agency-affirming scholarship. However, this does not mean that Du Bois, as well as the company he kept, were not moving in this direction. In 1962, Du Bois sent out what's known as *Information Report No. 2*, which was meant to report on the progress of the *Encyclopedia Africana*. In this report, we see the word Afro-centric being used for the first time in history when Du Bois states the project should be "unashamedly Afro-centric".[2] Kwame Nkrumah addressed the editorial board of Du Bois' *Encyclopedia Africana* in 1964 and stated that "the Project Africana must be frankly Afrocentric in interpretation of African history and the social and cultural institutions of the African and people of African descent everywhere."[3]

From this phrase we see one of the earliest strands of Afrocentric theory. In fact, this seems to be the natural evolution of Du Bois's philosophy toward

---

2 W. E. B. Du Bois, *Information Report No. 2*, September 1962, box Share069 GST/P/1/5, bound in ShareBox 069, Special Collections, Pennsylvania State University Archives, University Park, PA.
3 Molefi Kete Asante, "The Philosophy of Afrocentricity," in *The Palgrave Handbook of African Philosophy*, ed. Adeshina Afolayan and Toyin Falola (New York, NY: Palgrave Macmillan, 2017), 231–244.

Africa. Therefore, every stage in the scholarship of Du Bois, no matter the contradictions and limitations within, was a necessary step in the direction toward Afrocentric scholarship. Such work has provided us theoretical ideals that we may today identify and tease out those that are of use to African agency. If we understand that the theories of scholars such as Du Bois permeates not only the academy but also society at large, then it is only responsible that the continued refinement of such scholarship is done in order for their philosophies to better serve the communities they were created for. To be clear, arguably the most pervasive theories of Du Bois in the Western academy are *double consciousness, the talented tenth* and *the color line*. These come very early in Du Bois' intellectual development, yet many continue to regard them as defining ideologies. Therefore, we must critically examine and reveal the Eurocentric ideology present at all stages of Du Bois' intellectual development.

Du Bois, Socialism and Africa

As for the case of Du Bois and his call for Pan-African unity in the face of the continuing cultural war with Europe, in one article, "The Giant Stirs," he mentions that Western ideals are "historically slavery, caste, poverty, ignorance, and disease."[4] The context of this description sees William H. Ball, personal representative of President Dwight D. Eisenhower, assure an audience at an event celebrating Cecil Rhodes that one of the United State's major objectives is "to see that the peoples of Africa remain wedded to Western ideals."[5]

Interestingly, "Western ideals" were regarded as antithetical to "Soviet domination or influence," which Ball foresaw as the major threat. Du Bois seems to clearly regard Russia as Western, or at least European in culture. However, for Ball and the so-called "western bloc" of nations, I would argue that the establishment of China as a communist country, and perhaps even China's proximity to Russia, allowed the West to muddle the racial notions of Communism in order to garner more domestic sympathy toward wars against so-called "godless communism." China, naturally, was not and still isn't a Christian nation (though many Christians exist in the country) and Christianity is largely the hallmark of Western cultural influence or domination. Russia, for its part, didn't help these matters as the Soviet Union often persecuted Christians, even those of Russia Orthodoxy, in favor of Marxist-Leninist atheism. Russia was also the leader of the supposedly nefarious "eastern bloc" which, aside from the collection of Eastern European nations involved, included countries in Southeast and East Asia, as well as Africa and

---

4 Du Bois, *World and Africa*, 184.
5 Ibid.

Latin America. Thus, making it easier to paint a racialized East versus West dichotomy.

Nevertheless, Du Bois may have seen Russia as becoming somewhat less Western or, at the very least, evolving a more preferred form of Eurocentric ethos in their adoption of Marxism-Leninism. Du Bois seemed to have respected Karl Marx as he once stated that he regarded him "as the greatest of modern philosophers, and I have not been deterred by the witch-hunting which always follows mention of his name."[6] In his later years, Du Bois' opinions about the war between democracy and communism appears to have taken no sides, at least in regard to any political grandstanding on his part. He would argue:

> Men made cotton cloth and sold sugar; but between the two they stole, killed, and raped human beings, forced them to toil for a bare subsistence, made rum and synthetic gin, herded white labor into unsanitary factories, bought the results of their work under threat of hunger which forced down their wage, and sold the sugar at monopoly prices to consumers who must pay or go without. A process of incredible ingenuity for supplying human wants became in its realization a series of brutal crimes. There are people, and wise people, who have said that this can never be accomplished under the present organization of the world for business, industry, and profit; that in order to accomplish this we must establish a stern dictatorship of a few who hold to this idea of the commonweal. This is the theory of Communism. There are many who dislike the idea; there are some who fear and hate it for obvious reasons. But to these there is one clear answer: accomplish the end which every honest human being must desire by means other than Communism, and Communism need not be feared. *On the other hand, if a world of ultimate democracy, reaching across the color line and abolishing race discrimination, can only be accomplished by the method laid down by Karl Marx, then that method deserves to be triumphant no matter what we think or do.* [emphasis mine][7]

Russia, or the USSR, of course had at this time adopted the theories of Marx and Lenin as it advocated for a socialist reality. In early chapters I discussed Du Bois' description of Europe and their cultural ethos and he certainly included Russia. Therefore, there was no question in his mind of whether Russia was part of the particular "pattern of human culture" that has brought the world to ruin. Therefore, whether Du Bois absolutely believed

---

6 Ibid, xxxii.
7 Ibid, 163.

that Russia had better answers for the state the world was in isn't the point as much as whether Du Bois continued to value Eurocentric ideals as preeminent for solving African problems.

But if Du Bois is of the opinion that Western ideals are "historically slavery, caste, poverty, ignorance, and disease," then clearly he is speaking to Western politics. Why not then would Du Bois seek to further investigate precolonial African political and cultural paradigms? Was it because such had "lost" to European colonialism? Did he not see such paradigms as powerful enough to withstand Europe's cultural-political machine and therefore not worthy of further investigation? Or did Du Bois perhaps simply not have enough time to do the research necessary to come to such a conclusion?

The answers are more elusive than obvious as Du Bois appeared quite confused on the matter. Not in a sense of personal mental conflict, but rather he did not at all times seem to fully grasp the differing cultural modalities of Afrocentric and Eurocentric ethos. "Africa is for Africans," Du Bois decreed in 1955. "Hereafter it will no longer be ruled by Might nor Power; by invading armies nor police, but by the Spirit of all its Gods and the Wisdom of its Prophets."[8] These lines, if taken at face value, greatly contradict the need to ponder over which Eurocentric political reality, democracy or communism, would best suit Africans in their struggles for independence and power.

Though perhaps the issue is Du Bois' definition of socialism. He states in "Ghana and Pan-Africanism" that Africans should work together "to build a socialism founded on old African communal life."[9] Further, in "The Future of Africa" he states, "Africa has no choice between private capitalism and socialism. The whole world, including capitalist countries, is moving towards socialism [...]"[10] In the 1959 article, "Lenin and Africa," he suggested that maybe "Lenin had Africa as well as Europe in mind when he established the communist nation," adding also that, "this is the time the Soviet Union should spread Lenin on colonial imperialism to every African country and in every African language."[11]

This would seemingly suggest that he views the socialism of Russia and others as the standard of governance Africa should aspire toward. However, Du Bois also establishes, "There are many Negroes who regard the overthrow of the tribal system as a first step toward African progress. But there are others and I hope their number is growing who want to improve the tribal

---

8 Ibid, 185.
9 Ibid, 189.
10 Ibid, 196.
11 W. E. B. Du Bois, *1868–1963. Lenin and Africa, February 1959. W. E. B. Du Bois Papers (MS 312)*. Special Collections and University Archives, University of Massachusetts Amherst Libraries.

organization, but would preserve the main meaning of the tribe. *The African tribe was always and still is mainly a Commune; a socialistic organization where all capital goods belong to the tribe*; where work and trade was directed by the tribe [...]" (emphasis mine).[12] Of course, in *The World and Africa* he states something similar, "The African tribe [...] was communistic in its very beginnings."[13] This may lead us to now surmise that Du Bois viewed communism and socialism as universal traits of human civilization that expresses itself differently depending upon the culture that practiced them. If we entertain this possibility, perhaps the primary issue here is what Africologists refer to as utilizing "borrowed cultural terms."[14] Terms in this instance represent both the lexicon used, being socialism and communism, as well as the conditions or measurement by which a phenomenon is described. Living off of borrowed Eurocentric terms often means we describe African experiences in culturally inaccurate and unbefitting ways.

This is an issue germane to the African American experience. Despite our conscious and unconscious tethering to our own African linguistic paradigms, we have been forced to utilize the English and Latin lexicon; so if the historical examples of communal living among African people remind Du Bois of communism, then that is what he will call the practice. To be sure, there will be overlaps in the activities of various world cultural groups that people would recognize as similarities. However, it is quite dangerous to act on the same tendency as Du Bois' to simply consider the activity a different version of the same. Is it really the case that African history gives us examples of African socialism or African communism? Or is it that there are examples of African communal living that simply bears some similarity to what we refer to as socialism or communism? While this line of argument may seem to be a simple matter of semantics, consider the metaphor that while the American sweet potato and the African yam may often be confused for each other, they are both actually members of completely different botanical families. To assume that the typical European/American climate could produce a healthy yield of African yams would prove a fruitless endeavor. Likewise, the assumption that transplanting a European/American political climate would yield an Afrocentric political environment in Africa has proven to be likewise fruitless.

Nevertheless, his metaphor has another layer of meaning. Recall that Marx's bases for his economic and social theories derived from the events

---

12 Ibid.
13 Du Bois, *The World and Africa*, 197.
14 Mazama, *Afrocentric Paradigm*, 25.

surrounding the European Agrarian Revolution and the subsequent European Industrial Revolution.[15] Du Bois could have pointed out that Africa was swept into the historical circumstances produced by these revolutions, but he instead pointed toward the precolonial historical examples of African communal living. What were the factors that gave rise to those examples? What are the cultural bases for those examples? But more importantly, what were the agrarian circumstances and needs in Africa that informed the sociocultural needs of its people? Answering these questions will produce the need for different terms, both lexically and descriptively.

Du Bois was naturally not alone in the use of borrowed terms. Kwame Nkrumah, for example, introduces his readers to the term "communalism" in his book of decolonial philosophy, *Consciencism*. Though he suggests that communalism is the "socio-political ancestor of socialism,"[16] he would go on to say that "the restitution of Africa's humanist and egalitarian principles of society requires socialism."[17] Both Du Bois and Nkrumah appear to share the ideology of communism as a universal trait of human civilizations though perhaps expressed in different ways culturally. Nkrumah also believed that Marxism could and should be modified to meet the needs of Africans.

However, it remains my contention that the conflation of socialism or communism with the histories of African communal living will only continue to serve the proliferation of Eurocentric ideological hegemony. It is more accurate to say that the examples of African communal living show some similarities with the Marxist-communist theories, but they are fundamentally different cultural paradigms. Nevertheless, terminology remains the problem. Is it that we should discover a different and more accurate term to describe the history of African communal living? Further, could the heart of the issue be that we are using English terms, or "borrowed terms," to describe an African condition and as such there can never be an appropriate translation?

I agree with both of these suggestions and propose that it is best that we begin to utilize African terms from African languages in order to describe African phenomena. This may seem to be an obvious suggestion but it is one that will come with much sacrifice, ingenuity and exploration on the part of African scholars, particularly those in the Western Hemisphere. After all, very few of African descent have either the desire or, perceivably, the time

---

15 Ana Monteiro-Ferreira, *The Demise of the Inhuman: Afrocentricity, Modernism, and Postmodernism* (Albany, NY: State University of New York Press, 2015), 55.
16 Kwame Nkrumah, *Consciencism: Philosophy and Ideology for De-Colonization* (New York, NY: Monthly Review press, 1970), 73.
17 Ibid, 77.

to learn whole lexicons and enhance Ebonics languages with those of that of their mother tongues in Africa.[18] It is up to scholars and elders to present to the masses more appropriate terminologies and political positions that are useful and formed from epistemologies and theories that are culturally grounded.

With that said, I mentioned in previous chapters Ani's concept of *asili*, which she argues is a "conceptual tool for cultural analysis [that] refers to the explanatory principle of a culture. It is the germinal principle of the being of a culture, its essence."[19] It is interesting that the agrarian revolution in Europe represents a primary influence on Marx. For *class struggle* to become the hallmark of Marxist ideology there must be some understanding of a Pan-European *asili* as the recognition of European ethnic divisions, though certainly addressed by Marx and Friedrich Engels, does not hold much importance in the face of their philosophical dichotomy of classes and their struggles. However, as Marxism is grounded by an analysis of the cultural-historical realities of Europeans, applying it to Africa is an inherently agency-reducing exercise.

To be sure, Marx and Engels both apparently studied some degree of African history though there's sparse literature of their findings and opinions in comparison to the general body of their work. To their credit, they also appeared to disagree with the Hegalian notion of a static and non-historic Africa.[20] But they did fervently praise Louis Henry Morgan's, an anthropologist famed for the dubious theory that all human societies developed in three evolutionary stages: savagery, barbarism and civilization. Savagery and Barbarism was categorized and divided by stages of technological advancement. However, in Morgan's estimation, the designation of civilization can only be determined by evidence of a written language.

Of course, many anthropologists reject these notions today, just as the growing body of new scholarship rejects the notion of a single "cradle of civilization" in Mesopotamia. We now know that civilizations arose largely independently grounded by their own germinating matrices. However, as this information was not the scholarly consensus in their time, the scholarship and theories of those like Morgans appealed to Marx and Engels as the most

---

18 For the sake of clarity, my use of the phrase "Ebonics languages" here applies to languages such as African American Ebonics, Ayisyen (referred to as Haitian creole), Jamaican, Brazilian Ebonics and various other so-called patois languages spoken by African people.
19 Ani, *Yurugu*, 12.
20 Thomas Meisenhelder, "Marx, Engels, and Africa," *Science & Society* 59, no. 2 (Summer, 1995): 197–205.

probable explanation of the evolution of human societies. These theories not only influenced their work, but ultimately colored their opinion of Africa. Though one could argue that their characterization of races were based on sociological and historical circumstances as opposed to biological determinism, this did not stop them from espousing the rhetoric that European colonialism would bring about civilization to Africa.[21]

To be fair, they also wrote a great deal about the evils of colonialism, but it is clear that both Marx and Engels saw European culture as exhibiting an evolutionary superior stage to African culture, though based on their perception of sociological factors. Naturally, we could also point out some of Marx's and Engels' racist descriptions of African people, such as Marx's reference to enslaved Africans in Jamaica as "barbarians," and Engels' description of the Zulu as "Kaffirs."[22] However, while their language here is certainly something to be considered, the point of my argument is more so the implications of their theories when applied to African people. To think of African communal living, or communalism, as an antecedent to modern Socialism and Marxism is to suggest that they sprouted forth from the same germinating matrix. As we have now established that such a suggestion would be based on outdated assumptions about the evolution of civilizations, the perpetuation of such an idea would only further contribute to the already nocuous *eurocentric masquerade*, as we'd continue to be led to believe that modern European cultural ethos is the natural evolutionary aspiration of all human societies. Therefore, I argue that any sociological theory applied to modern African circumstances must be based on the germinating matrix of African culture. Furthermore, I believe that Du Bois himself was in the process of developing a theory that would serve Africa in a similar way Marxism has served Europe. This theory, "Pan-Africa," I argue to be a philosophical paradigm that holds a lot of promise if continued to be developed by DuBoisian, Pan-African and Afrocentric scholars.

Pan-Africa

As far as terminologies and theories are concerned, arguably the most popular theory in the Western academy which extends from DuBoisian thought is *double consciousness*. However, Du Bois only pens this construction of words once in all of his body of work. It is published twice, once in the 1897 issue of

---

21 Shlomo Avineri, *Karl Marx on Colonialism and Modernization* (Garden City, NY: Doubleday, 1968).
22 Meisenhelder, "Marx, Engels, and Africa."

the *Atlantic Monthly* and then most famously in *The Souls of Black Folk*. Though indicative of the very flowery prose of his earlier writings, double consciousness introduces a schizophrenic existence between two opposing patterns of human culture that Du Bois is quite clearly attempting to abandon by the end of his life. I have always found it curious as to how the Western academy could take the writings and thinking of one stage of a man's life and seemingly throw away or, at the very least, not contextualize it with the philosophies of his mature years. Du Bois lived another sixty-six years beyond the writing of this passage and, given the opinions of his later years, would perhaps be appalled to see African Americans decreeing that "America has too much to teach the world and Africa."

After all, Du Bois warns African nations in his essay "The Future of Africa" not to succumb to Americanism for "a body of local private capitalists, even if they are Black, can never free Africa; they will simply sell it into new slavery to old masters overseas."[23] Du Bois also admits his folly and that of other African Americans when he states, "Once I thought of you Africans as children, whom we educated Afro-Americans would lead to liberty. I was wrong."[24] Far from *double consciousness*, Du Bois in his later years, though still struggling with Afrocentric centeredness, was quite clear that he was of one cultural consciousness, which was exemplified by his stark allegiance to the African world. I argue that the theory of Du Bois that he himself most fiercely advocated and wrote and published the most on was that of *Pan-Africa*. This theory, in my estimation, was more resolute than Pan-Africanism and more demanding in sacrifice on the part of the Pan-African. In my estimation, Pan-Africa is the missing link for Du Bois in his search for unity. But instead of a focus on racial identity, this theory holds much more potential as a unifier under a paradigm of cultural identity.

What is cultural identity? Identity is expressed in many different ways. In the United States many refer to themselves as American. But the United States is a land of cultural heterogeneity. While many of its political leaders perpetuate the idea that America is a nation striving toward some notion of cultural homogeneity, this doesn't yet (and perhaps never will) represent reality. What then would people consider the aspects of their being that make them *culturally* American? Culture can be defined as the customs, motifs, aesthetics, arts, social institutions and achievements of a particular people. When it comes to national culture, often the customs of both dominant and marginal groups begin to assimilate to form national identity. Therefore, in order for a nation

---

23 Du Bois, *World and Africa*, 198.
24 Ibid, 200.

to become culturally homogenous there are often unique cultural aspects of certain groups that must either be left behind or assimilated in such a way that it no longer bears its uniqueness. Further, unless displaced by a once nondominant group that has gained the upper hand in power, the foundational cultural paradigm of that nation will remain that of the first powerful group. That being said, in order to produce what we may call a nationalistic culture, groups must either be willing, coerced or unwittingly duped into sacrificing their individual identities to the dominant cultural paradigm for the sake of cultural homogeneity.

In the United States, that dominant cultural paradigm is Anglo-American. No one can be obtuse about this as the standardization of the English language in the United States, both officially and culturally, is the primary indicator. Certainly, in its so-called "melting pot" phase many European groups came to the United States and added their cultural phenomena. However, this has never significantly eroded the cultural dominance laid out by those first Anglo-Saxons who came to power and the continuance of such under their descendants. No matter if we consider the existence of the cultural phenomena of Native Americans, African Americans, or Asian Americans, or any other racialized group in the country, this remains a truism. They have all significantly contributed; of that there is no doubt. However, America at its cultural foundation is an Anglo-Saxon country.

What then are African Americans without an America? The French, German, Anglo-Saxon and many other European ethnicities in America still have the cultural-historical tools that their respective motherlands afford them. Beyond that, through the shared histories of warfare, peace and exchange between them, a composite European identity affords some degree of identity fluidity for those of European descent. Such fluidity would assist them in some measure if, by extreme example, a tragedy befell the nation that was great enough to force a mass migration back to Europe. To be sure, this isn't a perfect scenario as there would certainly be those "white" Americans who would have a difficult time. I'd argue that this would be largely a result of the legacy of racism in America. The early to mid-twentieth century saw the shedding of European ethnic ties and the creation of "whiteness" as a racial bloc of opposition to the Civil Rights Movement. For some *white* families, this new racial identity may provide issues in juxtaposition to a *European* cultural fluidity.

Digressing, we can only imagine that Du Bois' understanding of history provided him the insight that while nations rise and eventually fall, culture has more longevity. Having received his degree in the field of history, Du Bois was sure to be endowed with the Western tradition of penning histories of civilizations and cultures with nationalistic ideals in mind which, depending on which European nation the writer held from, wouldn't shy away from noting how their nation represents the preeminent example of human progress. This tradition, with roots in Europe's Enlightenment era, had by Du Bois' time evolved into the modern Pan-European cultural construction that's extant today. This is what we may think of as the prototypical European, made up of the composite of cultural and national histories of Europe. But who or what is the prototypical African?

In a letter he penned to Nkrumah on the heels of Ghana's independence from Britain, Du Bois spoke of a future for the African world and described it as "Pan-Africa."[25] He coined this term as early as 1921 and used it frequently in various letters and publications.[26] As we know, Pan-Africanism has no set definition. There are many different approaches to the notion of Pan-Africanism. Certainly, "African unity" represents a simple definition with no real specificity in mind as to how that unity is gained. However, there are more specific definitions such as the push for the existence of a federated *country* of Africa. But, of course, not everyone who considered themselves a Pan-Africanist, or belonging to a program of Pan-Africanism, necessarily believed in the necessity of a federated state. We know this most infamously due to the rivalry between the mid-twentieth century group of African leaders who formed the Monrovia bloc and Casablanca bloc, which in later years led to the formation of the Organization of African Unity.

But Du Bois envisioned something between, and idealistically beyond, the petty rivalries of those two factions. Though coming short on illuminating the power of African cultural history, there is indication that he understood somewhat of what it took for an African nationalist cultural unity. Du Bois was to address the All-African People's Conference held in Accra, Ghana, on December 22, 1958. Being too sick to deliver the speech himself, he sent his wife, Shirley Graham Du Bois. She addressed the conference with Du Bois' speech aptly titled "The Future of Africa." In it, Du Bois had this to say of his Pan-Africa concept:

> As I have said, this is a call for sacrifice. Great Goethe sang, "Ent-behren sollst du, sollst entbehren"—"Thou shalt forego, shalt do without." If Africa unites it will be because each part, each nation, each tribe gives

---

25 Du Bois, *Autobiography of W.E.B. Du Bois*, 399–401.
26 Eugene F. Provenzo, Jr. and Edmund Abaka collect a number of these in their edited volume, *W. E. B. Du Bois on Africa*. B. (London, UK: Routledge, 2016.) The first published use of which was in the March 1921 issue of *The Crisis*, in an article of the same name, "Pan-Africa."

up a part of its heritage for the good of the whole. That is what union means; that is what *Pan-Africa* means: When the child is born into the tribe the price of his growing up is to give over a part of his freedom to the tribe. This he soon learns or dies. *When the tribe becomes a union of tribes, the individual tribe surrenders some part of its freedom to the paramount tribe.* When the nation arises, the constituent tribes, clans and groups must each yield power and much freedom to the demands of the nation or the nation dies before it is born. [emphasis mine][27]

Du Bois' vision of *Pan-Africa* was sure to fall on deaf ears. His words represented so much sacrifice on the part of African ethnic groups, both large and small. But Du Bois is perhaps right to suggest that there is no use in the identification as an African if Africans are not willing to sacrifice a part of their individuality for the sake of that composite identity. After all, this notion of what it means to be an African is a modern construction. There may be ancient cultural foundations to justify this identity, but there are no records of a nation known as Africa. This is something that will have to be created. Just as the United States is being molded into a national culture within the Anglo-Saxon mold-cavity, Africa must make the hard decisions and agree upon which mold-cavities are best for the molding of African cultural nationality. In the words of Du Bois, what groups should stand as "the paramount tribe"? Du Bois continues:

Your local tribal, much-loved languages must yield to the few world tongues which serve the largest numbers of people and promote understanding and world literature. This is the great dilemma which faces Africa today; faces one and all: Give up individual rights for the needs of the nation; give up tribal independence for the needs of Mother Africa. *Forget nothing but set everything in its rightful place*: the Glory of the six Ashanti Wars against Britain; the wisdom of the Fanti Confederation; the unity of Nigeria; the song of the Songhay and Hausa; the rebellion of the Mahdi and the hands of Ethiopia; the greatness of the Basuto and the fighting of Chaka; the revenge of Mutessa, and many other happenings and men; but above all-Africa, Mother of Men. [emphasis mine].[28]

From this passage we understand that Du Bois' notion of *Pan-Africa* wasn't necessarily the erasing of identities but the sacrificing of some aspects of

---

27 Du Bois, *World and Africa*, 198.
28 Ibid.

group autonomy for the sake of the whole. He encourages Africans to "forget nothing but set everything in its rightful place," and to above all consider the project that is Africa. But Du Bois is missing a key component to this argument. As a historian, he understood the historical dimensions of his arguments, but he failed to provide a proper analysis of the cultural basis for such a nationalistic stance. For example, to tell a people, as he did, to make their language secondary to others in Africa that were more widely spoken presents some fundamental misunderstandings. Though nations consisting of a variety of ethnic groups do not often form standard cultural foundations by peaceful means, history has shown that differing groups existing in the same space will vie for power over that space utilizing a litany of means that often leads to violence and domination.

This is not to say that differing groups cannot work together to compromise on issues that benefit the whole. For example, in 2022 the African Union adopted KiSwahili as an official working language. This is an amazing step toward unity but many divisive opinions on the decision remain. Nevertheless, over one hundred million Africans speak KiSwahili and it is the most widely spoken African language in the continent as well as throughout the African world. But I should point out that English, French, Portuguese and Arabic have been working languages since the AU's inception. Naturally, the differences between them and KiSwahili were the varying histories of war, domination and colonialism that follow these languages.

When I first conceived of the African World Antecedent Methodology (AWAM), I was determined to find a way to bring the African world closer together on our own cultural terms. I have never been content with the notion that the strongest argument for African unity was due to a shared history of oppression. That notion is quite superficial as a basis for unity. Certainly, there is value in realizing that unity should be achieved in order to end collective oppression. However, what makes it superficial is that if we remove the history of colonialism and slavery, all we are left with is some idea of connectivity via skin color. While phenotypical aesthetics is certainly a pillar of culture, it alone does not constitute *asili*. Those who espouse the rhetoric that the recognition of likeness in skin color alone is the germinating matrix of the culture of people of African descent entertain a philosophy that lacks the substance needed to unify African people in perpetuity.

There have of course been those who have recognized the cultural connections between people of African descent. Du Bois himself, though not drawing any real conclusions based on these connections, could not have possibly written about the Bantu, for example, without also developing an understanding that the centuries of history that make up that migration included the diffusion and evolution of culture. KiSwahili is in fact a Bantu language and, depending on how one views a language versus a dialect, shares a relationship with hundreds of other Bantu languages as far north as Cameroon, as far east as Kenya and the southern borders of Somalia, and as far south as Cape Town, South Africa. Further, though Du Bois would perhaps have had little knowledge of this fact, I have mentioned in a previous chapter that Bantu languages are but part of a larger and more ancient family of languages classified as Niger-Congo. Therefore, in advancing unity by assimilating culturally, as Du Bois was attempting to do in his speech for the All-African People's Conference, one must illuminate these ancient cultural ties. As language is a primary vehicle of cultural unity, it would make more sense for Du Bois to suggest a synthesis of languages instead of advocating the yielding of smaller languages to larger ones.

What I have sought to achieve with AWAM is to mend the old mold-cavities of traditional Africa with the dynamic cultural variations now extant throughout the contemporary African world. AWAM seeks to discover which cross-cultural phenomena are, using Du Bois' terminology, "paramount" and therefore useful for a philosophy of African unity based on cultural synthesis. Du Bois' notion of *Pan-Africa* would benefit greatly from such an approach. Mapping the cultural-historical matrix that exists throughout the African world solves many of the issues Du Bois faced trying to relate African Americans to African politics.

In "American Negroes and Africa's Rise to Freedom," Du Bois argued that during the period following the antebellum era "American Negroes learned from their environment to think less and less of their fatherland and its folk."[29] His assessment is that African American leaders began to adopt the moral shortcomings of Americanism and ignored the truth of the world around them. Du Bois' hope for African Americans was to learn from Africa's developing political situation. He quipped, "Would it not be wise for American Negroes themselves to read a few books and do a little thinking for themselves?"[30] Du Bois also had this to say on the matter:

> What effect did this have on American Negroes? By this time their leaders had become patriotic Americans, imitating white Americans almost without criticism. If Americans said communism had failed, then it had failed. And this of course Americans did say and repeat. Big business declared communism a crime and communists and socialists criminals. Some Americans and some Negroes did not believe this; but they lost

---

29 Ibid, 215.
30 Ibid, 218.

employment or went to jail [...] [Americans] said the American color line cannot be held in the face of communism. It is quite possible that we can beat communism if in America we begin to loosen if not break the color line [...] To the Negroes the government said, it will be a fine thing now if you tell foreigners that our Negro problem is settled; and in such case we can help with your expenses of travel. A remarkable number of Negroes of education and standing found themselves able to travel and testify that American Negroes now had no complaints.[31]

Though we may debate his defense of the rising adoption of communist and socialist thinking among African leaders, he is in my view nonetheless vindicated in his assessment of African American leaders and their servile relationship with American capitalism. However, is it really useful to focus on so-called leaders and their influence on a particular community? Certainly, the influence of leaders on community opinion and action is a fact that cannot be ignored. However, oftentimes we conflate the history of people admiring, listening to and acting upon the advice of community leaders as the complete history or the preponderance of events in a social history.

As I have detailed in previous chapters, while African American leaders may have pushed Americanism among the masses, African cultural ethos persevered among the very masses they were sent to evangelize. As such, Du Bois' arguments would have benefited from continued comparative analysis and assessments as he did in *The Philadelphia Negro*, particularly in his chapter "The Negro Family." While the chapter had some problematic language, he was on the right track with his brief comparisons of African and African American family structure and how that related to contemporary African American sociopolitical issues. AWAM, of course, is a more nuanced contemporary version of this type of process.

---

31 Ibid, 216.

CONCLUSION

This book set out to provide a critical Afrocentric analysis of Du Bois and his career-long engagement with Africa. It largely accounts for Du Bois' Eurocentric shortcomings and appraises his more Afrocentric positions. Performing this analysis required a fundamental reevaluation of his works under the lens of a number of mechanisms of analysis informed by the Afrocentric paradigm. I contextualized the experiences that shaped Du Bois' thinking about Africa throughout his life as well as provided commentary on influential events that shaped Du Bois' philosophy as early as his college years as well as experiences that continued to shape his opinions through the end of his life. Though I engaged with a number of Du Bois' writings that spanned the breadth of his career, the principal scholarship of Du Bois subject to review was his book *The World and Africa*.

In this study I have highlighted Du Bois' Eurocentric approaches to history in regard to African people. The significance of confronting these Eurocentric assertions is the fact that Du Bois is more or less considered the most influential African American intellectual of the twentieth century. Thus, my aim was to provide an analysis that is useful in illustrating the Eurocentric entrapments in regard to Africa and African people that have plagued even our most brilliant intellectuals. With that said, I have also demonstrated that Du Bois underwent an evolution of thought throughout his life which by his twilight years began to reveal early foundations for Afrocentric thought. I have argued that Du Bois' analysis of African history, and subsequent promotion of Pan-African unity, is limited by his primary use of the racial paradigm juxtaposed to utilizing a cultural paradigm—though he does make some ancillary mention of culture. As such, in *The World and Africa*, Du Bois often makes superficial and sometimes erroneous claims about what constitutes African identity. However, Du Bois himself in some ways has expressed his discontent with the racial paradigm, and though perhaps he himself wasn't aware, was on the verge of a revolutionary new philosophy in the form of what he describes as *Pan-Africa*. Du Bois' speech at the All-African People's Conference in Ghana charged Africans with the mission of unifying culturally. However, I speculated that his arguments for cultural unity were perhaps unfavorable among his audience as he called for smaller groups to yield their cultural autonomy to larger groups in forming a united cultural bloc. While this speculation is admittedly unsubstantiated by lack of any account from participants of that conference, mass skepticism of such a directive continues to be exemplified today among members of the African Union (formerly Organization of African Unity).

However, I argue that an appreciable understanding of the African *asili* would have instead armed Du Bois' rhetoric with the possibilities of a synthesis of cultural phenomena. To that end, my utilization of the African World Antecedent Methodology (AWAM) provided within this study some minor examples of the cultural patterns of African Americans compared with other African groups. In so doing, I established the existence of the cultural-historical phenomena of African Americans within the African cultural-historical matrix. Put another way, what was established is the fact that African Americans historically and culturally are within the lineage of the African *asili*. Of course, this isn't a novel argument as many across a variety of social science and humanities fields have made similar arguments. Thus, AWAM is but one in a long lineage of intellectual heritage established by scholars such as Du Bois, Cheikh Anta Diop, Molefi Kete Asante and many others.

Implications of Scholarship Utilizing AWAM

When Maulana Karenga founded Kwanzaa in 1966 he based it on his Kawaida theory, being, as he describes it, "an ongoing synthesis of the best of African thought and practice in constant exchange with the world." The worldwide popularity and practice of Kwanzaa represent the possibilities of Kawaida theory and likewise represents the unbridled possibilities of African unity under a cultural paradigm. Karenga's intensive study of African cultural history coupled with his firsthand knowledge of the social and political circumstances of African Americans and African nations under colonialism and apartheid, informed his desire to advance the African cultural project. In the creation of Kwanzaa, Karenga synthesized various African cultural phenomena such as language, customs, motif, aesthetics and philosophy and in so doing consciously and deliberately affected the course of African American and African-world culture as well as inspired people of African descent to unite on cultural grounds.

What I set out to accomplish in the AWAM sections of Chapters 2 and 3 of this volume was not to present an exhaustive record of comparative cultural phenomena but instead to inspire readers with the possibilities of its implementation. To be clear, without a praxis of making functional that which we have learned from the African cultural-historical matrix, there would be little effect on the social and political realities of African Americans with regard to Pan-African unity. Thus, while AWAM is intended to be a method of comparative analysis that illuminates and categorizes various cultural links, successful implementation of AWAM by scholars involves extrapolating the possible implications of the use of this research in praxis. In effect, the primary purpose of AWAM is to inspire the creation of more culturally unifying phenomena such as Kwanzaa. The synthesis of cultural phenomena provides endless possibilities for the further development of national culture among African Americans and Pan-African unity across the African world.

For example, in a few sections of the AWAM method I allude to African culture being, in essence, the germinating matrix of African American music. While there is general acknowledgment of the African origins of African American art forms, this often exists as an ambiguous origin in the minds of African Americans. Among the masses of African Americans, there does not exist a collective conscious understanding of how this lineage comes to be and therefore this presents a cultural (and potentially political) disconnect. However, if we were to establish a Pan-African holiday dedicated to celebrating those origins then we'd be able to bridge connections.

Imagine an African World Music Week that involves musicians of various African backgrounds releasing music and giving performances together that synthesizes their unique approaches.[1] Simultaneously, scholars of these musical genres host week-long colloquia meant to inform other scholars and the public at large about the origins and cross-cultural influences of these various musical forms. Further, from both of these praxes, institutions are created with the intent to train together scholars and artists (or even scholar-artists) from across the African world in order to produce future generations who deliberately and positively affect the course of African-world culture through the musical arts. Imagine further that instead of students being assessed by the standards of Western music theory (which is often expressed as just "music theory" due to the Eurocentric masquerade), they are instead initiated and charged with knowledge and tradition via a synthesis of the various rites of passage ceremonies such as those that exists among the djeli in West Africa as well as the incorporation of the rites and traditions of institutions such as the African American Jazz Caucus, the Universal Zulu Nation and the newly founded Zulu Union.

Similar types of holidays and institutions can be created around other forms of art such as cinema. Recall the discussion from Chapter 3 surrounding the

---

1 One contemporary example of this is Nas and Damian Marley's album, *Distant Relatives*.

history of African American film. The creation of similar holidays or platforms of awareness that draw in institutions like the African American Film Festival, the African World Film Festival and the African World Documentary Film Festival, as well as the creation of institutions meant to train interested parties would be beneficial to the African world. Imagine also colloquia as well as public-facing research that address cultural links in film such as the practice of libation in the film *Cooley High* and the significance of the phrase that followed: "This is for the brothers who ain't here."

Of course, while they present perhaps the most attractive and vivid of possibilities to imagine, this praxis isn't limited to the arts and neither does it require the creation of holidays to fulfill its purposes. There is a host of cultural phenomena to be explored that, when compared and analyzed, could provide the basis for the development of institutions and organizations whose members are endowed with a deep conscious understanding of the cultural lineage of their activities as well as the cultural bases for sociopolitical unity with other African groups. Attention should be drawn to fields as varied as economics, cuisine, psychology, history, mathematics, religion, architecture and physics. Thus, we'd find necessary the production of scholarship with topics ranging from an AWAM approach to analyzing African American and Yoruba food, or the aesthetics of homes in the African American south and that of the so-called Maroon towns in Accompong (Jamaica), or comparing Vodun in Benin and Vodou and Hoodoo in the African American south, or analyzing the political economy of west African susus and Harlem rent parties or even analyzing the continued shared influence between African American hip-hop and Afrobeat. The possibilities of comparative research are endless but the implications provided for the use of such research are vital to the continued development of Pan-African unity.

REFERENCES

Achebe, Chinua. "An Image of Africa: Racism in Conrad's Heart of Darkness." *The Massachusetts Review*, 57, no. 1 (2016): 14–27.
Adi, Hakim. *Pan-Africanism: A History*. London: Bloomsbury Academic, 2018.
Amadiume, Ife. *Male Daughters, Female Husbands: Gender and Sex in an African Society*. London: Zed Books, 2015.
Ani, Marimba. *Yurugu an African-Centered Critique of European Cultural Thought and Behavior*. Baltimore, MD: Afrikan World Press, 1994.
Asante, Molefi Kete. *The Afrocentric Idea*. Rev. and expanded ed. Philadelphia, PA: Temple University Press, 1998.
Asante, Molefi Kete. *An Afrocentric Manifesto: Toward an African Renaissance*. Cambridge: Polity, 2007.
Asante, Molefi Kete. *The History of Africa: The Quest for Eternal Harmony*. 3rd ed. New York: Routledge, 2019.
Asante, Molefi Kete. *Kemet, Afrocentricity, and Knowledge*. Trenton, NJ: Africa World Press, 1990.
Asante, Molefi Kete. "Locating a Text: Implications of Afrocentric Theory." In *Language and Literature in the African American Imagination*, edited by Carol Aisha Blackshire-Belay. Westport, CT: Greenwood, 1992.
Asante, Molefi Kete. *Lynching Barack Obama: How Whites Tried to String up the President*. Brooklyn, NY: Universal Write Publications, 2016.
Asante, Molefi Kete. "The Philosophy of Afrocentricity." Essay. In *The Palgrave Handbook of African Philosophy*, edited by Adeshina Afolayan and Toyin Falola, 231–244. New York: Palgrave Macmillan, 2017.
Asante, Molefi Kete and Mazama, Ama, eds. *Encyclopedia of African Religion*. Thousand Oaks, CA: SAGE, 2009.
Basu, Helene. "Music and the Formation of Sidi Identity in Western India." *History Workshop Journal*, 65, no. 1 (2008): 161–178. https://doi.org/10.1093/hwj/dbm069.
Beatty, Mario H. "W.E.B. Du Bois and Cheikh Anta Diop on the Origins and Race of the Ancient Egyptians: Some Comparative Notes." *African Journal of Rhetoric*, 8, no. 1 (2016): 45–67.
Blassingame, John. *The Slave Community: Plantation Life in the Antebellum South*. Rev., enlarged ed. Oxford, UK: Oxford University Press, 1979.
Blyden, Nemata Amelia, I. *African Americans and Africa: A New History*. New Haven, CT: Yale University Press, 2019.
Blyden, William W. *A Vindication of the African Race: Being a Brief Examination of the Arguments in Favor of African Inferiority*. Monrovia: G. Killian Publishers, 1857.

Breunig, Peter. *Nok: African Sculpture in Archaeological Context*. Frankfurt am Main, Germany: Africa Magna, 2014.

Broomfield, Matt. "The Research That Shows Europe Can't Be Getting "Full"." *The Independent. Independent Digital News and Media*, January 16, 2016. Retrieved From https://www.independent.co.uk/news/world/europe/more-people-europe-are-dying-being-born-research-finds-a6816651.html.

Brotz, Howard, ed. *African American Social and Political Thought: 1850–1920*. New York: Transaction Publishers, 1992.

Brotz, Howard, ed. *Negro Social and Political Thought: 1850–1920: Representative Texts*. New York: Basic Books, 1966.

Browder, Anthony T. *Finding Karakhamun: The Collaborative Rediscovery of a Lost Tomb*. Washington, DC: Institute of Karmic Guidance, 2011.

Burden-Stelly, Charisse and Horne, Gerald. *W.E.B. Du Bois: A Life in American History*. Santa Barbara, CA: ABC-CLIO, An imprint of ABC-CLIO, LLC, 2019.

Burgis, Thomas. *The Looting Machine: Warlords, Tycoons, Smugglers, and the Systematic Theft of Africa's Wealth*. New York: PublicAffairs, 2015.

Calls, Du Bois a traitor if he accepts post. *Afro-American (1893–1988)*, May 30, 1936. Retrieved From http://libproxy.temple.edu/login?url=https://www-proquest-. Retrieved From com.libproxy.temple.edu/historical-newspapers/calls-dubois-traitor-if-he-accepts- post/docview/531127178/se-2?accountid=14270.

Connah, Graham. *African Civilization: An Archaeological Perspective*. 3rd ed. New York: Cambridge University, 2016.

"CPI Inflation Calculator." U.S. Bureau of Labor Statistics. Accessed March 29, 2021. Retrieved From https://data.bls.gov/cgi-bin/cpicalc.pl?cost1=.25&year1=1918&year2=2017.

Cruse, Harold. *The Crisis of the Negro Intellectual: A Historical Analysis of the Failure of Black Leadership*. New York: The New York Review of Books, 2005.

Daaku, Kwame Y. "History in the Oral Traditions of the Akan" *Journal of the Folklore Institute*, 8, no. 2/3 (1971): 114.

Davidson, Basil. *Africa in History*. Rev. and expanded ed. New York: Simon & Schuster, 2005.

Davidson, Basil. *A History of East and Central Africa: To the Late Nineteenth Century*. New York: Doubleday, 1969.

Dawson, Michael C. *Black Visions: The Roots of Contemporary African-American Political Ideologies*. Chicago: University of Chicago Press, 2001.

Diop, Cheikh Anta. *The African Origin of Civilization: Myth or Reality*. Chicago: Chicago Review Press, 1974.

Diop, Cheikh Anta. *The Cultural Unity of Black Africa: The Domains of Matriarchy and of Patriarchy in Classical Antiquity*. London: Karnak House, 1989.

Diouf, Sylviane A. *Dreams of Africa in Alabama: The Slave Ship Clotilda and the Story of the Last Africans Brought to America*. Oxford, UK: Oxford University Press, 2009.

Diouf, Sylviane A. *Fighting the Slave Trade: West African Strategies*. Athens: Ohio University Press, 2006.

Du Bois, W. E. B. *1868–1963. Back to Africa. W. E. B. Du Bois Papers (MS 312)*. Special Collections and University Archives, University of Massachusetts Amherst Libraries.

Du Bois, W. E. B. *1868–1963. Lenin and Africa, February 1959. W. E. B. Du Bois Papers (MS 312)*. Special Collections and University Archives, University of Massachusetts Amherst Libraries.

Du Bois, W. E. B. *1868–1963. Letter from W. E. B. Du Bois to Leo Frobenius, February 9, 1937. W. E. B. Du Bois Papers (MS 312)*. Special Collections and University Archives, University of Massachusetts Amherst Libraries.

Du Bois, W. E. B. *1868–1963. Letter from W. E. B. Du Bois to Anson Phelps Stokes, March 10, 1937. W. E. B. Du Bois Papers (MS 312)*. Special Collections and University Archives, University of Massachusetts Amherst Libraries.

Du Bois, W. E. B. *1868–1963. Letter from W. E. B. Du Bois to Phelps-Stokes Fund, May 10, 1946. W. E. B. Du Bois Papers (MS 312)*. Special Collections and University Archives, University of Massachusetts Amherst Libraries.

Du Bois, W. E. B. *Africa in Battle against Colonialism, Racialism, Imperialism*. Chicago: Afro-American Heritage Association, 1960.

Du Bois, W. E. B. *Africa, Its Geography, People and Products; Africa: Its Place in Modern History*. New York: Oxford University Press, 2017.

Du Bois, W. E. B. *The Autobiography of W.E.B. Du Bois: A Soliloquy on Viewing My Life from the Last Decade of Its First Century. Third Printing*. New York: International Publishers, 1968.

Du Bois, W. E. B. *Black Folk: Then and Now*, edited by Henry Louis Gates. Oxford, UK: Oxford Univ. Press, 2007.

Du Bois, W. E. B. *Black Reconstruction in America: An Essay toward a History of the Part Which Black Folk Played in the Attempt to Reconstruct Democracy in America, 1860–1880*, edited by David L. Lewis. Oxford: Oxford University Press, 2007.

Du Bois, W. E. B. *The Conservation of Races*. Washington, DC: American Negro Academy, 1897.

Du Bois, W. E. B. *Dusk of Dawn: An Essay Toward an Autobiography of a Race Concept*, edited by Henry Louis Gates. New York: Oxford University Press, 2007.

Du Bois, W. E. B. *The Gift of Black Folk*. Oxford: Oxford University Press, 2014.

Du Bois, W. E. B. *The Negro*. Philadelphia, PA: University of Pennsylvania Press, 2001.

Du Bois, W. E. B. *The Negro Church*. Atlanta: Atlanta University Press, 1903.

Du Bois, W. E. B. *The Philadelphia Negro: A Social Study*. Oxford: Oxford University Press, 2007.

Du Bois, W. E. B. "Self-Righteous Europe and the World: Correspondence with W. M. Flinders Petrie" *Crisis*, 4, no. 1 (May 1912): 36–37 (New York: Crisis Publishing Co.), 1–6.

Du Bois, W. E. B. *The Souls of Black Folk*, edited by Brent Hayes Edwards. Oxford, UK: Oxford University Press, 2008.

Du Bois, W. E. B. *The World and Africa*. New York: International Publishers, 1965.

Du Bois, W. E. B. *The World and Africa; Color and Democracy*, edited by Henry Louis Gates. New York: Oxford University Press, 2017.

Du Bois, W. E. B. and Aptheker, Herbert. *The Correspondence of W. E. B. Du Bois*. Vol. 1. Amherst, MA: University of Massachusetts Press, 1973.

Dubow, Saul. *Scientific Racism in Modern South Africa*. Cambridge, UK: Cambridge Univ. Press, 1995.

Faraji, Salim. *The Roots of Nubian Christianity Uncovered: Triumph of the Last Pharaoh*. Trenton: Africa World Press, 2012.

Ehret, Christopher. *History and the Testimony of Language*. Berkeley, CA: University of California Press, 2011.

Farrar, T. "The Queenmother, Matriarchy, and the Question of Female Political Authority in Precolonial West African Monarchy." *Journal of Black Studies*, 27, no. 5 (1997): 579–597.

Feder, Kenneth L. *Frauds, Myths, and Mysteries: Science and Pseudoscience in Archaeology.* 10th ed. New York: Oxford University Press, 2019.
Floyd, Samuel A. *The Power of Black Music: Interpreting Its History from Africa to the United States.* New York: Oxford University Press, 1997.
Foster, Helen Bradley. *New Raiments of Self: African American Clothing in the Antebellum South.* Oxford, UK: Berg, 1997.
French, Howard W. *China's Second Continent: How a Million Migrants Are Building a New Empire in Africa.* 1st ed. New York: Alfred A. Knopf, 2014.
Garvey, Marcus. *Philosophy and Opinions of Marcus Garvey*, edited by Amy Jacques Garvey. Mansfield Centre, CT: Martino Publishing, 2014.
Gilroy, Paul. *After Empire: Melancholia or Convivial Culture?* Abingdon, UK: Routledge, 2004.
Gilroy, Paul. *Against Race: Imagining Political Culture Beyond the Color Line.* Cambridge, MA: Belknap Press of Harvard University Press, 2001.
Gilroy, Paul. *The Black Atlantic: Modernity and Double Consciousness.* London: Verso, 1993.
Gomez, Michael A. *African Dominion: A New History of Empire in Early and Medieval West Africa.* Princeton: Princeton University Press, 2019.
Gomez, Michael. *Exchanging Our Country Marks: The Transformation of African Identities in the Colonial and Antebellum South.* Chapel Hill, NC: The University of North Carolina Press, 1998.
Gruesser, John Cullen. *Black on Black Twentieth-Century African American Writing about Africa.* Lexington, KY: The University Press of Kentucky, 2015.
Gwaltney, John Langston. *Drylongso: A Self-Portrait of Black America.* New York: New Press, 1993.
Hale, Edward Everett. *The Queen of California: The Origin of the Name of California*, edited by Eric Jones and Eric M. Jones; Kindle Edition, Seattle, 2014.
Harms, Robert W. *Africa in Global History: With Sources.* New York: W. W. Norton & Company, 2018.
Hayford, Casely. *Ethiopia Unbound: Studies in Race Emancipation*, edited by Molefi Kete Asante. Baltimore, MD: Black Classic's Press, 2011.
Hochschild, Adam. *King Leopold's Ghost: A Story of Greed, Terror, and Heroism in Colonial Africa.* London, UK: Pan Books, 2002.
Horne, Gerald. *Black and Red: W.E.B. Du Bois and the Afro-American Response to the Cold War, 1944–1963.* Albany, NY: State University of New York Press, 1986.
Horne, Gerald and Burden-Stelly, Charisse. *W.E.B. Du Bois: A Life in American History.* ABC-CLIO, 2019. Retrieved From http://publisher.abc-clio.com/9781440864971.
Horton, James Africanus Beale. *West African Countries and People, British and Native: with the Requirements Necessary for Establishing That Self-Government Recommended by the Committee of the House of Commons, 1865: And a Vindication of the African Race.* Nendeln/Liechtenstein: Kraus Reprint, 1970.
Jackson, John G. *Introduction to African Civilizations.* New York: Citadel Press, 2001.
Kambon, Ọbádélé. "Africanisms in Contemporary English." In *The Sage Encyclopedia of African Cultural Heritage in North America*, edited by Kenya J. Shujaa and Mwalimu J. Shujaa, 192–198. Thousand Oaks: SAGE Reference, 2015.
Kambon, Ọbádélé. "X-Live FM: The Equal Sign Will Kill Our People." Interview with Ọbádélé Kambon. Abibitumi, April 29, 2018. Video, 1:04. Retrieved from https://youtu.be/DBhTdMSG8CQ.
Karenga, Maulana. *Kawaida Theory: An Introductory Outline.* Inglewood: Kawaida Publications, 1980.

Karenga, Mulauna. "Philosophy, Principles, and Program." Retrieved From http://www.us-organization.org. *Us Organization*. Last modified: February, 25, 2020, http://www.us-organization.org/30th/ppp.html.
Kenyatta, Jomo. *Facing Mount Kenya: The Tribal Life of the Kikuyu*. London: Mercury Books, 1965.
Kizza, Immaculate N. *The Oral Tradition of the Baganda of Uganda: A Study and Anthology of Legends, Myths, Epigrams and Folktales*. Jefferson, NC: McFarland & Co., 2011.
Knight, Mary. "Curing Cut or Ritual Mutilation?: Some Remarks on the Practice of Female and Male Circumcision in Graeco-Roman Egypt." *Isis; an International Review Devoted to the History of Science and Its Cultural Influences*, 92, no. 2 (2001): 317–338. https://doi.org/10.1086/385184.
Lewis, David Levering. *W. E. B. Du Bois - Biography of a Race: 1868–1919*. New York: Henry Holt and Company, 1993.
Lewis, David Levering. *W.E.B. Du Bois: The Fight for Equality and the American Century, 1919–1963*. New York: Henry Holt, 2001.
Lombardo, Paul A. *A Century of Eugenics in America: from the Indiana Experiment to the Human Genome Era*. Bloomington, IN: Indiana University Press, 2011.
Mackie, Gerry. "Female Genital Cutting: The Beginning of the End." Essay. In *Female "Circumcision" in Africa: Culture, Controversy, and Change*, edited by Bettina Shell-Duncan and Ylva Hernlund, 253–281. Boulder, CO: Lynne Rienner Publishers, 2000.
MacMaster, Richard K. "Henry Highland Garnet and the African Civilization Society." *Journal of Presbyterian History (1962-1985)*, 48, no. 2 (1970): 95–112.
Marchand, Suzanne. "Leo Frobenius and the Revolt against the West." *Journal of Contemporary History*, 32, no. 2 (1997): 153–170. https://doi.org/10.1177/002200949703200202.
Marck, Jeff. "Aspects of Male Circumcision in Subequatorial African Culture History." *Health Transition Review: The Cultural, Social, and Behavioural Determinants of Health*, 7 Supplement (1997): 337–360.
Martin, Tony. *Race First: The Ideological and Organizational Struggles of Marcus Garvey and the Universal Negro Improvement Association*. London, UK: Greenwood Press, 1976.
Masson-Oursel, Paul, Stern, Philippe, and de Willman-Grabowska, Helena. *Ancient India and Indian Civilization*. translated by M. R. Dobie. London, UK: Routledge, 2013.
Mazama, Ama. *The Afrocentric Paradigm*. Trenton, NJ: Africa World Press, 2002.
Mazama, Ama. "Cognitive Hiatus and the White Validation Syndrome: An Afrocentric Analysis." In *Black/Africana Communication Theory*, edited by Kehbuma Langmia and Ronald L. Jackson, 25–38. Cham, Switzerland: Palgrave Macmillan, 2018.
Mazama, Ama. "The Power of Institutionalized Disciplinarity: Molefi Asante's Visionary and Pioneering Contributions to African American Studies." *Journal of Black Studies*, 49, no. 6 (2018): 604–624.
Mazama, M. A. "Afrocentricity and African Spirituality." *Journal of Black Studies*, 33, no. 2 (2002): 218–234.
Mbiti, John S. *African Religions & Philosophy*. 2nd ed. Oxford, UK: Heinemann, 1990.
McGrath, Elizabeth. "The Black Andromeda." *Journal of the Warburg and Courtauld Institutes*, 55, no. 1 (1992): 1. https://doi.org/10.2307/751417.
Meriwether, James Hunter. *Proudly We Can Be African: Black Americans and Africa, 1935–1961*. Chapel Hill, NC: University of North Carolina Press, 2002.
Miller, Joseph C. "History and Africa/Africa and History." *The American Historical Review*, 104, no. 1 (1999): 1–32. https://doi.org/10.2307/2650179.

Monteiro-Ferreira, Ana. *The Demise of the Inhuman: Afrocentricity, Modernism, and Postmodernism*. Albany, NY: State University of New York Press, 2015.
Morris, Rosalind C. and Leonard, Daniel H. *The Returns of Fetishism: Charles de Brosses and the Afterlives of an Idea*. Chicago, IL: The University of Chicago Press, 2017.
Moses, Wilson J. *Afrotopia: The Roots of African American Popular History*. Cambridge: Cambridge University Press, 1998.
Moyo, Dambisa. *Dead Aid: Why Aid Is Not Working and How There Is a Better Way for Africa*. New York: Farrar, Straus and Giroux, 2009.
Mugo, Micere G. *African Orature and Human Rights*. Roma, Lesotho, South Africa: Institute of Southern African Studies, National University of Lesotho, 1991.
Ndlovu-Gatsheni, Sabelo J. *Epistemic Freedom in Africa: Deprovincialization and Decolonization*. New York: Routledge, 2018.
Nehusi, K. "From Medew Netjer to Ebonics". In *Ebonics and Language Education of African Ancestry Students*, edited by Clinton Crawford, 56–122. New York and London: Sankofa World Publishers, 2001.
Nehusi, Kimani S. K. *Libation: An Afrikan Ritual of Heritage in the Circle of Life*. Lanham, MD: University Press of America, Inc, 2016.
Obenga, Théophile. "Egypt: Ancient History of African Philosophy." In *A Companion to African Philosophy*, edited by K. Wiredu, 31–49. Hoboken, NJ: John Wiley & Sons, Incorporated, 2004. Retrieved from https://ebookcentral.proquest.com.
Obenga, Theophile. "The Genetic Linguistic Relationship between Egyptian and Modern Negro-African Languages." *The Peopling of Ancient Egypt and the Deciphering of Meroitic Script*. UNESCO (1978): 65–72.
Ogunyemi, Y. D. *The Oral Traditions in Ifi-Ife: The Yoruba People and Their Book of Enlightenment*. Bethesda: Academica Press, 2010.
Okafor, Victor Oguejiofor. "Toward an Africological Pedagogical Approach to African Civilization." *Journal of Black Studies*, 27, no. 3 (1997): 299–317.
Park, Robert M. "Tuskegee International Conference on the Negro." *The Journal of Race Development*, 3/1 (July, 1912): 117–120. Retrieved From http://archive.org/stream/jstor-29737946/29737946_djvu.txt accessed 3 January 2018.
Rabaka, Reiland. *Africana Critical Theory Reconstructing the Black Radical Tradition from W.E.B. Du Bois and C.L.R. James to Frantz Fanon and Amilcar Cabral*. Lanham, MD: Lexington Books, 2010.
Rabaka, Reiland. *Against Epistemic Apartheid: W.E.B. Du Bois and the Disciplinary Decadence of Sociology*. Lanham, MD: Lexington Books, 2010.
Rabaka, Reiland. *Du Bois: A Critical Introduction*. Cambridge, UK: Polity Press, 2021.
Rickford, J. R. and Rickford, A. E. "Cut-Eye and Suck-Teeth: African Words and Gestures in New World Guise." *The Journal of American Folklore*, 89, no. 353 (1976): 294–309.
Rodney, Walter. "African Slavery and Other Forms of Social Oppression on the Upper Guinea Coast in the Context of the Atlantic Slave-Trade." *The Journal of African History*, 7, no. 3 (1966): 431–443.
Rodney, Walter. *How Europe Underdeveloped Africa*. Baltimore, MD: Black Classic Press, 2011.
Samuels, Tristan. "Undoing the Hottentoting of "the Queen of Punt" A Jamaican Afronography on the Kemetiu Depiction of Ati of Punt." *Journal of Black Studies*, 52, no. 1 (2021): 3–23. https://doi.org/10.1177/0021934720945360.
Santos, Boaventura de Sousa. *Epistemologies of the South: Justice Against Epistemicide*. London, UK: Routledge/Taylor&Francis, 2016.

Shillington, Kevin. *History of Africa*. Basingstoke, Hampshire, UK: Palgrave Macmillan, 2012.
Shillington, Kevin. *History of Africa*. 4th ed. London: Red Globe Press, 2019.
Sjoberg, Andrée F. *Dravidian Language and Culture: Selected Essays*. Kuppam, India: Dravidian University, 2009.
Smith, E. and Crozier, K. "Ebonics Is Not Black English." *Western Journal of Black Studies*, 22, no. 2 (1998): 109.
Soyinka, Wole. "The African World and the Ethnocultural Debate." In *African Culture: The Rhythms of Unity*, edited by Molefi Kete Asante, and Kariamu Welsh-Asante, 13–38. Trenton, NJ: Africa World Press, 1990.
Stapleton, T. J. *A Military History of Africa. from Ancient Egypt to the Zulu Kingdom: (Earliest Times to ca. 1870)*. Santa Barbara, CA: Praeger, 2013.
Stearns, Jason K. *Dancing in the Glory of Monsters: The Collapse of the Congo and the Great War of Africa*. New York: PublicAffairs, 2012.
Stewart, Kayla. "Tracing Jambalaya." *Article 19* (2019). Retrieved From https://art19.com/shows/proof/episodes/31b81374-a953-47cd-9fba-2bccfdadbf2f.
Sudarkasa, N. "'The Status of Women' in Indigenous African Societies." *Feminist Studies*, 12, no. 1 (1986): 91–103.
Sultana, G. Sri Lanka after Rajapaksa: Can It Ignore China? *Strategic Analysis*, 40, no. 4 (2016): 245–254. https://doi.org/10.1080/09700161.2016.1184797.
Tavernise, Sabrina. "Fewer Births Than Deaths Among Whites in Majority of U.S. States." *The New York Times*, June 20, 2018. Retrieved From https://www.nytimes.com/2018/06/20/us/white-minority-population.html.
Thiong'o, Ngũgĩ Wa. "Notes towards a Performance Theory of Orature." *Performance Research*, 12, no. 3 (2007): 4–7. https://doi.org/10.1080/13528160701771253.
Thornton, John K. "Legitimacy and Political Power: Queen Njinga, 1624–1663." *The Journal of African History*, 32, no. 1 (1991): 25.
Tillotson, Michael. *Invisible Jim Crow: Contemporary Ideological Threats to the Internal Security of African Americans*. Trenton, NJ: Africa World Press, 2011.
Tishken, Joel E. "Indigenous Religions". In *Africa, Vol. 2, African Cultures and Societies Before 1885*, edited by Toyin Falola, 73–94. Chapel Hill, NC: University of North Carolina Press, 2000.
Tishken, Joel E., Fáló̩lá, Tóyìn, and Akínye̩mí, Akíntúndé, eds. *Sàngó in Africa and the African Diaspora*. Bloomington, IN: Indiana University Press, 2009.
Vansina, J. *Oral Tradition as History*. Madison, WI: University of Wisconsin Press, 1985.
Vansina, J. "Recording the Oral History of the Bakuba-I. Methods." *The Journal of African History*, 1, no. 1 (1960): 43–53. Retrieved from http://www.jstor.org/stable/179705.
Walker, C. E. *Mongrel Nation: The America Begotten by Thomas Jefferson and Sally Hemings*. Charlottesville, VA: University of Virginia Press, 2009.
Walker, C. E. *We Can't Go Home Again: An Argument about Afrocentrism*. New York: Oxford University Press, 2001.
Watson, Mary Ann. "Female Circumcision from Africa to the Americas: Slavery to the Present." *The Social Science Journal*, 42, no. 3 (2005): 421–437. https://doi.org/10.1016/j.soscij.2005.06.006.
Weinberg, Meyer. *The World of W.E.B. Du Bois: A Quotation Sourcebook*. Westport, CT: Greenwood Press, 1992.
Welsing, Frances Cress. *The Isis Papers: The Keys to the Colors*. Chicago, IL: Third World Press, 1991.
West, Cornel. *Race Matters*. Boston, MA: Beacon Press, 1993.

Wilderson, Frank B. *Afropessimism*. New York: Liveright Publishing Corporation, 2020.
Wobogo, Vulindlela. "Diop's Two Cradle Theory and the Origins of White Racism." *Black Books Bulletin*, 4, no. 4 (1976): 20–29, 72.
Woodson, Carter G. *The Miseducation of the Negro*. Trenton: Africa World Press, 1990.
Wright, Bobby E. *The Psychopathic Racial Personality and Other Essays*. Chicago: Third World Press, 2000.
Wright, William D. *Black History and Black Identity: A Call for a New Historiography*. Westport, CT: Praeger, 2002.
Zuckerman, Phil, ed. *Du Bois on Religion*. Walnut Creek, CA: Altamira Press, 2000.

INDEX

Achebe, Chinua 28
Adeyemi Alowolodu (Oyo empire) 1
Adventures of Esplandián, The (de Montalvo) 97–98, 98n79
Afrasian languages 94–95
Africa 8, 10; in 1940s 1–2; Afrocentric approach 5, 124, 127; Asian influence 91–94, 100; chronology system, history 49–51; circumcision practice 70–71; communal living 128; consciencism philosophy and 113; Du Bois' views 2–3, 47–49; early twentieth century 114–16; ethnic groups of 22; Europe's reign of terror 23, 48; Garvey's movement 116–18; history, distorted facts 47–49, 59, 61–62; humanitarian aid impact 33–34; Islamic influences 93, 101; old scripts, as resource 63; peopling of, Du Bois 51–55; race in 95n70; socialism and 125–31; use as setting and backdrop 28; and wars for conquest 48–49, 49n7; wealth of resources 114–15; "Western ideals" and 125, 127
Africa in Global History (Harms) 59–60
African achievements, history 44, 111
African American(s) 43; Afro-Caribbean culture and 102; Christians 38–40; Civil Rights 18; culture 101; ethnic unity 4; films 105–6, 142; identity 3; *kora, xalam/goje* instruments 103; leaders, and Americanism 137–38; music 103–5; self identity, perception 15; versions of American art and 103, 105
African cultural phenomena 6–7, 100–101, 124, 141–42
African ethnography and cultural history 76–77
African independence movements 121

African Myths and Folktales (Woodson) 108, 108n5
African Origin of Civilization, The (Diop) 6
African people: African American leaders impact 137–38; Arab phenotype 93; atrocities against Congolese people 28–31; classical civilizations (*see* Kemet; Kush); classifications 52–54; connections between, cultural 54–55; critique on Islam/Arabs 12; cultural identification 6, 132; cultural inferiority of 86, 98; cultural ontology and cosmology 18; domination of, in texts 27–28; as Egyptians 6; European culture, value 20; exploitation 27–28; Hebrews relationship ideologies 66; historical account 16; as "human factor" 28; ideas of religion 86–87; imposition of Euromodernity 36; level of education 23; nouveau-African cultures, in Americas 101–2; phenotype and cultural identity 92–93; plight, desensitization 28–33; racial attitudes 62–63, 131; relationship between Hebrews and 65–66; socialization, religion/education role 35–40; in South America 101; war against European forces 48–49; Western narrative in, props 28–29, 31, 33; *see also* African American(s); socialization of African people
African Religion and Philosophy (Mbiti) 87
African Survey (Hailey) 114
African Union 134, 136, 140
African World Antecedent Methodology (AWAM) 7, 67–69, 99–106, 136–37; African civilizations, comparative analysis 10, 45, 67, 140–41; Du Bois survey (*see* historical survey of Du Bois); *Fánna* concept 9–10, 70–73;

frame-working, for reconstructing past 10–11; *Kanna* method 9, 69–70; *Naani* concept 10, 74; spiritual similarity, evidence of 71; use of and aim 18
African World Film Festival 142
African World Music Week 141
Africanity: of African people 42; Arabic phenotypes 93; expressions 45; Kemet and Kush 68; suppression of, display 40
African-World Cultural Project 69
Africologists 4n4, 32
Afrocentric historiography 49, 51
Afrocentric Manifesto, The (Asante) 5
Afrocentric Paradigm, The (Mazama) 8
Afrocentric theory 124
Afrocentricity 97; father of 5, 50; influence 5, 7
Afromodernity 35–37, 44
Against Epistemic Apartheid (Rabaka) 21
Agency Reduction Formations 47n1
Aime, Hurbert 54
Akan 22, 102
Almoravid dynasty 95
Amazigh 94–95, 95n70
American Civil War 26
"American Negroes and Africa's Rise to Freedom" 137–38
Andromeda myth 12, 110–14
Anglo-Saxon cultural ethnocentrism 38–39, 133, 135
Ani, Marimba 5, 16, 44
Arabic phenotypes 93
Armattoe, Raphael 99
Asante, Molefi Kete 5, 16–17, 21, 48, 50, 83–85, 95, 103, 108, 112–13
Ashwood, Amy 117
Asian influence, in Africa 12, 91–94, 100
Asili concept (Ani) 9, 11, 44, 99, 130, 140
Atlantis 76, 81

"Back to Africa" article 117
Bakongo faith 72
Ball, Charles 102
Ball, William H. 125
Baltimore Afro-American 78
Bambara 22
Bambenga 22
Banjo 103
Bantu: chiShona language 90; Du Bois on 89–90, 99; groups, and languages 53, 136–37; history of migration 12, 123; migration, cultural influences 16, 89–91, 99–100; term 89; in Zimbabwe 90–91
Barbosa, Duarte 100
BCE, (Before Common Era) 51
Benin Kingdom 1, 12, 83–84
bilād as-sūdān 94–95
Black Church 40
Black film genre 105
Black Hebrew Israelites 66
Black nationalism 34
Black Skin, White Masks (Fanon) 5
Black Sudan: *see* Sudan
Blassingame, John 38
Bleck, Wilhelm 89
Brexit 41–42
Burgis, Tom 27, 31–32, 35
burials, and personal effects 73
Bushmen 53

Carnegie, Andrew 79
Caucasoids 52
CE, (Common Era) 51
Chicago Tribune 2
China 125
Christendom 12, 17, 49; in Africa 37–40; chronology as developed 50–51; hallmark of Western cultural influence 125; religious superiority complex 50; theory of "vague force" 50
Christian conditioning 39–40
ciKam language 57
cire-perdue process 83–84
civilized Africans 113
cognitive hiatus, concept 8, 98
"Cognitive Hiatus and White Validation Syndrome: An Afrocentric Analysis," (Mazama's essay) 8
Cold War 18, 41
collectivism, culture 99
color line, notion 47–48
Communism 126, 128
Congo 27
Congolese people, exploitation and oppression 27–31
Conrad, Joseph 27
conscienism ideology 112
Cooley High (film) 73, 142
Coupland, Reginald 100
crania, studies of 59–60
Crisis, The 77
cultural continuity, phenomena 9, 54–55, 99, 101
culture, defined 132

INDEX

dances, African 105
Dancing in the Glory of Monsters (Stearns) 27, 29–30, 32
Darwin, Charles 51
Darwin, Leonard 51n15
dating system 49, 51
de Brosses, Charles 71–72
de Montalvo, Garci Rodríguez 97
Dead Aid (Moyo) 34
deities, African 50
Delafosse, Maurice 88, 99
Delany, Martin R. 38
democracy *vs.* communism 126
Diagne, Blaise 20
Diop, Cheikh Anta 5–7, 16, 68
double consciousness theory 4, 13, 26, 98, 107, 109, 125, 131–32
Dravidians 92
Du Bois, Shirley Graham 134
Du Bois, William Edward Burghardt 15, 119; Afrocentric analysis 139–40; argument for saving Africa 5, 124; article, self-determination principle 20–21; "color line" 47–48, 112, 125; Darwin influence 51–52; "double consciousness" theory 4, 13, 98, 107, 109, 125, 131–32; education, experiences 108–9; Eurocentric ideological entrapments 3, 16–17, 20–26, 123, 127, 139; Future of Africa, speech 134–35; Hayford's critique 107–8; historiography Afrocentric 5, 49, 51, 54; intellectual development 21–25, 119; opinions of, European imperialism 27; "rape of Africa" 43–44; reference to Africa 21–22; religious background 39–40; significance 2, 4; talented tenth theory 51, 125; views on, collapse of Europe 19–20, 41; vision of *Pan-Africa* 2, 5, 8, 12–13, 124, 132, 135–36, 139; on West Africa 12, 81–88; Western ideals 125, 127; white scholars/philanthropists, conundrum with 76–81, 108–9; *see also* historical survey of Du Bois; *World and Africa, The*
Dusk of Dawn (Du Bois) 39
dynastic race theory 59, 67, 77, 81, 85

Ebonics languages 130, 130n17
education, socializing phenomenon 35–37
Egypt 6
Eisenhower, Dwight D. 125

Encyclopedia Africana (Du Bois) 12, 77, 80, 120, 124
Encyclopedia of African Religion, The (Asante and Mazama) 103
Encyclopedia of the Negro 108–10; development 77–78; Du Bois thoughts, on whites 76–80, 108–9; Europeans perspective, on African people 110; Frobenius' interest 77, 80; funded by Phelps-Stokes fund 77, 110; Woodson views 78–79, 108–10
Engels, Friedrich 130
Engels, Marx 130
English language 35
Eschenbach, Wolfram von 97
Ethiopia 11, 48, 61, 75, 110
Ethiopia Unbound (Hayword) 107
Ethiopianism 107
eugenics 51n15
Eurocentric ideology/Eurocentricity 16–17, 25, 40–45
Eurocentric masquerade 17, 25–35, 44, 113, 131; black skins in white masks 43; cultural war 17, 32–34, 42, 44, 58, 113, 125; domination philosophy 26–27; Eurosupremacy, and African inferiority 43–44; exploitation and oppression 27–35, 34; false universalism 25, 48, 113–14; humanitarian aid 33–34; literature role, in desensitization 27–30, 33; social engineering and 27; Stearns' words, and Eurocentric biases 30–31
Eurocentric paternalism 22
Eurocentric socialization 32
Euromodernity 25
Europe: civilization history and 82; cultural connections in 68; cultural war with 17, 32, 34, 42, 44, 58, 113, 125; history of 82
European Agrarian Revolution 112, 129–30
European atrocities, and social engineering 26–27
European ethos 16–17, 23, 25
European Industrial Revolution 112, 129
European powers and control over Africa 19
European trade of enslaved Africans 1, 10, 29, 55, 61, 66, 88
European world, collapse 18–20, 41–42

Fanna: burials, personal effects placement 73; cultural diffusion, from Nile Valley

70–71; dishes creation, and origin 104–5; fetishes 71–72; practice of libation 73; similar African phenomena 9–10; similarity concept 9, 70, 104; spiritual similarity, evidence 71–72
Fanon, Frantz 5, 43
Father of Egyptology (Petrie) 59
fetishes 71–72
Fisk University 109
Fortunes of Africa, The (Meredith) 115
Foster, Helen 102
French language 35
Frobenius, Leo 12, 76, 80–81, 84–86, 99
From Babylon to Timbuktu (Windsor) 66
Fuess, Harald 24
Fulani 53

Garnett, Henry Highland 38
Garvey, Marcus 18, 38, 117–20
Garveyism 24
Ghana 41, 116, 120–21
"Ghana and Pan-Africanism" 127
God concept 38–39, 50, 87
Gomez, Michael 73, 102
Great Depression 1–2, 18
Great Lakes region 89
Great Zimbabwe 59, 90–91
Greco-Roman figures 59
Gregorian calendar 49
Griot tradition 73
Guiding Hundredth, The essay 51n15
gunpowder weapons 48–49

Hailey, Malcolm 114–15
Haitian Revolution 96
Half Has Never Been Told, The (Baptist) 115
"Hamitic race" theory 90
Hansberry, William Leo 11–12, 75
Harms, Robert 59
Hayford, J. E. Casley 115–16
Heart of Darkness (Conrad) 28
Hebrews, and Africans 65–66
Herero-Ovambo 53
Hindu culture, origins of 93
historical survey of Du Bois: from African American historians 75–81, 84; on African civilization history 21; antecedent methodology 99–106; artifacts 84; Asian influence in Africa 91–94; Bantu migration 89–91; correspondence with Petrie 77; European scholars, inputs from 75–77; Frobenius works, reliance on 76–77,

80–81, 85–86, 94, 99; orature 82–83; Sudanic empires, ancient 94–98; on West Africa (*see* West Coast of Africa); Woodson views and 78–80; written account 75, 82–83
Historically Black Colleges and Universities (HBCUs) 108–9
History of Ashanti (Claridge) 114
Hoodoo spiritual systems 72
Hope, John 79–80
Horchschild, Adam 28–29, 31, 33
Hottentot 53
How Europe Underdeveloped Africa (Rodney) 116n25
human societies evolution 130–31
Hunhu/Ubuntu philosophy 37
Hurston, Zora Neale 101–2

Ibn Battuta 95–96
identity, cultural 132
Iliad 62
individualism 99
Indo-Aryan migration, into India 92–93
Indus Valley civilization 93
The Instruction of Amenemope 73
Invention of Women, The (Oyèwùmí) 35
Islam 101

Jambalaya 104
Japan 23–24, 24n30, 93
Jesus 50
Johnson, Harry H. 89, 99
Jollof 104

Kabila, Joseph 32
Kanna 101–4; antecedent sameness analysis 9, 69–70, 101–3; folklore, origins in Africa 104; religious culture continuation Kush/Kemet 66, 69–70
Karenga, Maulana 5, 7
Kasaï-Oriental region 85
Kawaida theory 7, 140
Kemet 6–7, 11, 16; Africanity 68; as ancient Egypt 55–56; "Black Queen" Nefertari 61; chronological assessment 11; circumcision practice 70; dancing/music significance 72–73; Du Bois views on 55–61; dynasties, historical survey 60–61, 64, 66–67; "Golden Ages" 60; Het-heru deity 92; hierarchical separation in 57–58; history, and links to Kush 64–67; Kushite culture influence 66, 69–70;

INDEX

new year/*wepet renpet* in 49; practice of libation 73; racial identity 55–57, 60; religion 56; studies of crania 59–60; use *sistrums* and *djabara* 73; vitality from, the South 60, 63–64; women 56
KhoiKhoi 53
King, Martin Luther Jr. 18, 34, 38
King Leopold's Ghost (Horchschild) 27–28, 32
Kingdom of Monomotapa (Mutapa) 90
KiSwahili 136
Kitchener, Herbert 48
Kitwara kingdom 90
Krishna 92, 92n63
Kush civilization 92; biblical passages, Hebrew's views 65–66; capital, Meroë 63, 67, 69; circumcision practice 70; connection to Kemet 64–67 (*see also* Kemet); Du Bois views 61; Ethiopia or 11, 61, 75, 110; Greek's reverence 62; history, and African inferiority false notion 61–62; Kandakes 67; Meroitic script, as resource 63; Negroid phenotypes 64; religious culture, between Kemet and 66, 69–70
Kuyafana 9
Kwanzaa practice 140
kya and *ybp*, conventions 51

Lam, Aboubacry Moussa 84
Lane-Poole, Stanley E. 98, 100
League of Nations 25
Lee, Spike 105
"Lenin and Africa," article 127
Leopold II 27
Libation: An Afrikan Ritual of Heritage in the Circle of Life (Nehusi) 71
Looting Machine, The (Burgis) 27, 31–32
Luschan, Felix von 19

Maasai 22
MacIver-Randal, David 11, 58–59
Mandela, Nelson 34
Mandingan empire, of Melle 95–96
Marke, George O. 118
Marx, Karl 126
Marxism 112, 129–31
Marxism-Leninism 125–26
Mazama, Ama 5, 7–8, 16, 98, 103
Mbiti, John 87
Meiji era, Japan 24
Meiji Restoration, The (Hellyer and Fues) 24
Melanesians 92

Meroitic script 63
Mesopotamia 130
Michaux, Oscar 105
minkisi, interpretation 72
Miseducation of the Negro (Woodson) 109
Mongoloids 52
Moorish conquest of Spain 94
Moors 98
Morel, Edmund 28–29
Morgan, Louis Henry 130
Mossi people 88
Moyo, Dambisa 34
Mugabe, Robert 32, 35
music, African American 103, 105, 141–42

Naani: African American phenomena 105–6; concept of uniqueness 10, 74, 105; distinguishing cultural phenomena 10
National Association for the Advancement of Colored People (NAACP) 2
Nationalistic cultures 6–7, 132–33
natives, views on 3, 11, 22–23, 52n15, 86, 114
Negrillos (pygmies) 52
Negro, The (Du Bois) 8, 54, 77, 80
Negro Nation within the Nation, A (essay, Du Bois) 4
Negro with a Hat: The Rise and Fall of Marcus Garvey (Grant) 118
Negroes: *see* African American(s)
Negroids 52, 64
Nehusi, Kimani S. K. 71
"*New Raiments of Self*" (Foster) 102
Ngũgĩ wa Thiong'o 83
Niger-Congo languages 53, 90, 137
Nile Valley culture/people 70, 75
Nkrumah, Kwame 34, 37, 112–13, 120, 124
Nok culture 84
Ntuli, Pitika 83
Nubia 16, 58

Obama, Barack Hussein 42
Okafor, Victor 9
On the Origin of Species by Means of Natural Selection (Darwin) 51
oral literature and oral tradition 82; *see also* historical survey of Du Bois
orature 50, 82–83
Ottomans 93
Oyèwùmí, Oyèrónkẹ 35

Pan-African Congress, 1919 20–22; education, in self-knowledge 25; Eurocentric language, of resolutions 24–25; language of resolutions 24–25; list of resolutions 22–24; native, as underdeveloped 25; participants 22
Pan-African theory 2, 121, 131–32, 134–36
Pan-African unity 5, 55, 134, 139; African Americans and 141; based on cultural foundations 68; composite African identity for 124, 133, 135; paramount tribe 135, 137
Pan-Africanism, notion 2, 24, 54, 115–21, 134
Parsifal story 97–98
Patois languages 130n17
Payne, Bishop Daniel Alexander 40
Peace Conference 1918 2, 20
Petrie, Flinders W. M. 11, 59, 63, 67, 77
Phelps-Stokes fund 77
phenotype and cultural identity 92
Philadelphia Negro, The (Du Bois) 138
Plato 69, 76
pre-Dravidian negrillos 92
Pyramids 60

Rabaka, Reiland 21
race relations, gaps in 97–98
racial classifications, of Africans 52–53
rapid-fire rifles 49
religion in schools 38–39
religious celebration, dancing in 40
Rhodes, Cecil 125
ring shouts 72, 102–3
Rodgers, J. A. 98, 100
Russia 125–26

Sankara, Thomas 37
Sankofa term 7
Schweinfurth, Georg 100
self-determination principle 20–21
self-knowledge 25
Semitic languages 94
shabtis 71n68
Shakespeare plays 98
Sheppard, William 29
Shona 22, 37, 53
Shona language 35
Siculus, Diodorus 63
skull shape, and racial classification 52, 59
slave trade 88, 121
Smuts, Jan 33

Snowden, Frank 12, 75, 80
Social Darwinism movement 51
social engineering 26–27
socialism, defined 127
socialization of African people 35, 37, 40; behaving as an African 40–41; Christianity and 37–40; by education 35–37
Souls of Black Folk (Du Bois) 107, 132
Space Race 18
Spanish Flu 1
Stearns, Jason 27, 30–32
Stewart, Kayla 104
Stokes, Anson Phelps 77, 80, 108, 110
Sudan 58, 100–101; cultural cohesiveness and continuity 100; Du Bois on 94–98, 100; Mali cultural customs, Battuta views 96; race relations, tensions of 97–98; Sudanic empires, ancient 16, 95
Suto-Chwana [Soto-Tswana] 53

Tamazight 95
Tilltson, Michael 47n1
Tip, Tippu 93
Townsend, Robert 105
tribe, meaning 128
Trump, Donald 33, 42
twentieth century, Africa 114–16

United Nations 25, 33
United States: Anglo-Saxon, cultural paradigm 38, 133, 135; cultural heterogeneity 132; funding to African countries 33–34
Universal Negro Improvement Association (UNIA) 117–19

Vansina, Jan 82
"Vodou" (Voodoo) 72, 72n71, 103

Wagadu (Ghana) 61, 95
Washington, Booker T. 18, 29, 79, 121
W.E.B. Du Bois: A Life in American History (Burden-Stelly and Horne) 120–21
West Coast of Africa: architecture 88; art/tools in 83–84; bronze statues discovery 84; customs/ideals, value of 82–83; Du Bois views 76, 81; Frobenius opinions 12, 76, 81–87; history notion 82; ideas of religion 86; individualism *vs.* collectivism 99; Kassai-Sankuru, description 85–86; Lam's work 84–85; slave trade 88; term *Atlantis* 76, 81

western bloc of nations 125
Western education 17, 25; Christian conditioning 38–39; foreign aid 35; imposition of European languages in Africa 36; languages taught 35–36; removing prayer out of schools 38–39; socialization by 35–37; in United States 38–39
Western ideals 125
white scholars/philanthropy: concerns of Woodson 77–80, 85–86; Hope's response 79–80; mistrust of 78–80, 108–9
white supremacy 32, 42
Williams, George Washington 29
Wilson, Woodrow 20
Windsor, Rudolph R. 66
Wolof 22
Woodson, Carter G. 76–80, 85–86, 108–10, 121
World and Africa, The (Du Bois) 2, 18, 26, 44–45, 47, 75, 80, 96, 139; "Andromeda" myth, metaphor 108, 110–14; Asian influence in Africa 91–94; Bantu migration 89–91; "The Black Sudan" 94–98; "color line" 47–48, 125; comparisons with European culture 86; composite African ontology, notion 4–5, 123; Europe critique 16–17; "*natives*" views on 3, 11, 22–23, 52n15, 86; Pan-African struggle, reasoning 2–4, 10, 108, 115, 121; "pattern of human culture" 3, 16–17, 58, 113, 126; problematic, language 21–22, 25, 123, 128; West Africa, "Atlantis" 76, 81–88; world history, from African point of view 21–22
World War 18
Writings on Africa essays (Du Bois) 8
written account 82

Yorùbá 22; English language and 36; idea of gender 36; religion 87; society 35
Yurugu (Ani) 9

Zimbabwe: Asiatic influences 91; Bantu migration to 90–91; Christianity in 37; Western forms of education in 35–36
Zirimu, Pio 82–83
Zulu 22, 53

www.ingramcontent.com/pod-product-compliance
Lightning Source LLC
Chambersburg PA
CBHW021143230426
43667CB00005B/237